The
SEARCH
FOR
WHY

The SEARCH FOR WHY

A REVOLUTIONARY NEW MODEL FOR
UNDERSTANDING OTHERS, IMPROVING
COMMUNICATION, AND HEALING DIVISION

BOB RALEIGH

TILLER PRESS

New York   London   Toronto   Sydney   New Delhi

An Imprint of Simon & Schuster, Inc.
1230 Avenue of the Americas
New York, NY 10020

First Tiller Press hardcover edition January 2021

TILLER PRESS and colophon are trademarks of Simon & Schuster, Inc.

For information about special discounts for bulk purchases, please contact
Simon & Schuster Special Sales at 1-866-506-1949 or business@simonandschuster.com.

The Simon & Schuster Speakers Bureau can bring authors to your live event.
For more information or to book an event, contact the Simon & Schuster Speakers
Bureau at 1-866-248-3049 or visit our website at www.simonspeakers.com.

Interior design by Jennifer Chung

Manufactured in the United States of America

1   3   5   7   9   10   8   6   4   2

Library of Congress Cataloging-in-Publication Data
Names: Raleigh, Bob, author.
Title: The search for why : A revolutionary new model for understanding others,
improving communication, and healing division / by Bob Raleigh. Description:
New York : Tiller Press, 2021. | Includes bibliographical references and index.
Identifiers: LCCN 2020041370 (print) | LCCN 2020041371 (ebook) |
ISBN 9781982130558 (hardcover) | ISBN 9781982130565 (ebook) Subjects:
LCSH: Human behavior. | Developmental psychology and motivation. | Motivation
(Psychology) | Choice (Psychology) Classification: LCC BF199 .R265 2021 (print) |
LCC BF199 (ebook) | DDC 150.19/43—dc23
LC record available at https://lccn.loc.gov/2020041370
LC ebook record available at https://lccn.loc.gov/2020041371

ISBN 978-1-9821-3055-8
ISBN 978-1-9821-3056-5 (ebook)

Credits for illustrations on page 194: family: https://stock.adobe.com/images
/male-and-female-playing-with-children-outside/140239444; road:
https://unsplash.com/photos/rRJ0aA6AIpQ.

Jessica Raleigh
My daughter, colleague, and collaborator. You have gone above and
beyond the call of duty with your support, enthusiasm, and dedication
to this project. Simply put, this would have not been possible
without your steadfast resolve and commitment to excellence.
Thank you

CONTENTS

INTRODUCTION

Science is a funny thing. At times it can be bone dry—unless you love immense amounts of detailed work, repetition, and frequent failure. But it can also be exhilarating, if you enjoy the challenge of unsolved mysteries and are motivated by making the unknown known.

I have always been fascinated by how science tells a story to make sense of the world. Even if we don't understand all the machinations involved, we identify with the journey of the heroes—the scientists. Where do their ideas come from? How do they persist in their pursuits? How do they survive the journey?

I don't have a special affinity to astrophysics, but a June 24, 2020, headline in *Nature* caught my eye because it demonstrated so perfectly the power of scientific narrative. "Neutrinos Reveal Final Secret of the Sun's Nuclear Fusion,"[1] it read. For more than one hundred years, this particular study of the sun's energy has inspired countless theories and kept many teams of scientists busy. In the article, science reporter Davide Castelvecchi writes, "By catching neutrinos emanating from the Sun's core, physicists have filled in *the last missing detail* of how nuclear fusion powers the star." I was floored. The last missing detail. Scientists had solved a riddle conceived of more than a century ago—in an article by Arthur Eddington in the *Observatory*, "The Internal Constitution of the Stars,"[2] which speculated for the first time on the source of stellar energy.

Such dogged pursuit, and ultimate revelation, strikes me as a rare success for humanity, and gives me hope for the future. In our current haze of widespread illness, institutional racism, and economic doom, the story showcases the collaborative power of science to build upon the insights and proof points of those who have come before. It's like fitting the last piece in a thousand-piece puzzle—if the puzzle then sprang to life in your living room. The whole is, ultimately, so much more than the sum of its parts.

Understanding that process is the mission of this book, *The Search for Why*. My goal is to explain *why we do the things we do*. Admittedly, it's a highly complex question that we can't fully answer today. But we can advance the mission by using what we know *so far*. In these pages, I offer an actionable model based on sound theory and real-world research, meant to help us tackle the big problems we face.

I propose that we are all born with a particular "instinctual profile," which then comingles with our life experiences to create our worldview. If we can identify and understand another individual's instinctual profile, we can move beyond polarization to a form of reconciliation—first at the interpersonal, and then the societal, level.

These are the kinds of questions this book will explore:

1. In 2020, we saw nearly every issue—including a deadly and indiscriminate virus—politicized, with different groups of people subscribing to vastly different realities. How far will this go, and what can we do to stem the tide? Are these learned behaviors, or something more systemic? Are we doomed to fight these battles every day?

2. Why do so many people seem to vote against their interests? Why do those who live with rural poverty vote against the Affordable Care Act? Why did so many women vote for President Trump, in spite of numerous rape and assault allegations? Why do some affluent citizens vote to raise their own taxes?

3. Why, for various issues, do so many people hold so many opinions that are immutable to reason? Abortion. The death penalty. Border control. Climate change. Why does new information or logic rarely seem to change the public split on these subjects— and how can we hope to bridge that divide?

In the grip of so many concurrent crises, it's getting harder to recognize our once can-do country. When everything is a source of conflict, civil society is paralyzed. How can we get back to a common interest, a common good? The Model of Why will explain what has gone wrong, and what we can do about it.

When, despite polls showing a strong lead for Joe Biden in the 2020 presidential election, Donald Trump performed surprisingly well—including among Black and Latino men—we were forced to admit, as a country, that polls are no longer a reliable predictor of voting behavior. But at PathSight, we weren't surprised. Because demographic data like age, gender, ethnicity, education, income, and location, while useful, have never been the only determinants of human behavior—in the voting booth or anywhere else. The key piece the polls miss is the impact of our *biological instincts*—how people innately feel about concepts like fairness, loyalty, and authority. These instincts are hugely influential in how we decide what's important to us. Social justice, climate change, the economy, and even the workings of democracy itself—our responses to all of these issues can be traced directly back to how our biological instincts shape our beliefs.

CONTEXT IS KING

Importantly, we believe that no single area of science—social, physical, or biological—has all of the answers. Rather, we think that the only way to truly uncover why people do what they do is to borrow from various strands of psychology, including social, clinical, evolutionary, and neuropsychology, as well as the related fields of sociology, economics, anthropology, data science, conflict resolution, and political science. We also seek to transcend the psychology of individual differences. That is, we don't believe a person is simply a collection of traits that can be parsed to suss out their motivations. In fact, we often find that these individual differences—for instance, age, ethnicity, and gender—explicitly do not shed light on the causes of our behavior. There are certainly plenty of companies that mine demographic data for insight on how people will vote, shop, or join. But these insights rarely hold up under scrutiny.

Other models, like Social Identity Theory, suggest there are motivational differences for the individual and social domains of one's identity—that is, the "I" identity and the "We" identity. Social psychologist Campbell Leaper writes, "Social identity theory addresses the ways that social identities affect people's attitudes and behaviors regarding their ingroup and outgroup. . . . Examples include sports teams, religions, nationalities, occupations, sexual orientations, ethnic groups and gender."[3] This sounds simple and straightforward, but it gets complicated quickly.

Let's consider age and its consequences on our ingroup and outgroup status. What does it mean to be a member of the Greatest Generation? A Boomer? What about Gens X, Y, and Z?

How about your sexual identity? The U.S. Census asks us to check Male or Female. But what about transgender, nonbinary, or gender-nonconforming?

Now layer in where you live. Rural, Urban, Suburban, or Exurban.

What about income? Are you poor, working poor, middle class, affluent, or one of the elusive 1 percenters?

When you fill out the census, what box do you check: Caucasian? Black or African American? Hispanic, Latino, or of Spanish Origin? Asian? American Indian? Alaska Native? Native Hawaiian? Or Pacific Islander?

Who do you love? Are you a husband? Wife? What about LGBT or Q? Head of household? Divorced? Remarried? Oh, by the way, are you a parent?

Do you identify as a Democratic voter? Republican? Independent? Christian Conservative? Socialist Democrat? Tea Party? Feminist? Second Amendment loyalist or an advocate for the "Rent Is Too Damn High" party?

Do you carry a stigma or badge of honor? Are you differently abled? Overweight? A New Yorker? A Veteran? Retired? Autistic? Are you on welfare? Mentally ill? Other?

Thus, a seemingly simple idea becomes a monumental challenge to map. Where do you draw your boundaries about what is important and what is inconsequential?

In our Model of Why, the merging of our biological and social attributes gives us a window into why these memberships occur, and how they impact our lives. We are all equipped at birth with certain cards—not just the physical attributes that indelibly mark who we are, but also Instinctual Patterns that influence how we filter and make sense of our life experiences.

To be clear, we don't see this hardwiring as predetermining the direction of one's life, in the way that a knee propels your foot forward when struck by a physician's hammer. That couldn't be further from the truth. But we do think these patterns matter enough that we can predict how a given adult might adapt to life's circumstances and challenges. For example, if you are a thirty-two-year-old white female living in New York, and we know your Instinctual Pattern, we can largely understand why you vote the way you do, buy what you buy, and join certain groups. Likewise, if you are a forty-five-year-old black male living in a suburb of Atlanta, we should be able to do the same thing. The story is never complete, but we believe we've added invaluable insight into one of humanity's most enduring riddles—and, we hope, a tool to help people reconnect in our fragmented world.

THE AGE OF ADHOCRACY

The world is in the throes of transformation. In many ways, humans have come a long way—we've enjoyed great progress and our future is brighter. We have successfully avoided a world war for more than seventy-five years. In the last decade, the world has seen, on average, a ten-year improvement in life expectancy. Worldwide literacy rates have grown from 42 percent in 1960 to 86 percent in 2015. And we are making seismic progress on poverty, as the global middle class expands.

In other ways, and especially in the past few years, we don't feel especially hopeful. We are in the middle of a pandemic that is straining our democracy to its limits, while people are suffering and dying, as well. Our culture has splintered into tribes that don't even pretend to want the same things anymore. And America's original sin, racism, has now come home to roost in the form of mass protests after the death of George Floyd in Minneapolis, Minnesota, at the hands of a white policeman.

As social beings, we react to change at the population level in much the same way we do at the individual level. Over the past hundred years or so, as America has migrated from an industrial economy to a service and knowledge economy, many lives have been disrupted. But busy with two world wars and a depression, there was no time to focus on the stressors of everyday life. In retrospect, Americans' long-simmering discontentment is like the fable of the frog in a warming pot of water. We couldn't have predicted that when the water boiled, the toxicity of today would be the result.

In the early 1960s, a group of enterprising social scientists began to chronicle the decline of American civic life. The trend was steadily downward, and in 2000, Harvard sociologist Robert Putnam made waves with his book *Bowling Alone: The Collapse and Revival of the American Community*.[4] According to Putnam, since 1960 "our stock of social capital, the very fabric of our connections with each other, has plummeted." His reporting showed that membership, or participation, in community organizations has dropped by 58 percent, the occurrence of family dinners has dropped by 43 percent, and every ten minutes we commute reduces all forms of social capital by 10 percent."[5] The result is the resegregation of our neighborhoods, the stratification of the opportunity gap, and a permanent schism between the haves and have-nots. It manifests in virtually every area of modern life: life expectancy, healthcare, education, income, and environment, not to mention a near permanent digital divide.

Tom Friedman, opinion writer for the *New York Times*, coined the phrase "the world is hot, flat, and crowded,"[6] to which he added "connected" to describe the challenges of modern life. To me, that last word—connected—changes everything. As humans, we have always grappled with ingroup and outgroups, but we've never before been connected to 1.3 billion other humans, as we are currently on Facebook, for example. It has changed all of our points of reference, along with our expectations. The original pact that we made as a country—to embrace the "united" in the United States, and the institutions it inspired, doesn't seem so permanent when Twitter and Facebook are the new sources of social identity. And with our carefully tended social media identities, how many of us are willing to abandon the moral high ground in order to compromise with a fellow human being?

Where do we turn to now for a sense of security? By all reports, public opinion of our government, our media, and our politicians is as low as it has ever been. We are living in the Age of Adhocracy—a term coined by organizational consultant Warren Bennis in his 1968 book *The Temporary Society*. It refers to an organizational model characterized by "adaptive, creative, flexible, interpretive behavior based on non-permanence and spontaneity."[7] In our fast-changing, ever-evolving world of information overload, we are aimlessly searching for a new connective tissue to bind us to our country, a rejuvenated set of institutions that deserve our respect, and most important, a shared set of expectations. We must realize that, while the connective wizardry of modern life makes us *feel* like we have the power to control everything, there are now 7,847,855,749 of us out there who expect the same privileges. That means we need to get on the same page—and quick.

That is ultimately why I wrote this book. I believe that great breakthroughs come at the dynamic intersection of data and theory. Naturally, we employ advanced data learning, artificial intelligence schemes, and advanced tool sets that exist today. But in this book we will not be emphasizing this technology phase of our work; instead we focus on the deeper reasons our Model of Why works. Our research has shown that people aren't convinced to alter their behaviors through logic, "likes," or a snappy one-liner. Rather, we have found that the alignment of messaging—words, images, and themes—with triggers that emanate from the nonverbal parts of a person's brain is the most reliable way to break through the deadlock. The whole purpose of the Model of Why is to identify what these triggers are for a given individual, and determine what images and themes will resonate most deeply with them, facilitating connection and, even, occasionally, behavioral change.

In short, we don't need more data to be mined. We just need it to answer the right questions.

WHY ME?

My interest in human motivation goes back to my first job, as a youth worker at the Huntington Family Center in Syracuse, New York. I knew all about the center because my grandmother was one of the people who established it in the middle of one of the poorest neighborhoods in Syracuse.

My grandmother was wise, fair, and compassionate—my first, and most important, role model and teacher. In 1947, after her husband died, my grandmother took a brave and unusual step for women of her generation: She went to Syracuse University and got a degree in Social Work. Around the same time, she met a couple who had emigrated from Germany and wanted to open a settlement house to serve the urban poor. The Huntington Family Center adhered to the ethos of the Progressive Era's settlement movement, bringing support services to poor inner-city families—not just food and necessities, but everything from childcare to healthcare to education to job training. The center served mostly what now would be called marginalized populations: Native Americans, Black Americans, Latinos, and whites living with poverty. It was the perfect place for my grandmother to work, given how much she valued fairness, justice and caring, and I am pleased to report that Huntington Family Center still operates in Syracuse today.

As you might imagine, it wasn't just a nine-to-five job. Throughout my childhood, I watched my grandmother confront social ills on behalf of her whole community: poverty, racism, illiteracy, homelessness, and hunger. She believed that everyone deserved to love and be loved, that everyone needed and wanted to work, and that we should all reasonably expect happiness—or at least satisfaction—from life. When I myself made the journey to Syracuse to study, I kept my grandmother in the loop. No matter how esoteric my schoolwork became, she always reminded me not to forget the lessons of humanity, and never to underestimate the impact that one person can have on another. To this day, those two concepts underpin everything I do.

I thought of my work at Huntington as a quasi-formal training program, where I reviewed protocols with a caseworker before engaging with anyone. We met our clients wherever they were, most often in the street. We did not apply any clinical terms to them, like delinquent or pre-delinquent, no matter what their records showed. By getting to know them, without preconceived ideas or labels, we developed a clear view of each person in their totality and earned their trust in return. Our job was simply to participate in their lives, provide support, and offer genuine care and compassion. Over time, this method produced some real successes.

At the center, I found that I could enter a world that was foreign to me and become a fleeting part of it, without forsaking anything about my own emerging worldview. Somehow, my values and life experiences comingled to guide me through. And I gained confidence in my ability to impact someone else's life. I didn't know anything yet about the formal study of behavioral change; I was working solely by instinct.

This is where the story gets more predictable. I ended up earning a doctorate in psychology, and though the training didn't hugely excite me at the time, it did provide me with a lens through which to process the world. I chose to do my dissertation with a research group building on the early promise of prescriptive therapy, a new approach that had begun tailoring psychotherapy to a client's unique needs. Drawing from a wide range of effective techniques—for instance, talk therapy, somatic therapy, and skill development training, to name just a few—this client-focused approach asked us to determine, "Which patient meeting with which therapist for which treatment would yield which outcomes?"[8] Rather than subscribing to a certain single treatment and believing it to be the panacea for all that ailed a client, this nontraditional, personalized approach appealed to me.

As I learned in graduate school, and in the applied arena over the next ten years, meaningful behavioral change is one of the most complex areas of science. The practice of psychology, executed in a controlled setting, can do remarkable things. But rarely, in the real world, is the setting in any way controlled. As my experience at the Huntington Family Center taught me, the challenges we face often require more than one-to-one input.

This insight came thundering back to me when the mother of all transformations—the Internet—came on the scene. We were all suddenly connected, all the time—and all bets were off. I felt instant déjà vu. It felt like we were entering a new universe without a road map. Shortly thereafter, I left a career in television and returned to my psychology roots, eager to explore full-time how we were going to adapt to this new flat world. With that, my company, PathSight Predictive Science, was born. We were focused on the same question that had driven me since my days at Huntington: Do we know why people do what they do? Can we hope to understand each other's motivations and use that understanding to build a better world, as my grandmother had sought to do in her own work, too?

This book is my attempt to answer these questions. It's imperative, now more than ever, to find common ground.

My objectives for writing this book are as follows:

1. To show why, at a time when culture is fluid and changing by the day and we're experiencing an unprecedented global health and economic crisis, we need new narratives, new messages, and new models to understand human behavior, especially in the disciplines of market research and customer insights. Who's going to tell these future stories? Who's going to enjoy rights and who won't, if we're not careful?

2. To introduce a model for understanding human behavior that helps frame, deeply and holistically, why people do what they do. This has become more and more important as the population has grown; we've become more polarized, and problems are so massive, that global collaboration is required.

3. To address the polarization of our country by showing how we can better communicate with one another and bridge our divides.

4. To teach marketers, activists, writers, and artists (and anyone in need of honing persuasion skills) to craft messages that meet people where they are, with a willingness to listen and respect strongly held beliefs on all sides of an issue.

5. To ensure the foundational model works with existing thinking—implicit and explicit knowledge—but layers and blends in new research and intelligence. The model must grow and build as our culture grows, providing a framework for this work in progress—because this story is not yet finished.

We'll talk theory in these pages, but I am more interested in practice, in everyday situations. I've read the research, surveyed people directly, and helped clients trying to reach new markets or audiences. Throughout it all, I've found the theory-and-practice combo is the ideal way to understand why people do what they do. It was no mistake that my grandmother instilled in me the values I still live by today. At this turning point in history, those values have never been more salient. I invite you to join me on this journey, in the hope that it will not only enrich your work, your life, and your relationships, but also give you new insight into yourself.

• **PART ONE** explains the history of the model and theories explored—everything leading up to our development of the Model of Why at PathSight. *The Search for Why* did not begin in a vacuum. Part One of this book details the context of this pursuit. I had been fascinated by the science of predicting human behavior for many years before my interests were formalized within this search. I have always believed in understanding the characteristics of who we are talking to as a starting point. This portion of our journey explains this context. (Chapters 1–2)

- **PART TWO** explains the Model of Why. I explain the basics of our model and the evolution of the many points of view that we have incorporated into it. (Chapters 3–6)

- **PART THREE** shows how we've put the model into practice, with relevant case studies. We have begun to use this functional model across subsections of many different markets and have collected some noteworthy insights and experiences. We are aware of the enormous potential of our work but do not minimize the complexity of the task. (Chapters 7–8)

- **PART FOUR** shows how you can move beyond conventional thinking to harness this model to change the world. We are at the beginning of being able to appreciate the impact we can have at the personal, social, and population level. As such, we are excited about our trajectory, but mindful of the work required to chip away at the incivility of our culture and the tribalism of our discourse and hasten the return to the optimism of believing in each other once again. (Chapters 9–10)

Let's get started!

CHAPTER 1

WHY ASK WHY?

W hy do we do what we do? Let that question sink in. Over time, the search for an answer has inspired journeys both mundane and profound. Since the dawn of civilization, the greatest thinkers in the world have debated the origins of choice and motivation, and the tug-of-war between reason and emotion.

I'm not sure at what point in my childhood I realized that not everything was knowable. I was also surprised to learn my parents and my teachers didn't have all the answers. But as much as possible, I was determined to understand why people behaved a certain way and why they made the choices they made, both good and bad. How did we decide between "right" and "wrong"? I poured myself into the philosophies of Aristotle, Plato, Locke, Kierkegaard, Confucius, and Kant and explored the scientific theories of Darwin and Einstein. I read Marx, Freud, Thoreau, and even the debates of the Founding Fathers. History proved instructive as I read story after story about wars, peace, civilizations being built and destroyed, from pre-civilization through ancient and medieval times and into modern times. The more I read, the more I appreciated the complexity of human motivation and morality, and I had a strong desire to translate whatever answers I could find into action, even if the pursuit was a work in progress.

There are countless theories and approaches that underpin the fields of psychology, sociology, anthropology, economics, biology, and neuroscience. In the past sixteen years, I've read about many of them in hopes of understanding human behavior. I have sought to synthesize all the information we have—and can act upon—to make sense of our ever-changing world and benefit from its many possibilities. Ultimately, I believe no single discipline owns all of the answers. But I do think we are entering an era of breakthroughs, as we increasingly bring concepts from one discipline into another, to innovate and enhance each other's work. I've embarked on this journey with one eye on the past and studying history and another on the future of humankind, including understanding the impact of great technological changes brought on by data science and, in particular, artificial intelligence, which is getting better at revealing how our minds and emotions work.

Understanding why people do what they do is not a straightforward business. I agree with neurobiologist and primatologist Robert Sapolsky when he says: "If you were interested in the biology of, say, how migrating birds navigate, or in the mating reflex that occurs in female hamsters when they're ovulating, this would be an easier task. But that's not what we're interested in. Instead, it's human behavior, human social behavior, and in many cases abnormal human social behavior. And it is indeed a mess, a subject involving brain chemistry, hormones, sensory cues, prenatal environment, early experience, genes, both biological and cultural evolution, and ecological pressures, among other things."[1] In short—understanding human behavior, is a *complex* endeavor.

There is a significant difference between a *complex* and a *complicated* problem, and we turn to the science of complexity not only to explain the difference, but also to provide a necessary lens in our pursuit of *why*; otherwise, any answers we arrive at are little more than guesses, or extensions of our individual biases. I first learned about complexity science while working with the Institute for Scientific Interchange (ISI), one of the world's foremost data science laboratories, headquartered in Turin, Italy. Since their founding in 1983, the ISI has participated in several of the greatest breakthroughs in data science—chaos theory, quantum computing, and complex networks, to mention a few. They continue to break new ground with their research every day.

In 2014, I was hired as an advisor to help them prepare for the next chapter of their growth. It was very important to them that they preserve their organizational culture during this time of expansion. The ISI was founded on the principle of "curiosity-inspired science"—defined as an interdisciplinary pursuit of the answers to really hard questions, without preconception.

My work with ISI taught me to recognize the balance between data and theory. Inspired by their "borderless attitude," which they assert "allows them to draw an endless arc through time, space, disciplines, and the research domain,"[2] I learned that answers can come from any arena. The institute shares its perspective as follows: "Within the overarching domain of Complexity Science, the ISI Foundation leverages the competing contributions of Data and Theory to avoid the silos of science too prevalent elsewhere. The combination of data, theory and impact is the founding essence of all the ISI research domains."[3] I have often wondered whether striking this balance between data and theory is just a sneaky way to apply self-analysis via the scientific method. If either data or theory wins the battle, we risk losing a little bit of our humanity.

For those of us not steeped in complexity science, it is helpful to learn from the experts how to differentiate between a task that is *complicated* and one that is *complex*. Dr. Mario Rasetti of the ISI has often illustrated the difference with this anecdote: If one were to take all the parts of a Boeing 777 and spread them across a football field, the job of reassembling the plane and its millions of parts would make for a very complicated, difficult (and tedious!) task. But that assembly itself, especially if it came with a user's manual, would not be considered complex. The solution is a linear process. By contrast, predicting the global migration pattern of an infectious disease is a *complex* problem: It requires understanding the intersection of networks (e.g., weather, transportation, wind, disease transmission rates and incubation times) across an extremely large number of variables to create a set of predictions that include time and location as outputs. The contagion rate, whether or not the virus is airborne, and the population of the outburst are all examples of variables that one might consider. Another example of this contrast might be understanding the dynamics of weather (complicated) versus predicting the exact future of weather patterns (complex). Complexity has nothing to do with difficulty. It simply means that a system is driven by many forces and that causality is nearly impossible to prove.

In simple terms, dynamic tension is found between what we expect to be true and what real data say is true. That tension is what guides the pursuit of all knowledge, and no single discipline has a broad enough perspective to fully define all answers to our questions. We must take a multidisciplinary approach to our research in order to truly learn anything.

Sapolsky has something to say about this point, too, when he argues it doesn't make "sense to distinguish between aspects of a behavior that are 'biological' and those that would be described as, say, 'psychological' or 'cultural.' Utterly intertwined."[4] In other words, we must look to biology in understanding human behavior, but not rely on it to give us the full picture.

Another hallmark of complexity is the acknowledgment of incomplete knowledge. That is, we assume that any solution to a complex problem will, in the long run, be wrong, or at least incomplete. As more knowledge is gained, it leads to new insights and a more complete understanding of the problem. Think of it as arriving at successive hills of increasing elevation. Each hill improves your perspective, but none actually supply complete knowledge of the future.

As an example, consider our desire to understand the invisible world of pathogens and their effect on our health. First, determining causality in human biology is a classic *complex* problem because there are many variables to consider in our intricate biological systems. Turns out, building a tool that allows scientists and researchers to observe, at the tiniest level, the world of bacteria, viruses, fungi, and parasites that cause illness is also a complex problem. To understand just how complex, let's go back to about 1590 when Zacharias Janssen[5] and his son Hans created the first microscope using a stack of lenses in a tube. The amplification wasn't great, but it laid the groundwork for future iterations of the microscope, including advances in magnifying power. In 1665, the physicist Robert Hooke used a simple single-lens microscope; he was the first person to identify the construction of a cell. The science began to expand rapidly as microscopists had to learn the limitations of conventional optics, to better understand how light works, and to ultimately develop electromagnetic lenses capable of discerning the individual particles that make up our world. And the world took note. In 1986, the Nobel Prize in Physics was awarded for the scanning tunneling microscope. In 2014, again the Nobel Prize was awarded for a microscope, the super-resolved fluorescence microscope which allows microscopes to "see" matter smaller than 0.2 micrometers.[6] Does anyone think that this journey is at its endpoint? I believe that the complexity of the human interface and consequent behavior is the most complex node on the most complex network ever, it might be wise to prepare for a long journey ahead.

A THREE-PART SYSTEMS APPROACH

Back when I started studying Psychology at Syracuse University, I was confronted by something I hadn't anticipated. After the first few years of general study, the department engaged in the not so subtle process of attaching students to standard philosophical schools of thought with which to guide their next phase of training. Most students naturally gravitated to one philosophical point of view on how best to help people. There were Fritz Perls loyalists for Gestalt Therapy, Carl Rogers loyalists for Client-Centered Therapy, and Albert Ellis loyalists for Rational Emotive Behavior Therapy, and the Freudians were there for Analysis. I didn't realize it at the time, but this was an act of self-classification. Students' decisions were made, in part, by how they felt that these philosophies aligned with their own worldviews. In hindsight, I should have thought of this as a first step in my inquiry into why we do what we do. (For the record, I thought the Analysis model seemed to be the most complete, offering more ways to solve real human problems.) But I did not participate in that process. Instead, I joined a group of colleagues whose goal was to look at treatment as a prescriptive concept. In other words, adapt the therapy treatment to the unique needs and characteristics of an individual patient. It sounds obvious now, but it wasn't then. We were asked to consider the following:

1. **PATIENTS:** What specific characteristics is the patient bringing to their treatment?

2. **TREATMENT:** What treatments would we recommend based on those characteristics?

3. **OUTCOME:** What expectations could we anticipate that might signal success, or at least progress?

When evaluating the success of any treatment, each one of these factors needs to be considered. This focus on the interaction effect of each of these variables certainly helped prepare me for the concept of intersectionality that is reviewed later in this book.

Because of my belief that no single theory could possibly answer all of my questions, my objective was to build an approach where we would evaluate how any foundational theory or model would work with the tools in use at the time. What other models could we learn from and integrate into the model we were building? If we applied a holistic systems model, how well would any other model integrate with ours?

DIGGING INTO THE BUSINESS OF DIGGING

Even with multiple perspectives to explain why people do what they do and an appreciation for the complexity of the endeavor, it's not easy explaining human behavior. First, the challenge for any broad-base theory to supply holistic insights on any topic related to people is the tendency to regress to the situational. It is very difficult to find any trait not qualified by at least some subset of the population. For example, often a theory will we presented as a cure-all for the habits that derail your career. What looks like a universal cure may turn out to be only appropriate for people who think of the world with very clear-cut stimulus-and-reward motivations. Those that don't need not apply. This is not to say that this cure is not effective, just that it does not reflect something that is universal.

FAULTY HEURISTICS OR WHY WE'RE
HARDWIRED TO DELUDE OURSELVES

One area where the research does hold up as a universal trait is in the area of cognitive bias. Extensive research on how people make decisions has proven to address this important but self-contained area of work: People do not always make rational decisions or act in their own best interest, as classical economists have believed. Our cognitive biases, including selective memory, attention limitations, interests, dislikes, etc.—all attempts to simplify information processing—affect our thinking, interpretations, judgments, and decision-making. The Rational Choice Theory assumes, in fact, that people are predictably illogical and incapable of making good decisions. Economist and professor Richard Thaler built upon the work of psychologists Daniel Kahneman and Amos Tversky to launch the science behind the field of Behavioral Economics (I highly recommend his book, written with legal scholar Cass R. Sunstein, *Nudge: Improving Decisions About Health, Wealth, and Happiness*).* It answers

---

*For more on behavioral economics read *Predictably Irrational* by Dan Ariely.

a lot of questions about human economic behavior and goes into depth about the effects of cognitive bias on decision-making, challenging the belief that the market knows best. If we want to make better decisions in our personal lives, we need to be aware of our biases and false reasoning. One example is the negativity bias, where people fear loss more than they appreciate gain, or they focus on negative more than on positive experience. Just think about a time when someone complimented you on a job well done, but then gave you one tiny bit of feedback to help you improve. Guess what you focused on? The negative comment more than the positive one, so next time you perform you may not do so as confidently. In Kahneman's book, *Thinking, Fast and Slow*, he talks of our innate tendency to be risk averse as we are hardwired to "treat threats as more urgent than opportunities,"[7] thereby revealing the crucial link between economics and psychology. Historically, this particular bias has increased our odds of survival, and we've passed those genes along to our descendants so they, too, can win the "survival of the fittest" contest.

Another type of cognitive bias, confabulation, has humans pulling together a justification and rationale for the decisions they make, *after* they've made them, not before. In neuroscientist Michael Gazzaniga's *Who's in Charge?: Free Will and the Science of the Brain*, he writes, "When we set out to explain our actions, they are all post-hoc explanations using post-hoc observations with no access to nonconscious processing. Not only that, but our left brain also fudges things a bit to fit into a makes-sense story."[8] Psychologists would call this an act of inference. These rationales feel totally reasonable to us and so natural it's hard to know it's happening. Gazzaniga may be saying here that we might never know *why* we do the things we do!

In his book *The Moral Animal*, Robert Wright leans on Darwin and his theory of evolution, along with evolutionary psychology, to say the brain's role in forming and expressing opinions is to basically confirm what it already believes. A person's brain will even reject ideas counter to its own, especially when someone is trying to get it to change its mind.[9] Wright argues: "The reason the genetic human arguing style feels so effortless is that, by the time the arguing starts, the work has already been done. The human brain is, in large part, a machine for winning arguments, a machine for convincing others that its owner is right—and thus a machine for convincing its owner of the same thing."[10] Our emotions and values, honed through millions of years of evolution, are there for us, front and center. Bringing this back to Gazzaniga again, "moral reasoning is good for human survival."[11]

So the good news is that cognitive bias is believed to be a universal trait. The bad news is that bias makes it harder to understand people—and we all have the potential to delude ourselves. Cognitive biases cloud our thinking, and when you're trying to understand why people do what they do, thinking they'll act rationally and without bias is not a given. In fact, the opposite is often true. It's common for people to choose options that confirm their beliefs or neatly fit within their already formed worldview instead of seeking views that could challenge their thinking. People also would rather reach consensus than make the time to review multiple options. Smart and thoughtful companies implement practices to mitigate this faulty thinking across the company, including staffing innovation and research teams whose job it is to think differently and take risks, encouraging a free exchange of ideas across departments, and not assuming the status quo is the best or only option.

Another way to help with cognitive bias involves technology. Powerful machines can parse through millions of points of data and detect patterns, identify anomalies, and remain objective, where humans could not. Presumably computers eliminate personal bias and negative associations, are not shaped by natural selection, and don't get overwhelmed by so much information that they can't home in on what's important. It's worth noting, however, that these days, I don't believe machines are completely without bias, because humans built them. But data scientists put measures in place to mitigate this, through more transparency and clear explanation in how data is collected and analyzed, starting with more representative data sets, and employing a more diverse engineering team. Fortunately, computers don't get confused or exhausted by large amounts of data. Unlike humans, their performance doesn't decrease with the amount of data collected or when it experiences time pressure—at least not yet!

Big data is also especially effective at capturing and identifying nuanced differences well beyond broad philosophical foundations. Because the sweep of our individual differences has many more points of data to consider than any philosopher could even begin to imagine, our modern tools serve to extend these philosophical points of view. This doesn't mean the work of philosophers, social scientists, marketers, and market researchers should be forgotten. Quite the opposite, as you'll see in the following pages. Big and small "expert" data work together to make sense of it all—their convergence can help us make better insights. Piles of data are of little value if not turned into key insights on what drives people to do what they do (that eventually inform a marketing strategy or campaign). We were looking for a foundational theory to ground what we already had, to have a seat at the table, as it would help us set the stage for the comprehensive approach we envisioned.

There is a chance that none of the theories above aptly consider the factors that help determine how we form our worldviews. And depending on data science to extract what factors determine our *why* is also not a lock, as much as marketers hoped it would be the magic bullet. Many marketers viewed it as a panacea. Data can be descriptive in identifying a set of circumstances where a result occurs, but it doesn't shed any light on whether those are the *only* times the result appears, if the circumstances *cause* the result to appear, or if the result is simply a random occurrence. We need a foundational theory to explain as best as possible *why* an event occurs. For this reason, we were uncomfortable relying on a data-only approach with no way to define the connective tissue that holds this point of view together. Even today we view data with a healthy skepticism—yes, it can get us closer to the answer, but not 100 percent there.

THE ROLE OF CUSTOMER INSIGHTS AND RESEARCH

Unsurprisingly, a multibillion-dollar industry has sprouted to codify how we define each other. Understanding people's motivations, what they might consider valuable, and how they behave is complicated and can be difficult to pin down, but it's not impossible. Companies like Experian, Equifax, Accenture, Capital One, Nielsen, and myriad new companies that advance similar methods have amplified their power and influence in the marketplace with the emergence of big data and advanced data science modeling. They now seek a competitive edge in advertising, marketing, politics, and product development. Can you imagine a political candidate today who would not be thoroughly analyzed and researched by a host of consulting firms, to ensure their viability and competitive advantage?

Ironically, despite the huge amount of money involved, most of these research techniques and models are not very good at understanding *why* people do what they do. The chart below shows how customer research and observation has evolved over the past one hundred years.

THE EVOLUTION OF HOW WE DESCRIBE PEOPLE	
THE VIEW OF PEOPLE	HOW MESSAGING RESPONDED
Undifferentiated	One voice for everyone
Life Stages	Accommodations were made for age
Gender	Male / Female within traditional roles
Multicultural Differences	Black, Asian, Latino were referenced
Different Attributes	Lifestyle differences by attributes
Big Data Segmentation	Complex profiles are possible

ONE SIZE DOES NOT FIT ALL

The science of marketing and communications began with an undifferentiated, simple, "one size fits all" paradigm because its goal was to understand the mass market. Because the mass market was fairly unified, most models were rooted in the tradition of demographic sorting and included age, gender, and ethnicity. These were the anchors of every segmentation system, even when companies also looked at family size, education, and income. Age, gender, and ethnicity were the key factors when trying to define populations of customers and to influence human behavior toward a preferred outcome.

Consider the Nielsen Company, perhaps the best-known ratings company, which has more than ninety years of experience in describing audiences.[12] Before Nielsen was known for selling its advertising research, it measured audience size and composition for radio, live events, and eventually television programs and digital platforms. The company gave media a "Nielsen rating." In 1965, Nielsen launched a new product called the Station Index Service, which was designed to sell TV time to advertisers in the U.S. Not surprisingly, it was organized around demographics. The first demographic used was age. Total audiences were broken into various age brackets like 18–49, 25–54, and 55 plus. Then the service differentiated between men and women, and ultimately education, ethnicity, and income. This logic was revolutionary at the time and allowed Nielsen to assume a global presence. In 1979 the company developed another product, Scantrack, which gave clients the ability to track specific market trends, produce custom reports, and develop better marketing and distribution plans.

This is as close to ground zero as we will get in the search for why. It wasn't so much curiosity-inspired science as necessary work. When these ratings books were published, the industry expanded to include a whole new service: finding correlates—or connections—that could link an advertising campaign with an audience predisposed to purchase a specific market basket of goods. The "basket of goods" was a standard set of goods, such as a set of groceries, toys, or clothing, that one might purchase in a given market. Marketers would want to know how much media, and what kind of media, was needed to motivate a shopper to buy that particular set of goods. The media was quantified in these ratings books. To be clear, these lists of data tables that show the frequency of a trait in a particular segment of the population, e.g., education, are still a mainstay of the segmentation business. There is a certain simple logic to their permanence, but they don't tell us *why* any of these traits would cause someone to buy a certain product.

These companies and other types of research firms made a lot of money, yet some very complex factors of human motivation never made their way into the matrix. It turns out that the elusive "human factor" cannot actually be captured by a cross-tabulated analysis of age and income. Psychographic segmentation widened the research lens and introduced personality traits, interests, hobbies, attitudes, and other lifestyle factors into the mix. In other words, qualitative data. The work of social scientists was brought in to help marketers group people into segments based on shared worldviews. The internet had made it easier for people to find and engage with like-minded folks who shared their values, goals, interests, and affinities. These hyper-engaged communities and fandoms encouraged members to identify more and more with their tribe, rather than people who were the same age or ethnicity, or who lived in the same neighborhood. (Such levels of personalization have significantly contributed to the current state of polarization we're seeing today. More on that later.) Understanding particular segments—the more narrowly the better—would be useful.

In the last ten years, behavioral segmentation has given companies real-time data on customer actions, path to purchase, and other digital behavior. Still, this additional segmentation has not provided an adequate level of data to answer the question of *why*—necessary to drive communications strategy. Only with the relatively recent advent of big data and complexity science have we begun to push back against the dominance of demographics and all other forms of segmentation. For example, social listening, one type of data analytics, has introduced customer opinions, behaviors, and motivations into the equation, so now we can understand what someone truly feels about a product, topic, brand, or celebrity.

Customers freely give their opinion—no one is shy about it. The challenge with this type of intelligence is identifying which online communities hold the most accurate data. The Model of Why makes room for this kind of data, though, like all easily accessible and public data, it is more valuable considered alongside the dynamic influence of one's worldview, rather than purely on its own merits.

Coincidentally, product marketing and advertising evolved in much the same way—from communicating functional, emotional, and utilitarian consumer needs to expressing the more complex reasons people purchased products, such as satisfying a need to belong or to self-actualize. In the early stages of advertising, ads typically described what a product was or how it was to be used. The virtue of a product was all about its utility or the emotion it evoked—this mouthwash makes me feel attractive, this detergent will help me take care of the house (and my man), or this soup in a can is convenient, inexpensive, and nourishes my family. For example, in 1904, early Coca-Cola ads featured in the *Saturday Evening Post* told us that Coke was "Delicious and Refreshing." One of the brand's longest running slogans—for thirty-four years[13]—the simplicity was brilliant, and an easy sell. Compare this with owning a Cadillac (a Tesla today) or a Leica camera, where the motivation to buy is likely status or pride in using a product viewed as "for rich people," "cool," "eco-conscious," or one a famous person uses. Again, to tap into higher-order values, marketers and advertisers looked to the rigor of the social sciences to provide insights about segments they could target with different messaging.

There was an attempt to use gender as a differentiator in the 1960s. Products were touted as having the attributes of a man (e.g., "How do you handle a hungry man? The Manhandlers") or a woman (e.g., "You've come a long way, baby. Virginia Slims"). Of course, gendered ads did not represent a serious study in identity. Products and their messaging could be perceived to be stereotypically male (sports, cars, beer, male hygiene) or female (fashion, makeup, romantic comedies) within patently mainstream themes. It was only much later that there was any empathy paid to the true nuances of femininity or masculinity (and even then, a far cry from today's sexuality and gender-identity spectrum). It was an era of hints and naughty sexuality, but only between a man and a woman, who were usually of the same race.

Once the industry began to pay attention to life stages, the notion of motivations became more important. Yet it was still largely one-dimensional. Customer profiles, voter profiles, job applicant profiles all still began with age, gender, and race. All discussions of intent were linked to demographic predictions. But when it came to the most important questions, the data fell flat. Does mental illness abide by the taxonomy of demographics? How about the traits of loyalty or compassion or fairness? Does knowing one's race let you predict who is empathic? When a public relations executive, advertiser, politician, or cause or movement organizer sits down to define the ideal person that they wish to reach, it typically even now starts with one of these descriptors. Millennial? Boomer? Income or Education? Black American? Latinx? We have to do better than this. How can we create a vision of people that acknowledges the realities of demographics but is not bound by them either?

BRINGING IT ALL TOGETHER

Understanding why people do what they do is an all-hands-on-deck endeavor. This is a complex problem we're solving, and we'll need to use all the tools we have to examine the problem from all sides until we get to the real story. It's how we'll build a sophisticated model that is flexible enough to take on new perspectives and more data as technology enhances our capabilities. Even today, while some capabilities are relatively new, they draw on longstanding histories of consumer insights and market research work. Human insight is not a single-source product.

We've seen that there are many ways to gain insight into why humans behave the way they do. To date, most significant breakthroughs in our understanding of how people function in the world and engage with others have come from the world of academic research. Our discussion of cognitive bias above, for example, gave us a taste of how our minds work when we're making decisions. Theorists who study evolutionary and cognitive development or behavior change are especially instructive. Many of us are at least somewhat familiar with scientific theories that have been proven over time—Pavlov's classical conditioning, Piaget's cognitive development in children, Darwin's theory of evolution. These theories have made it out of the labs and into our lives, in various ways. But they were years in the making. First, they were subject to rigorous methods of investigation, data collection, analysis, testing, and refinement in controlled scenarios. Then they were put to the test, again, in real world applications. Finally, only after systematic experimentation, the commercial marketplace deployed these breakthroughs.

It's common today to see references to Darwin's "survival of the fittest" in business and in advertising. It's now understood that children are not mini adults, as they were thought of before Piaget's theories challenged that notion. Clinicians, educators, and parents are all aware that the brains of young people develop in key stages on the way to adulthood and autonomy. And, of course, as consumers, many of us are just as conditioned as Pavlov's dog. Black Friday, anyone?

These scientists, and many others, provided foundational new theories for understanding human behavior that have shaped the potential for what we can know in our pursuit to understand human behavior today. The field of behavioral change continues to be one of the most complex areas of study for understanding why we behave the way we do, and how we can change our behaviors. And the recent advances of big data and complexity science can help us recognize the true scope of what is possible. We might track multitudes of pathways to attract different types of people by using different analytical starting points. For example, consider a product being sold to homeowners.

- For some, the overarching need is to be responsible when caring for your home. If something is broken, you fix it. You have to keep a rainy-day account to pay for things.

- Others are more motivated making sure they have a reasonable budget on which to live on. A house is just one of many expenses.

- These two motivations can also exist simultaneously in the same person.

- Likewise, we can conceive of a range of people who want the product but prefer different sales experiences, media mixes, or campaign messaging.

However, the process of understanding human behavior and thinking about how to affect behavioral change is a humbling and frustrating endeavor, in part because people are very quick to deny the complexity of the pursuit; they seek to boil it down to simple causes and effects by narrowing the scope of inquiry. For instance, the original market basket analysis model promised to deliver on a very complex behavioral outcome with a very straightforward approach: A schedule of thirty-second television advertisements and print newspaper ads was determined sufficient to increase sales of a certain shoe in the Cleveland market. If shoe sales went up, the media mix was deemed correct. The market basket analysis model is the most common model used to determine the products that customers regularly purchase together—think of the mix of products in a shopping cart—so as to predict future sales. Some frequently purchased products go hand in hand ("Would you like fries with that sandwich?"). Others aren't quite so obvious: diapers and beer?[14]

With today's multiplicity of media, however, the customer embarks on different pathways to purchase. The customer journey has ceased to follow a linear path, so now marketers need to develop more sophisticated tools to predict what a customer might do. The new media schedule might be spread across websites, social media, and traditional media. Often the outcome, such as sale of a product, and the sequence of behavior that leads up to the sale are different from market basket analysis. As such, we might be convinced that this is a better measure of the target's buying behavior. Likes, recommendations, and button pushes typically make the sequential steps easier to quantify with digital analytics. In this case, the big data analytics lower the bar of success by offering button pushes as a proxy for sales.

These are all examples of *how* media is used to facilitate sales. They are still not examples of *why* we do what we do.

In 2007, Simon Sinek, a former advertising executive turned author and motivational speaker, gave an influential TED Talk about why people buy things. His clear-eyed observation was that people don't buy things because of *what* the products are, or even *how* they are made. Rather, consumers gravitate toward goods and brands because of *why* they are made.[15] According to Sinek, most people/organizations/companies "know *what* they are doing. Some know *how* they do it. But only the most successful know *why* they are doing it."

These are the leaders in the marketplace, distinguished by their ability to inspire. Consider Apple. Sinek explains how Apple's mission has always been to "challenge the status quo, to think differently, to make great products that are user-friendly." That is *why* Apple exists, *why* its products are continually superior, and *why* consumers remain loyal to the brand. The most loyal Apple customers will buy virtually any product Apple puts out—even a slightly different version of a phone they already own. The same applies to causes, movements, and other leaders in different spheres of influence, like Martin Luther King, Jr., or the Wright Brothers. Causes, inventions, and creations are palpably inspirational when they are founded on a clear purpose or belief—a *why*.

CHAPTER 2

LAYING THE FOUNDATION: BIOLOGIC INSTINCTS

W hen we truly understand why people do what they do and the life experiences that have brought them to that point, we might be more empathetic toward them, feel less threatened by them, and be better able to work together to find shared dreams and achieve common goals.

Our understanding of others will come from a confluence of places. It will arise from an awareness of how they see the world, how they see themselves in the world, an anticipation of how they will react to the world, and an understanding of how they judge the world. Knowing why they do what they do will enable us not just to influence certain behaviors (buying, joining, voting), but also to communicate more effectively, with civility, empathy, and compassion. When we speak to others in a language that they can hear and *understand*, we have the beginnings of dialogue—and positive change.

I worked in television and media for years, at Spelling Entertainment and Carsey-Werner. My work included overseeing research and marketing services. At the time, I thought we could do a fine job marketing, for example, the release of a show to its intended core audience, but the lack of a generalizing effect, or appeal, to a broader population confused me. I wondered why we had not tapped into any universal truths that would allow us to reach a broader swath of people; why we were not drawing on any more foundational models for understanding human behavior. At the time, it felt like we were building a custom software program for every show we launched—ultimately successful, but very expensive and time-consuming.

As I worked to apply the lessons I had learned, I realized that even without overarching universal truths or an overarching theory to ground our work, we needed to direct our work differently. I quickly learned the value of knowing exactly whom we were talking to in the television marketplace and speaking to them directly.

We built some creative campaigns for award-winning, critically acclaimed television shows in the 1990s, like *Judge Judy*, *3rd Rock from the Sun*, and *That '70s Show*. In syndication, we were charged with repurposing the off-network shows and building a whole new audience for the first-run shows. Our goal was to reach new audiences with messages that were directly attuned to them, in order to engage them and gain their viewership.

Judge Judy is one of the all-time leading shows in syndication, a courtroom program in which judge Judy Sheindlin presides over real-life small claims disputes with a no-holds-barred approach that is smart, irreverent, and authentic. In 1996, at a time when the television audience was already fragmenting, we were asked to deliver an audience for a show that featured an unknown family court judge from New York. Success meant pulling together enough of an audience to break out in the first twelve weeks of the first season. We decided to go after a hybrid audience of general market adult women, as they were called by the industry (read: Caucasian) and Black Americans, the logic being that daytime audiences were largely dominated by women; and Black Americans, on average, consumed 50 percent more television than other audiences.

At that time, the network ratings for the general market and Black Americans only had two crossover elements: the NFL and *60 Minutes*.[1] We did our due diligence, searching for reasons why these particular audiences might care about *Judge Judy*—a tall order, on its face. We found that the general market audience was most interested in the fact that Judge Judy was a real judge, and that these were real cases. So our marketing campaign focused on the tagline "Real People. Real Cases. Real Judge at 4 o'clock."

When we marketed the show to Black American households, though, we found them to be most interested in the fact that there would be a conflict and a resolution. With this in mind, we invited them to join *Judge Judy* with the message: "Got a Grudge? Take it to the Judge. The gavel drops at 4 o'clock." When the show debuted, it appealed to those in Black American households by 100 percent more than the audience of the show it replaced and went on to begin a twenty-five-year run of success. We chalked this up to great talent, specifically Judy Sheindlin and a talented creative team to make a show worth watching, and *the power of knowing to whom you are speaking*. It is interesting to note that we were able to accomplish this with the minimal data readily available to us, in contrast to today's data troves, which make parsing audiences much easier.

Another show from which we tried to uncover some kind of generalized insight was *3rd Rock from the Sun*, a number one show on NBC. It was a critically acclaimed, award-winning, and decidedly odd sitcom about an alien expedition that landed on earth, with aliens and earthlings sharing life experiences and grappling together with some controversial topics. When that show went into syndication, it had great expectations, but it did not perform well in markets with a high rate of Black American viewers. We did a study to test whether or not it mattered who did the inviting. Did it matter who promoted the show? If we created promos that reflected Black American sensibilities would there be an increase in viewership?

To wit, we constructed a double-blind study that matched stations with the same lineup of shows in the same daypart—or time segment purchased for the airing of television shows, commercials, and radio spots—and we created two types of promos. One had a quirky general-market theme, which played off the show's general story line. The Black American version played off culturally relevant, audience-tested radio ads, posters, flyers, and postcards. Our partner, MEE Productions, suggested we feature a melody from Parliament's "P. Funk (Wants to Get Funked Up)" and use the slogan "Make My Rock the 3rd Rock" in our radio ads. When the promos were tested in the matched markets, the culturally relevant campaign showed an increase in viewership. Later, when those promos were switched to the generic campaign, viewership receded back to the previous ratios. We did not think this was a great universal trait, but rather another version of the value of "knowing your customers" and speaking to them in ways that might capture their attention, using cultural references that would likely resonate with them.

One last example of my early efforts in trying to understand how people respond to the ways in which information is delivered to them was when we brought *That '70s Show* to market. *That '70s Show* was not a great hit to start out; it had been ranked seventy-fifth in network television by virtue of being on the Fox Network. At that time Fox was breaking through as a network and did not have the benefit of the powerful network affiliates of NBC, CBS, and ABC.

Interestingly enough, though, after we rolled out an integrated, multi-platform campaign aimed at attracting the target audience of eighteen- to thirty-four-year-old men, first and foremost, but inviting all audiences online to experience several layers of interaction, 1.2 million people visited the website in just six weeks. This was in 2001, the early years of internet marketing and at the time not common practice. Using a multi-platform distribution system—broadcast and cable TV, online and direct response, print, radio, narrowcast, grassroots, and PR—with several contextually relevant entertainment points—including a seventies nostalgia translator and an online sweepstakes—coordinated over time, we reached a much wider and more engaged audience. In its first two weeks of syndication, the show was ranked number one in syndication and had a 4.1 Nielsen rating. Thus our initial search proved that inviting people to your show is helpful, promoting it in culturally relevant ways is crucial, and delivering it via the media they prefer is the coup de grâce.

In 2001, while I was at Carsey-Werner, in an attempt to understand this new market, we began a digital experiment that was way ahead of its time and that turned out to be prescient. We took outtakes from filming and even table reads of comedy productions (e.g., *The Cosby Show*, *Roseanne*, *3rd Rock from the Sun*, *Grace Under Fire*, *That '70s Show*), and after capturing clips, we aired them on high-traffic websites and other portals, adding a commercial on the front and back for revenue. In 2001, we generated a million dollars in revenue. Please remember, back then less than 25 percent of the country had access to broadband modems. The lessons about the transformation of consumers—where they were going and what they were open to—was powerful.

—

While I felt we had used the tools available to us in television to make insightful decisions on how to serve content to people in ways that had deeper resonance, I also knew there was a deeper layer of understanding that our existing methods weren't reaching. In 2014, I founded PathSight Predictive Science with a mission to interpret and predict the behavior of our clients' core audiences so that we could help our clients improve communication and increase efficiency. My goal was to bring together all I had learned in a career of media and marketing industries research with the new possibilities of complexity science in an era of big data. But I also wanted to find those foundational areas of research that could connect the work of each project to those deeper universal truths. As I looked for additional methods in my search for why, I became increasingly fascinated by the work of social psychology in the field of moral development.

Jonathan Haidt published his influential book *The Righteous Mind: Why Good People Are Divided by Politics and Religion*[2] in 2014, the same year I founded PathSight. In the book, Haidt synthesizes key research in the development of the field of moral psychology. One section of the book details his and Craig Joseph's Moral Foundations Theory. Drawing on the work of Richard Shweder and Alan Fiske, as well as researchers like Robert Trivers, Muzafar Sherif, and Mark Schaller, Moral Foundations Theory (MFT) posits that much of human behavior is the result of five foundational instincts, which vary in strength from person to person (and sometimes from culture to culture). They are Care/Harm, Fairness/Reciprocity, Loyalty/Betrayal, Authority/Subversion, and Purity/Degradation.[3]

I still remember my reaction on first reading the book. We were building our new approach to research at PathSight, and the field of moral psychology outlined in the book had exposed me to what felt like the foundational layer missing from typical consumer and market research practices. I wanted to explore it more, see what more it could deliver. While I had occasionally seen moral psychology referenced by research in professions like political strategy, such research rarely made its way into the hands of the applied researchers shaping so many types of influential communication. Cutting-edge academic fields are often not translated to the real world in a way that promotes seamless adoption by practitioners. And the even greater challenge seemed to me that utilizing the insights of moral psychology would require professional communication researchers to take a risk, and to admit that some of the old ways of doing things weren't working.

I wondered if we might start by drawing on the exciting findings in the field of moral psychology to illuminate and expand on our search for why. They did seem to have the breadth to anchor many of the questions we were pondering. The field also blended well with the theories and tactics that we knew had served behavior change specialists well in the past. Moral psychology could add a broader perspective to the latest in segmentation research. In practice, if people were grappling with how to infuse the values of their worldviews with a moral basis, we surmised that these universal truths might impact even the most basic of everyday life choices. This point of view might offset the current tendency for data science to dominate the complexity of why we do what we do, by giving a voice to humanity regarding the real world. Remember, a strong blend of data science *and* theoretical points of view is where the "ahas" are found.

As PathSight grew, we drew on the field of moral psychology to both explore ways in which it could anchor our work and to measure how our work might impact the field of market research and marketing communications. We also drew upon Moral Foundation Theory categories[4] to see if there were broader uses for them out in the culture, beyond those implied by moral reasoning—the thought process for how one determines right and wrong. And does that reasoning apply to purchasing decisions, too? Think of a parishioner of the United Church of Christ, known to be a very liberal church, in which congregants highly value fairness and compassion. Do those same values extend to their decision-making processes when looking to purchase a new car? Through our work, we have sought to explore whether there are relationships between the way we approach our moral decisions and our lifestyle choices, the news that we ingest, and the transactional decisions we make.

Building on work from the field of moral psychology, we were convinced we'd see lots of opportunities emerge to help in our search for why, and that is exactly what happened. We have organized this work into a model that has detected how these five foundational instincts are distributed within five Instinctual Patterns. This provides us with a means to understand how people see the world and how the world reacts to them. We believe this model will help to understand how populations, companies, and people in general understand one another in a deeper and more profound way. This process of applying one's instincts and instinctual patterns across the following three layers of focus will drive our inquiry throughout the remainder of this book:

1. **PERSONAL.** What are the building blocks of these Instinctual Patterns, and how do they influence our worldviews?

2. **THE SOCIAL ECOSYSTEM.** While we live in groups and associate across very diverse realities, how do we gain insights for ourselves and others?

3. **POPULATION.** If we can map the national and global distribution of our worldviews, what can we learn about

the opportunities before us as a society—or how to solve the problems that affect us all?

Before we go into the work of PathSight, though, let's review more from the field of moral psychology, and Haidt and Joseph's Moral Foundations Theory, in particular. I'll integrate aligned insights from my work as we go along.

I have worked in the fields of psychology, data, and media. Each has revealed a different, invaluable perspective on life. Psychology provided a basis for understanding myself and others. Data added a feeling of being able to predict what was possible. Media instilled a sense of the world as interconnected. Sure, traditional ways of gathering information about consumer needs and preferences—including demographic and the broader set of psychographic data such as education or income level, hobbies, and interests—provide some measure of variety, new inputs, and increased accuracy. Just not enough. When I discovered the field of moral psychology, it felt like a true, holistic starting point for how we might organize our understanding of the world, a strong counter to the report cards of data we were being fed.

With the Moral Foundations Theory, Haidt and Joseph introduce the concept of five foundational influences, rooted in human biology and evolution. They posit that these foundations are integral to the formation of our worldviews and our cultural and personal identities.[5] For a thorough understanding of the theory and the work surrounding it, you should read *The Righteous Mind*. I suspect you will find it as transformational as I did. However, here I will provide a quick overview of MFT, enough to give you what you need to understand how it relates to the argument put forward in this book and the work we have done at PathSight.

There is a popular meme in evolutionary biology that you may have heard: "You can take people out of the Stone Age, but you can't take the Stone Age out of people." Is it true that our current behavior is influenced, or controlled, by our primitive selves? Well, to avoid rehashing the voluminous research record on this topic across dozens of disciplines—for example, Darwin's natural history or E. O. Wilson's biogeography—suffice it to say that science is moving toward a more integrated model, rather than the nature versus nurture debate that held sway for so long.

At PathSight, we acknowledge that there are both universal human traits *and* a full array of individual differences that influence how we, as people, turn out. The key is to understand the interaction *between* nature and nurture for any particular behavior or trait. As you might imagine, the number of combinations influencing a trait or behavior is myriad. So, while it's possible that "remnant DNA" from our primitive past plays a part in our motivations, it is difficult to prove its direct impact on any specific behavior.

According to Merriam-Webster, instincts are the largely inheritable and unalterable tendencies of an organism to have a complex and specific response to environmental stimuli without involving reason—in other words, an automatic response. The so-called fight-or-flight reflex is the classic example for good reason, since for a trait or intuition to be considered an instinct, there must be an observable link to an improved chance of survival. But most instincts have a much more nuanced impact on our behaviors, harder to separate from environmental factors.

The Moral Foundations Theory, according to Haidt, was created "to understand why morality varies so much across cultures, yet still shows so many similarities and recurrent themes. In brief, the theory proposes that several innate and universally available psychological systems are the foundations of 'intuitive ethics.' Each culture then constructs virtues, narratives, and institutions on top of these foundations, thereby creating the unique moralities we see around the world and conflicting within nations, too."[6] The foundations that Haidt and Joseph outline are as follows:

- Care (Care/Harm)
- Fairness (Fairness/Cheating)
- Loyalty (Loyalty/Betrayal)
- Authority (Authority/Subversion)
- Purity (Purity/Degradation)

CARE   FAIRNESS LOYALTY PURITY* AUTHORITY

* Purity is also referred to as sanctity / degradation.

What makes this theory so interesting is that it incorporates both our instinctual starting points and the influence of real-world experiences on how those instincts are expressed. In it, Haidt draws on the work of Gary Marcus, who writes about the mind as if it were the manuscript of a book: "Nature provides a first draft, which experience then revises. . . . 'Built-in' does not mean unmalleable; it means 'organized in advance of experience.'"[7] Haidt and his colleagues further summarize that genes provide the "first draft" from the fetal stage into childhood, and then the experience of life during childhood (and even adulthood) acts as the continuing revisions to that draft.[8]

As I work on this book, that metaphor seems particularly apt. Our search for why begins with a first draft, written into the neural tissue. The instincts are not hardwired or determinative. Rather, they *influence* how we engage with the world.

The **Care/Harm instinct** originated in response to our need to protect and nurture children. When our ancestors moved off the plains and started living in groups, the suffering of children—sickness, hunger, threat, neglect, poverty— aroused those with a heightened instinct on the Care/Harm index to respond. If they were successful, more children would survive and become viable members of the group. Thus, the group would succeed. A larger, more viable group yields improved odds of survival for everyone. Thus, we all have this instinct in our profile, but it varies in strength and potency from person to person.

Over the millennia, this process has evolved, but it is still rooted in those original triggers. As Haidt explains in *The Righteous Mind*, your Care/Harm instinct can be aroused by the sight of toys and cherished childhood items, photos, or even images of helpless animals, like baby seals.[9] The emotional responses might be characterized as compassionate, protective, or nurturing—we all have the capacity to care for others and feel their pain and joy. These responses may also spark anger toward a perpetrator of harm. As such, this instinct is one of the most frequently targeted by marketing forces. Consider the triggering imagery used by charitable outreach campaigns, pet adoption sites, and pediatric cancer foundations. PETA's "Do unto others as you would have them do unto you"; American Heart Association's "Healthy for Good"; Save the Children's "No mother should have to watch her children starve."

The **Fairness/Cheating instinct** answers the adaptive challenge of reciprocity in relationships (versus going it alone). If there is a mutual benefit to an individual relationship, it leads to more efficient and effective functioning of the larger group as a whole. The original triggers were likely rooted in cheating, deception, and inequitable outcomes of these behaviors, hence introducing the ideas of justice, individual rights, freedom, and autonomy. A modern trigger might be marital infidelity. When we experience these kinds of situations, the response is often anger and resentment if we are the victim of a triggering act, or gratitude and appreciation if we are the beneficiary of mutual respect.

The **Loyalty/Betrayal instinct** functions to encourage us to form cohesive coalitions. The "us vs. them" dynamic originates here, with triggers based on perceived threats to the group. The instinct to identify with one's group of origin has plenty of modern equivalents, of course. Loyalty to one's country, sorority/fraternity, sports team, religion, or family is an example of something that might motivate this response, as is self-sacrifice for the group.

The urge to align with ideas of hierarchical order is reflected in the **Authority instinct**. The ability to make and sustain relationships within hierarchies goes a long way toward creating smoothly operating groups. Those for whom this instinct is strongest have total comfort within the natural order of leaders and followers, or winners and losers. In early times, the triggers would have been signs of high and low rank, whereas today they manifest between bosses and employees, politicians and constituents, etc. The emotion engendered is respect for power, expressed via deference to the boss and obedience to the rules.

Purity/Degradation is an instinct that evolved from the imperative to avoid disease. At its core, it's a cleanliness instinct. The original triggers were food that might be contaminated, waste products, and visibly diseased people. Today, this instinct is triggered by such things as immigration, sexual practices that are seen as deviant, and things that generate a sense of disgust. Deeming things "not natural" makes them potentially subject to forms of disgust or derision. Those for whom this instinct is strongest tend to value temperance, piety, and the general idea of cleanliness.

—

The field of moral psychology supplies a cogent and extremely useful view of morality: as not absolute, but dynamic. With this book, my goal is to build upon these truths, using everything we know about motivations and behavioral change to prepare for the demands of a connected age, fueled by the speed of technology. Our situations may shift, but we can rely on our Stone Age instincts to sort them out. Within the Moral Foundations Theory offered by Haidt, Joseph, and their fellow researchers, there's a process to filtering these inputs.[10]

1. **NATIVISM:** There is a "first draft" of the moral mind, organized in advance of experience.
2. **CULTURAL LEARNING:** The first draft gets edited during development within a particular culture.
3. **INTUITIONISM:** Intuitions come first, strategic reasoning second.
4. **PLURALISM:** There are many recurrent social challenges, so there are many moral foundations.

In short, the evolution of our morality is not simply a question of right and wrong. It extends to our worldview, which considers things like motivation: the reasons *why* we vote, join, buy, love. How does our sense of fairness in relationships—e.g., how we care for the vulnerable—influence what car we buy? Or the groups we prefer socially? Or the shampoo or smartphone we choose?

Morality is complex, and can offer competing explanations for the same behaviors. For instance, great philosophers might infer that an individual man is moral because he acts in a certain way, constrained by common values or traits such as honor or loyalty. Others, however, will favor more collective explanations, such as "Morality-as-Cooperation,"[11] which suggests that morality arises from the mutual benefits of cooperation across humanity. They will consider different types of cooperation, such as family support, mutual advantage, and conflict resolution, and their sources, such as family values, reciprocity, bravery, and respect, to name a few.

First, as we proceed, we need to understand the context within which these instincts operate. For starters, they are biologically transmitted. At their core, these are not learned or socialized points of view. In the following chapters you'll see how this model also accounts for things such as socialization. Instincts and the complex behaviors they trigger are closely entwined. The relationship between individual instincts and the traditional demographics of age, gender, and ethnicity is quite weak. If one *only* knew a person's age, gender, or ethnicity, it would be difficult to predict with any degree of certainty the pattern of instincts that person would possess. What we believe is that these foundational instincts shape how we think about things like one's cultural, lifestyle, and age/life stage, as well as the gender and ethnicity markers through which one's individual identity is formed. Most models in the segmentation world start with, and give precedence to, age, gender, and ethnicity—the three legs of their stools. But, at Path-Sight, we believe that you have to know more than that. In fact, the comingling of one's instinctual patterns with the traits of age, gender and ethnicity results in how you evolve and understand the reality of your worldview. It is not imposed upon you, it evolves.

These instincts surface in both the social and physical sciences. Their effect on our actual personalities and values depends on where their impact is coded by the brain. For example, in 2011, a study by Gary J. Lewis and Timothy C. Bates using fMRI technology demonstrated that there are two different dimensions of moral values, associated with different parts of the brain. "The two clusters of moral values assessed were 'individualizing' (values of harm/care and fairness), and 'binding' (deference to authority, in-group loyalty, and purity/sanctity),"[12] Lewis and Bates write. Meanwhile, a 2011 study by Allison Lehner Eden found specific evidence that suggested "that moral content activates distinct neural areas based on moral relevance. In line with past moral neuroscientific findings, morally relevant content versus morally irrelevant content activated a 'moral judgment' network in the brain."[13] This research implies that the processing of moral judgments, as opposed to other general neural activity, is functionally accounted for by the brain.

Luckily, you don't need to be a neuroscientist to understand some functional details about our brains and our instincts. We are constantly learning more about how the brain works. The limbic system is a prime example. First identified in 1939 as an area of the nonverbal midbrain solely responsible for managing our emotions, it is now understood to be a complex system that includes areas like the amygdala, the hippocampus, the thalamus, the hypothalamus, and the fornix.[14]

We have long known that the limbic system catalogues our emotional reactions, including moral judgments. Recent research has shown that this cataloguing is not just for the purpose of sorting our memories, but also for predicting what might happen next. A recent paper by neuroscientist, psychologist, and author Lisa Feldman Barrett makes this clear and direct: "The unique contribution of our paper is to show that limbic tissue, because of its structure and the way the neurons are organized, is predicting. It is directing the predictions to everywhere else in the cortex, and that makes it very powerful."[15]

As Joe O'Connell writes in the online publication *News@Northeastern*, "In recent years, scientists have discovered the human brain works on predictions, contrary to the previously accepted theory that it reacts to the sensations it picks up from the outside world. Experts say humans' reactions are in fact the body adjusting to predictions the brain is making based on the state of our body the last time it was in a similar situation."[16] This reflex is instinctual, and immediate.

Barrett shows that your brain is not wired to be blindly reactive. It's wired to ask, the last time I was in a situation like this, what sensations did I encounter, and how did I act? "What your brain is trying to do is guess what the sensations mean and what's causing the sensations so it can figure out what to do about them," Barrett says. "Your brain is trying to put together thoughts, feelings, and perceptions so they arrive as needed, not a second afterwards."[17]

We also know that from birth to five years of age, the structures of the brain are being constructed and are evolving. The imprint of these five foundational instincts at the core of MFT begins in childhood. Think of the words, images, and themes that dominate our toddlers' lives. They start with the family, then preschool teachers and classmates. By the time they enter kindergarten, our kids have a robust set of ways to organize their perceptions and interactions. Think of these emerging experiences as the start of a lifelong feedback loop answering the question: "How does the world react to me and my instinctual point of view?" They are the earliest example of experience editing our mind's "first draft." This dynamic interplay continues throughout our lives.

This brings us back to the difference between an instinctual point of view and a demographic one. Typical psychometric testing that often measures peoples' values, affinities, and aptitudes does not go deep—it merely mines the stories we tell ourselves, that we've developed through the continual editing of our "first draft"—the interplay we have described above. These "self-narratives" become our personalities, and our values are heavily biased by our aspirations: Who do we

want to be? How do we present ourselves to the world? When we are asked probing questions, these biases—how we wish to be perceived by others—influence
our answers. It's only when we understand someone's instinctual foundations
that we can see through that veneer, to the less-sanitized version. We get a clearer
picture of who they are and what their intentions might be.

So how are our worldviews influenced by these instinctual foundations?
And how can we use this knowledge to engage more effectively with others?
One route is considering how images, themes, settings, and words appeal to
particular instincts. In 2009, Jesse Graham, Jonathan Haidt, and Brian A.
Nosek created a "Moral Foundations Dictionary"[18] for the research community, organized by virtue and vice. Here are examples of the seed words used for
each foundation.[19]

FOUNDATIONAL SEED WORDS PER MORAL FOUNDATIONS DICTIONARY					
	CARE	FAIRNESS	LOYALTY	AUTHORITY	SANCTITY
VIRTUE	Kindness Compassion Nurture Empathy	Fairness Equality Justice Rights	Loyal Team Player Patriot Fidelity	Authority Obey Respect Tradition	Purity Sanctity Sacred Wholesome
VICE	Suffer Cruel Hurt Harm	Cheat Fraud Unfair Injustice	Betray Treason Disloyal Traitor	Subversion Disobey Disrespect Chaos	Impurity Depravity Degradation Unnatural

Jeremy Frimer, "Moral Foundations Dictionary 2.0," OSF (OSF, April 11, 2019), https://osf.io/ezn37/.

But tone and context can likewise trigger instinctual responses. Consider a
news anchor charged with delivering an important news story. If their delivery is
fast-paced, with an amplified tone and uneven tempo, they may overwhelm the
copy and contribute to the anxiety they are trying to quell. On the other hand,
an evenly paced, sonorous voice, speaking with self-assurance, can enhance even
a poor narrative. Our research suggests that the literal words we use to influence
people are often overrated as a variable.

In 2016 and 2020, the electorate was offered a stark choice between candidates who personified these instincts, which is why they inflamed our passions
so effectively. Donald Trump appealed to those who deeply valued authority and

loyalty; Joe Biden emphasized fairness and our need to care for all Americans. The 2018 midterms, on the other hand, were almost entirely about policy. Without Trump (or Biden) on the ticket, there were no triggering slogans or media caricatures—and the outcome was much less surprising to the political class.

—

This chapter was meant to summarize some of the key concepts within contemporary moral psychology that have been instrumental to the research approach I've taken in building PathSight's Model of Why in the past few years. As we proceed, we will refer back to this moral psychology research as a foundation for a deeper understanding of why we all do what we do. As we identify some of the most-common patterns of moral instincts and share findings from our work to identify them in people, it will not only provide a deeper understanding of the "why" behind people's decision-making, but it will also demonstrate the power of connecting these Meta Worldviews to what data are more traditionally used in applied communication research, such as age, gender, ethnicity, income, affinities, and purchasing behavior. What results is a model that provides rich, complex ways of understanding how people make decisions through connecting insights from such groundbreaking research into why people do what they do, as well as all of the big data available to us in our digital age. As we do so, we will also seek to understand how our decisions and loyalties are impacted by advertising, communications campaigns, and the media. Finally, we will suggest insights into how we might see our way forward into the world of tribalism, failing institutions, and a new perspective on the choices we can make to continue to thrive.

CHAPTER 3

BUILDING THE MODEL: THE FIVE META WORLDVIEWS

Before I began researching the field of moral psychology and applied its thinking to our PathSight model, my work used a variety of tools to impact people. My first mission was always to define the target audience, so we could best determine the optimal message for that audience. In each research project we'd use the variables of age/life stage, gender, and ethnicity as base markers for each population, then we'd analyze which media platforms were best suited to reach that audience. It was a conventional marketing approach, albeit backed by a sophisticated data model. Today, we use these same variables, but filter them all through the rich lens of instinctual foundations, inspired by Haidt and Joseph's MFT framework. This layered approach allows us to design very powerful, specific marketing campaigns and communications.

Our first step toward adding this moral psychology approach to our model was a survey we sent to more than a thousand people, which sought to explore how the core MFT instinctual categories connected to fundamental aspects of U.S. culture. We asked a sample of random questions, on topics ranging from entertainment to health to education to politics to finances to sports to business to family and relationships. We saw enough confirmation of our suspicion that these instincts could apply to a broad array of behaviors, to be intrigued. Shortly thereafter, we deployed a larger national survey to 3,345 people. We also had a team of data scientists and software engineers on hand to help us make sense of what we found.

Over the next five years, our team at PathSight continued to build on this body of research by administering nearly fifty thousand research questionnaires to a broad sample of people. Each study had a focus. Some sought to measure the impact of the core instinctual categories on individual people, while others sought answers to broader social questions, like: Why do people go to casinos? How do people make music selections? How do donors pick charities? What do people think about health? Some surveys were taken by fifteen hundred people, some by fifteen thousand. Each study was tied to census variables of age, gender, ethnicity, region, and the like. From there, we expanded to document the attributes, attitudes, and affinities of our subjects. We reaped plenty of insight from these studies, including a clear distribution of instinctual characteristics across the sampling, which helped us hazard some preliminary answers as to *why* we do what we do. They included answers to the following:

- Who are the most likely people to consult a financial broker?
- Who is most likely to donate to charity?
- What trait is most significant to Americans: Accomplishments, Gender, Ethnicity, Religion, Generation, or Family?
- What are the best predictors of political affiliation?
- Who is more likely to be murdered or to not have access to clean water?
- Who is more likely to travel internationally vs. domestically?
- Who ignores their medical test results from doctors?
- What are the most significant predictors of a successful outcome for a hospital stay?
- Who believes that health is a gift and, therefore, there is not much we can do about it?

Shortly thereafter, we launched a series of studies hoping to reveal a link between how we conduct modern life and our Stone Age instincts. We explored how several subjects—music, movies, health, finances, food, travel, gambling, voting, hospitality, sports, architecture, culture, and causes—drove different reactions among the five MFT profiles. I look forward to sharing what we have learned in the pages to come.

According to Allison Eden, a professor at Michigan State University, the MFT framework suggests that there are two different networks of the brain that respond to issues of autonomy versus community. In "The Influence of Moral Behaviors on Person Perception Processes: An fMRI Investigation," Eden writes, "The autonomy domain includes violations which take away others' personal freedoms (such as volition or health; i.e. Haidt's harm domain) and virtues which emphasize giving or expanding others' personal freedoms (i.e. Haidt's fairness domain); whereas the community domain involves violations which go against society, specifically duty, hierarchy, interdependency, and group values including normative behaviors that are not explicitly involved in denying or upholding the personal rights of others."[1] The presence of these two regions has been verified by neuropsychologists, often using fMRI in their research, and further substantiated in other studies by social scientists.

We wanted to understand how this insight could predict how a given individual might see the world. And we wondered whether knowing that worldview would help us more effectively engage with that person. For example, we surmised that those more inclined toward the autonomy side might find the traditions of American culture restrictive and resist their nudges towards conformity. The community side might view traditions as the natural way to build a cohesive culture, and view that same conformity as a virtue.

THE SOCIAL BINDING SPECTRUM

As we pursued these hunches, patterns began to emerge. These patterns represented the full spectrum of worldviews, from those most fully committed to the *autonomy* point of view to those who fully embrace a *community* point of view. This spectrum became foundational to our PathSight Model of Why. Going forward, we'll refer to it as the *Social Binding Spectrum (SBS)*. Those firmly on the autonomy end, we'll classify as having *Individuist* tendencies. Those on the community end exhibit what we'll call *Social Binding* tendencies.[2]

We have also identified a group that sits directly in between. Yet it has a unique point of view that is more than just a compromise between the two poles. In short, this group fully endorses the status quo. They come to this point of view honestly, as they certainly don't feel that they have settled for it. They see moderation as a choice they validate every day—with empathy for individual differences, kept in check by a keen appreciation for the traditions of their culture. For them, the right choice is always a question of balance.

This *Centrist* group is typically the largest in any given population. Within it, centrists are differentiated by how aware they are of certain individual differences. The group at the upper end has a very keen awareness of how individual differences are manifested. The group at the lower edge is decidedly less concerned with these differences; they take a more holistic approach in their social interactions. We'll explore all these nuances in the following chapters.

THE ROLE OF STORY IN OUR MODEL OF WHY

In our journey to why, we bounce between the academic and the applied worlds of behavioral science, and we use terms that have taken on specific meanings in each. Sometimes this can lead to confusion, so I want to take a moment to clarify how we reference three key descriptors: *worldview*, *narrative*, and *story*.

We consider one's *worldview* as the sum total of their physical, personal, and social identities. This includes genetics, foundational instincts, age, gender, ethnicity, lifestyle, personality, spirituality, and life experiences. So, there is a potentially infinite array of variations.

We now have advanced data models that can separate people along very fine points of difference, but when it comes to mining these differences for insights as to why people do what they do, they rarely yield much. Rather, we tend to agree with Maya Angelou, who famously said: "We are more alike, my friends, than we are unalike." Through our research, we have determined that though morality may widely vary across cultures and groups, there are broad similarities between how people describe their own worldviews. We've organized them accordingly, into five *Meta Worldviews*.

Again, worldviews are highly personal, and thus not up for debate. The challenge with them as data points is that they are only partially available for public viewing. Not everything a person considers is shared with the world. We are left to infer the rest.

Think of it like a house. If the house has a big front porch, the implication is that the building is accessible to the public. But however big the porch, we don't know how many stairs are behind it. It is sometimes difficult for you to know if even your own worldview reflects the *authentic* you, or only the version you aspire to be.

That brings us to the next layer of interest, the *narrative*. Narrative is a very common term in academia and the applied sciences, and the idea of using a narrative to describe one's own personality has long been of keen interest to psychologists, especially those studying cognitive, behavioral, and moral psychology. In 1989, Dan P. McAdams, a Northwestern University Psychology professor, described his work on the subject in the article "The Development of a Narrative Identity":

"My own research and theorizing over the past ten years may be situated within that maverick tradition in the social sciences called 'the study of lives' or 'the personological tradition'—historically associated with the approaches advanced by Murray (1938), White (1966, 1981), and Tomkins (1987), among others. As Murray envisioned it over fifty years ago, the personologist should endeavor to study the whole person and to comprehend the structure and the content of his or her life in its full socio-historical context. Following Murray's (1938) lead in *Explorations in Personality*, personologists have traditionally placed prime emphasis on motivation and biography in their own empirical explorations of the whole person."[3]

When the Moral Foundations Theory emerged, it was ready-made for McAdams's approach, which had homed in on three elements of a narrative: motivational and affective themes, autobiographical reasoning, and structural aspects.[4]

This discovery—that one's worldview is far more accessible than much of the commercial market had recognized—has been a boon to our work. As we developed the Model of Why, we came to view narrative as the key to unpacking a given worldview. By linking someone's foundational instincts with their age/life stage, gender, and ethnicity, we get the core building blocks of their worldview, which is a good start. But a carefully constructed narrative offers a much more nuanced understanding of the whole life of a person.

In the commercial market, we generally have incomplete access to data. So as we present the information that may go into these narratives, it will come from several different layers. We'll use publicly available data, a second broad category called psychographic data, and a third layer of more intimate and protected data, to provide insights on how the five Meta Worldviews are formed.

The final term that needs clarification is *story*. For our purposes, the story is really just a short version of the narrative, one we use primarily to understand and influence one another. More often than not, we will only be concerned with an incomplete piece of someone's narrative; after all, for most people with whom we interact we will not require an in-depth understanding of their operational history. Rather, if you're looking to improve or influence a relationship, it helps to narrow the scope from the broader narrative to the situation-specific story. This function of story appears often in marketing, communications, and even human resources.

So how do these layers of information fit together? Imagine you wanted to find out how many people are likely to buy a particular product. At the population level, we could identify a particular Meta Worldview possessed by those who would probably be interested in trying the product. Within that set, we could investigate why some people are more likely to like the product than others, based on their narratives (and our available data and modeling). And when we finally tried to convince someone to buy it, we would use the narrower focus of story. This same structure applies well beyond consumer products—to voting, joining, "liking," inspiring loyalty, and changing behavior.

In fact, we've found that this process illuminates not only specific behaviors, but also the way we *discuss* those behaviors. As humans, we're predisposed to embrace narratives as a way to communicate ideas. Acclaimed economist and Nobel laureate Robert Shiller put it like this:

"The human species, everywhere you go, is engaged in conversation. We are wired for it: the human brain is built around narratives. We call ourselves *Homo sapiens*, but that may be something of a misnomer—*sapiens* means 'wise.' The evolutionary biologist Stephen Jay Gould said we should be called *Homo narrator*. Your mind is really built for narratives, and especially narratives about other humans."[5]

Our findings certainly support this. In fact, we believe that what really brings people together along the Social Binding Spectrum is the story they respond to as they organize their worldview, not a cluster of static attributes like age or ethnicity they happen to have in common. This is how we choose our friends and partners; our relationships are based on shared stories that create bonds of affinity.

For instance, a person who is passionate about ensuring individual rights might believe that "if we spend all the money in the budget [on a particular social program] and save one family, it will be worth it." Yet an equally empathic person could easily disagree. This difference might be due to a variation in their sensitivity to the Care/Harm instinct. Farther down the spectrum, a third person might object to allocating any money to the program at all.

This story focus is what gives nuance and heft to our Model of Why. Unlike traditional segmentation models, we don't think that knowing someone's income or education level necessarily provides a differential insight as to why they do what they do. And we know that a strong story can transcend all kinds of differences, including race, class, and generation.

We already have the capacity to define normative expectations, or predictable outcomes, about different populations (e.g., how many Individuists there will likely be in a given market segment). But our goal is to go deeper. We believe that understanding *why* we do things is far more significant and impactful than simply knowing *what* we will do.

THE MODEL OF WHY

Before we go further, let's go back to the building blocks of our model—the five core instincts of the Moral Foundations Theory framework.

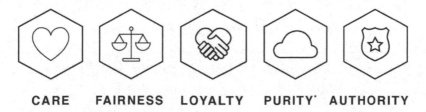

CARE   FAIRNESS   LOYALTY   PURITY*   AUTHORITY

* Purity is also referred to as sanctity / degradation.

The Model of Why is built on finding relationships among the five foundational instincts of MFT (Care/Harm, Fairness/Cheating, Loyalty/Betrayal, Authority/Subversion, and Purity/Degradation).[6] As we studied how these instincts manifest in the decision making of our survey participants, we identified five unique Instinctual Patterns (IPs), shown in the graphic below. Individual behavior within each pattern is influenced, in predictable ways, by certain themes, words, and images. The vertical axis signifies each IP's sensitivity to individual differences, as measured by loyalty scores. High loyalty scores typically are for people who are highly aware of differences, like age, gender, ethnicity, lifestyle, and religion. Low loyalty scores signify a sense of universality; these individuals are likely to feel we all have equal access to the benefits of our culture.

THE MODEL OF WHY: DISTRIBUTION OF THE META WORLDVIEWS IN THE USA

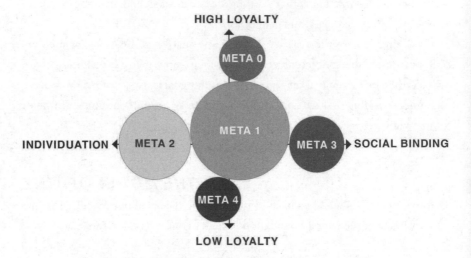

The five Instinctual Patterns we've identified are as follows:

- Instinctual Pattern 0: The Balanced, Meta Worldview 0
- Instinctual Pattern 1: The Centrist, Meta Worldview 1
- Instinctual Pattern 2: The Individuist, Meta Worldview 2
- Instinctual Pattern 3: The Social Binder, Meta Worldview 3
- Instinctual Pattern 4: The Fatalist, Meta Worldview 4

The next section of this book will detail what we know about each. From that base of knowledge, we can explore how these patterns play out against various demographic, psychographic, and behavioral markers. We find that, with these IP profiles assigned, the plethora of available data yields much richer, more complex insights, especially for advertising, marketing, communications, human resources, and general behavior management (as we will see shortly). In the model below, we track the profile of the Meta Worldview 2 from this new starting point.

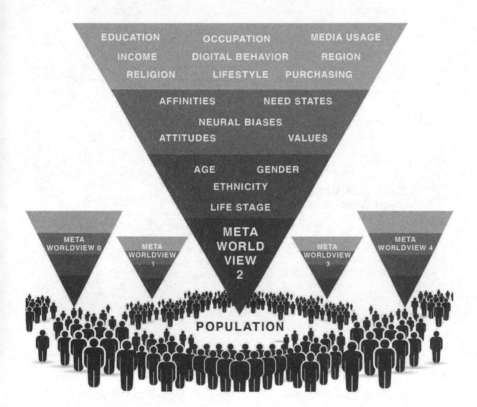

Each Instinctual Pattern represents a different starting point. Rather than looking to more traditional models, this pyramid of inputs, unique to each pattern, will provide a more complete picture of what drives individual tastes, preferences, and habits—and most importantly, *why*.

As mentioned in Chapter 2, many companies have spent many decades competing to categorize people in the most effective (and lucrative) way. The following chart captures how the modern marketplace organizes these processes. In most cases, marketing campaigns across media platforms focus on delivering the likes, joins, loyalty, loves, votes, and buys of particular demographic clusters. This is represented by the upper layer on the chart.

In other words, if you want someone to respond to an offer, the traditional model suggests accounting for their biology (age, gender, race), description (education, income, lifestyle), behavior (attitudes, personality, habits), and location (physical, digital). But while demographics have proven useful in defining *who* we are, or *what* we do, they have not proved helpful when it comes to *why*.

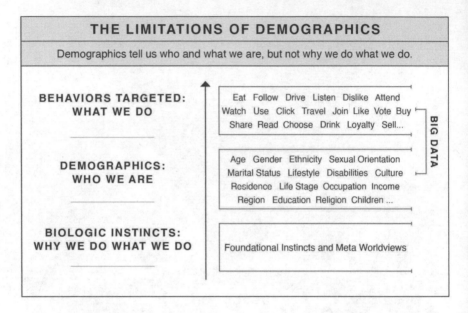

These demographics, whether separately or in an integrated model, are still inadequate to deliver on the "market basket" of goods that Nielsen sold so many decades ago. Contemporary moral psychology research, best encapsulated by the Moral Foundations Theory, promises that understanding our higher moral concepts will ultimately have a broader impact on the ways we engage the world than the correlations of age, gender, or income. If you have a strong instinct to pursue fairness, it will probably be a better predictor of your behavior than, say, your birth order. That's why these five Instinctual Patterns form the base of our model. As we explore the research around our Model of Why, let's see what we can learn about ourselves—and more important, others.

CHAPTER 4

TO EACH THEIR OWN:
THE INDIVIDUIST WORLDVIEW

I n the previous chapter, I outlined the five Meta Worldviews we've developed at PathSight. I hope, at this point, you've seen how more traditional segmentation models, while useful, have not been able to offer us a complete picture of why people do what they do. Before we dig into each Meta Worldview, let's review our inverted pyramid with the many different sources of information we have to understand why people do what they do.

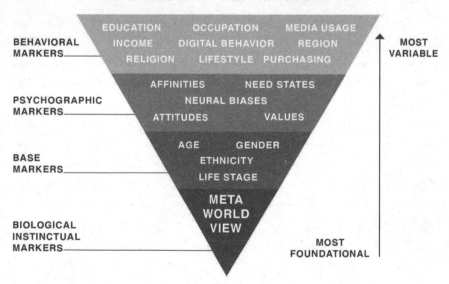

THE BLUEPRINT FOR A NARRATIVE

BEHAVIORAL MARKERS — EDUCATION OCCUPATION MEDIA USAGE INCOME DIGITAL BEHAVIOR REGION RELIGION LIFESTYLE PURCHASING — MOST VARIABLE

PSYCHOGRAPHIC MARKERS — AFFINITIES NEED STATES NEURAL BIASES ATTITUDES VALUES

BASE MARKERS — AGE GENDER ETHNICITY LIFE STAGE

META WORLD VIEW

BIOLOGICAL INSTINCTUAL MARKERS — MOST FOUNDATIONAL

Starting at the bottom, the most influential and impactful data grounds our model. It is the most difficult to discover or mine. Here, at the point, sit the Instinctual Patterns. The descriptive demographic data, beyond age, gender, and ethnicity, sit at the other end of the triangle and are the easiest to observe, but also the least reliable and meaningful when it comes to producing deep insights. Think of the model as made up of layers of data, insights, and variables that are organized and triangulated to help us understand people deeply and thoroughly. Starting at the bottom, we gather information for the instinctual markers by surveying people or assessing the data that describe them. As mentioned earlier, PathSight has sent out more than fifty thousand survey-based questionnaires in the last five years specifically to collect this data. In our search for why, we believe this layer is the most influential of all because it impacts every other layer. To reiterate, instincts reflect our biological "first draft," and all other markers are viewed through this instinctual marker lens.

Next comes age/life stage, gender, and ethnicity, all present at birth, for the most part. As those cornerstones of our sense of self evolve, they do so with the neural imprint of our instincts. These two layers, we've seen in our work, have primacy over the succeeding elements that make us who we are. There's a pattern here—the higher up you go on the inverted pyramid, the less foundational the marker.

The layer in between the base markers and the behavioral markers is a broad category called psychometric markers. This is where many segmentation models start. Psychometric markers include information about an individual or a population's attitudes, affinities, opinions, achievements, and personality quirks. Again, in our model, we believe that these psychographic data points are significantly enriched when understood through the lens of a person's core Instinctual Pattern, a glimpse of human nature in the raw. This psychographic information is gathered using standard instruments like personality tests, value clarification questionnaires, and correlational measurements of attributes and affinities (e.g., if you love this movie, you'll likely love this one too).

Now, with the layers of identity in our inverted pyramid in mind, let's meet our first Meta Worldview—the Meta 2 Individuist.

THE META 2 WORLDVIEW

The Meta 2 worldview consists of those who see the world in terms of how people are treated. How do we care for one another? Do we have equal access to opportunity and justice? This instinct can be expressed in a variety of ways, but the common thread is tolerance for differences and an instinct to push back against conformity.

CHARACTERISTICS OF THE META 2 WORLDVIEW

Anchored by an Individuist point of view, the Meta 2 Worldview values individuality, compassion, fairness, and justice. The Meta 2 is inclined to give others great latitude in their personal behaviors, unless one is causing harm. They want to protect and nurture the vulnerable, and those unable to provide for themselves. They are not especially judgmental. They tend to prefer a life of variety, stimulation, and personal freedom. Rather than seeking expensive signifiers to communicate their success, they take pride in being the first to find and endorse a trend or product, to move beyond the status quo. Meta 2 individuals (like most of us) are validated when the world conforms to their values and they get to celebrate that natural alignment. When culture demands conformity, on the other hand, they are the first to resist, often via ironic or satiric

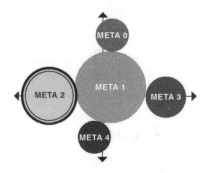

The Meta 2 worldview lies on the left side of the Social Binding Spectrum (SBS) in our Model of Why.

META 2 WORLDVIEW

PRIMARY INSTINCTUAL DRIVER

- Care
- Fairness

THE META 2'S STORY

As we saw earlier, each Instinctual Pattern is represented by a narrative that reflects how that particular pattern of instincts may be triggered in daily life. Here's a narrative for a typical Meta 2 profile:

> When I look at the world around me, I see one that is filled with new things, lots of choices and ways to express oneself. We get to push the boundaries with new technologies in almost every facet of life. That is thrilling to me, and something I embrace. It is easy to get carried away when the world is at your fingertips. I happen to love art and music and can explore them easily and in every conceivable form.
>
> What concerns me is how judgmental the world has become. I see a whole section of society that wants everyone to do things their way, or else. That concerns me, because I think if it isn't affecting you, you should keep your opinions to yourself. People have a right to be able to express themselves as they see fit. I also look around and see that there are lots of people in a bad way, and I don't think we do enough to make sure that everyone has a safety net beneath them. There are too many examples of people not having equal protection under the law, and that is just not right. It is our obligation to make sure that is not happening.

Let's peel back the layers of this narrative, so that we might understand it more completely.

THE SEARCH FOR WHY

ENJOY DISCOVERING NEW THINGS

The Meta 2 individual is curious by nature. For example, our research on music consumption shows that this kind of consumer samples a wide variety of music, across a number of genres. (Interestingly, the genres themselves don't appear to matter; it is the *number* of genres that is predictive.) Over a total of twelve musical genres we tested, Meta 2 consumers enjoyed an average of nine. By contrast, the Meta 3 worldview (the Social Binder) preferred an average of just three musical genres.

In an interesting article entitled "Secret Lives of Liberals and Conservatives: Personality Profiles, Interaction Styles, and the Things They Leave Behind,"[1] psychologist and associate professor of Business at UC Berkeley Dana Carney highlighted some fascinating details about partisan self-sorting, which closely tracks the patterns of the Meta 2 and 3 worldviews that we have identified in our research. Carney notes an array of traits that have, over time, sorted into consistent patterns for each. In one such observation, liberals (largely Meta 2 worldview) preferred a wide array of books, whereas conservatives (often Meta 3 worldview) preferred a narrower selection.

Philosophically, the Meta 2 looks forward to newness, a potentially better way of doing things. But they don't necessarily coalesce around a single idea of what "better" means. In fact, as a social function, this group supplies our culture with an endless variety of perspectives. They are often the ones to search for and discover new, emerging ideas that can drive change in the world. Think of disruptive innovations like Airbnb and Uber, which take an existing service or product and cast it in a whole new light. Someone has to go first, and it's often a Meta 2.

A JUDGMENT-FREE ZONE

This is another key element of the Meta 2 narrative. They worry that some people and beliefs exert undue spheres of influence. As our sample narrative states, their core belief is: "If it doesn't affect you, you should keep your opinions to yourself." In terms of rulemaking and governance, this translates to "do no harm."

This group is not strongly aligned with the Authority instinct of the Moral Foundations Theory, with its focus on traditions, order, and rules. Rather, fairness, which is rooted in reciprocity and mutual respect, is much closer to the heart of someone with a Meta 2 worldview—with its focus on the individual, rather than the group. The idea of the lean and agile start-up is a perfect example of the Meta 2's mindset—collaborative product and scrum teams; peer networks; a flat, more egalitarian organization; and of course, radical innovation. And think of Stephen Colbert's opening monologue, most often about the hypocrisy of politicians, the overreach of culturally puritanical morals, and our collective intolerance of freedom. In a recent study we conducted on the appeal of different television shows, we found that people with the Meta 2 worldview were far and away the most ardent fans of this show.

EQUAL PROTECTION

The notion of equal protection, a subset of the fairness instinct, is also central for the Meta 2 group. They typically demonstrate widespread compassion, and as a result, a high tolerance for diversity. They also believe that the culture needs to make sure that all its members have equal access to every opportunity. In the Individuist version of America, we can't guarantee equal outcomes, but we should be able to guarantee equal access. Perhaps unsurprisingly, many of the other worldviews disagree on this point, at least sometimes. When push comes to shove, this is the belief that separates this group from the others.

Equal protection is also driven by the high Care instinct. The importance of caring about every human individual can't be underestimated as a core belief of Individuists. The Meta 2 has the most pronounced Care influence of any of the Instinctual Patterns, but caring, as an instinct, is present in every Instinctual Pattern. As we know, this instinct originally arose from the biological need to protect children, but it can apply to all stages of human empathy—identifying, projecting, and ultimately demonstrating resonance with the feelings of others—with sensitivity and compassion. In some other worldviews, caring may be muted, or secondary to other instincts, but it is the closest we have to a universal characteristic.

THE ELEMENTS OF THE META 2'S IDENTITY

From this brief and basic narrative, we can glean an amazing amount of insight about this group. In order to see how the array of data attributes, or demographics, are filtered through the Meta 2 worldview, let's begin with the foundational traits of age, gender, and ethnicity (other demographics are helpful, such as urban vs. rural, or socioeconomic status, but not foundational, as are age, gender, and ethnicity).

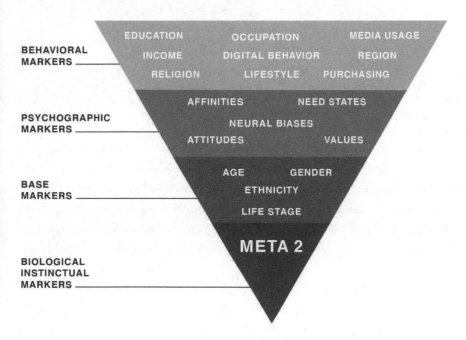

BEHAVIORAL MARKERS —
EDUCATION   OCCUPATION   MEDIA USAGE
INCOME   DIGITAL BEHAVIOR   REGION
RELIGION   LIFESTYLE   PURCHASING

PSYCHOGRAPHIC MARKERS —
AFFINITIES   NEED STATES
NEURAL BIASES
ATTITUDES   VALUES

BASE MARKERS —
AGE   GENDER
ETHNICITY
LIFE STAGE

META 2

BIOLOGICAL INSTINCTUAL MARKERS —

Before we do so, here's a brief explanation of what each of these slices mean (in market research both demographics and psychographics provide insights into the customer).

- **BASE MARKERS:** The core traits that have long been the standard in identifying the characteristics of a target audience. Typically, these include, age/life stage, gender, ethnicity, income, education, family size, religion, and location (rural versus urban is a relatively new data point). These traits are considered easiest to measure.

- **PSYCHOGRAPHIC MARKERS:** Interests, hobbies, motivations, opinions, and attitudes. This psychological information is less measurable and is typically gathered through surveys, questionnaires, and formal psychometric instruments.

- **BEHAVIORAL MARKERS:** These markers are generally available through observation of someone's behavior. Readily accessible, they are frequently referred to as characteristic of demographics, and typically variable. These are publicly available data points that are integrated into our model as a means of adding personalization.

First, back to age/life stage, gender, and ethnicity. We discovered earlier that these attributes do not necessarily predict someone's sensitivity to a specific instinctual trait. Rather, at PathSight we are interested in how these base markers mix with particular Instinctual Patterns, resulting in unique worldviews. Adding layers of demographic data, observation, and psychometric scores to the melding of instincts will provide us with much more holistic, impactful, and predictable insights in the long run.

From 2015 to 2017, PathSight asked more than twenty thousand people how likely they were to emphasize age/life stage, gender, or ethnicity when describing themselves to others. This seemingly straightforward question generated some very complex responses, which we will revisit when we discuss the concept of intersectionality. These three descriptors, when understood in the context of one's Instinctual Pattern, form a whole new starting point for the idea of identity.

The chart below shows how the U.S. population as a group rated the relative impact of these attributes. We have to note that approximately 76.5 percent of this audience identifies itself as Caucasian. This obviously skews the result at the population level, but you will see when we get to individual groups that these generic impressions tell a different story. However, they are still a pretty good barometer for America's cultural sentiments. These were calculated as "net" affinity scores—

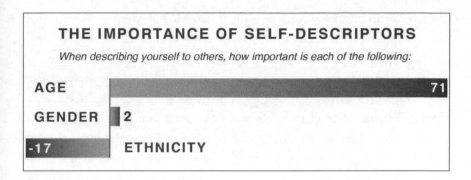

that is, subtracting the negative scores from the positive scores displays the relative strength of these traits. This population considers their generation the most accessible issue by far when describing themselves to other people. Gender was rated an almost neutral attribute, while ethnicity was a less important indicator when people described themselves. Again, this is a population finding that tends to obscure important individual differences on these particular and important reference points.

AGE/LIFE STAGE AND THE META 2 WORLDVIEW

The impact of this generational filter cannot be overestimated. It has proven convenient, easy to use, and hard to get rid of. Witness the U.S. marketing obsession with generational names—Millennial, Gen X, Baby Boomer, Gen Z. This phenomenon is not nearly so prevalent in other countries.

Of course, where these generational groups truly differ is not in their essential elements, but in how they are managing the demands of their lives in specific sets of historic circumstances. The instinctual traits that they bring to these demands are reasonably the same from generation to generation. What changes is the set of situational experiences, providing a set of challenges unique to each generation. We then mistakenly ascribe these solutions as generational traits. For example, there has been much written about millennials and their unique relationship to the world of work—demanding video games in their employee lounges, specialized new job onboarding with meet-and-greet set up, clear job expectations outlined, or increased flex time. But this generation came of age during the Great Recession and had to deal with a number of financial issues arising out of it. Given the job market, student loan debt, a higher cost of living, and needing to save more for longer life spans, what we think of as millennial "traits" may just be the effects of an unstable labor market that substitutes frivolous benefits for true job security.

How is one's generational expression influenced by one's Instinctual Pattern? The simple answer is that it depends on one's life stage and specific Instinctual Pattern. After all, each Instinctual Pattern is formed by the interaction of one's instincts and their life stage and experiences. It is useful for us to think of life stage as a predictive indicator of a person's preferences or behavior, not just a simple data point. This allows us to examine how a particular Instinctual Pattern responds to age-related situations. For instance, a Meta 2 Worldview is likely to not be constrained by the cultural norms of what a typical sixty-year-old might do, say, and look like though they might. In contrast, a Meta 3 might be more predictably traditional. The Meta 2 may take offense at conventional expectations of middle age, whereas the Meta 3 might expect them. All along the lifespan, your feelings about your chronological age—and, in turn, society's perception of you—will be filtered through your particular Meta Worldview.

There have been several studies on this topic. For example, in *Age Differences in Moral Foundations Across Adolescence and Adulthood*, Ece Sagel hypothesized different ways that individualizing and social binding traits are expressed longitudinally over the course of one's life.[2] Sagel suggests that the demands of various life stages tend to feature either an individualizing or a social binding theme. For example, in late adolescence, there are lots of challenges around rules and conformity: curfews, driver's license exams, school rules, religious and social norms. These milestones share a social binding element, in that they are rites of passage designed to transition children to the adult world. Shortly thereafter, though, a new set of challenges pushes a distinctly Individuist perspective: a first job, first lease, first experience with insurance. This is also the time when most people begin to define their boundaries and lifestyle—choices that will likely define their lives for a long while. Finally, as one enters full adulthood, the challenges shift back in the social binding direction, with school loans to be paid back, mortgages to handle, family to support, and retirement to save for.

These shifting demands offer different challenges for one's particular Instinctual Pattern. When approaching a new life stage, there are at least two separate factors to consider. One, whether the challenges will have a social binding theme or an Individuist theme. Two, how a person's Instinctual Pattern will manifest in the face of those changes.

For example, in young adulthood, a Meta 2 may embrace life's "firsts" with a risk-taker's delight. Perhaps you leave college and head to a new city for a new job. You make new friends and new habits, like a new workout routine. All of this can be stimulating, piquing interests and passions you never knew you had, whetting your appetite for more.

A Meta 3 individual, or Social Binder, may feel quite differently, given their natural instinct for rules, social conformity, traditions, and security. We will explore the Social Binder's experience of life stages in Chapter 5.

GENDER AND THE META 2 WORLDVIEW

According to our surveys, gender seems less important than generations in most people's concept of themselves—in America, at least. But we do know a lot about how different Instinctual Patterns think about gender.

At the population level, it might seem insignificant, given that gender rates just above zero on the chart. This, however, is more likely an effect of the *range* of feelings on this topic, and the polarization that spreads out sentiment in equal parts positive and negative. For example, consider this graph, which compares the ratings of total females and total males. There is a 28 spread between them, with

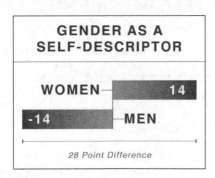

GENDER AS A SELF-DESCRIPTOR

WOMEN — 14

-14 — MEN

28 Point Difference

women showing a positive rating of 14 and men a -14. In other words, women in total do think that their gender is important to their self-description. It has a net-positive sentiment. Men, on the contrary, rate gender as a negative factor. It is because in U.S. culture, men are perceived by many as occupying a consistent position of power. It may be that men, when given the opportunity to rate gender as an important trait to use as a self-descriptor, simply don't consider it as important, especially when we compare that to women. Women clearly feel differently on the whole, but there are differences across worldviews. Gender is of particular relevance to the

Meta 2 women. They tap into their dual instincts of Care and Fairness and view Gender as more than a fixed role, bringing it into their conversation when they choose and defining the role as they see it. It would be interesting to generate this data across a whole range of subcategories paired with other power-related attributes of privilege, income, education, sexual orientation, religion, ability, and occupation to see if this disparity remains. This way, when we refer to gender, we would be using the broadest definition of its socialization—how it relates to personality and behavior—as well as its implications economically, legally, and politically.

ETHNICITY, RACE, AND THE META 2 WORLDVIEW

Ethnicity is another core trait that factors heavily in how we think about and relate to one another. As we discussed earlier, the Meta 2 is generally quite tolerant of differences and inclined to regard them as an asset. Overall, Black Americans, Latinx, and Asian-Americans with this Instinctual Pattern express similar sentiments about ethnicity as a self-descriptor. Whites, however, rated ethnicity as a characteristic that they would not likely include in a self-description. Similar to men in their rating of gender, this result may indicate that race is not a char-

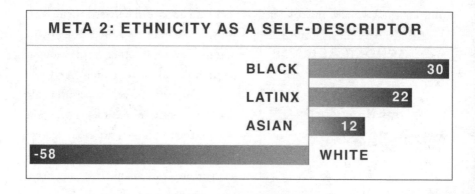

acteristic they would feel compelled to instinctually share with someone. This certainly has implications for the state of racial tolerance. We might surmise that whites don't intuitively think of race as representing a different point of view when it comes to the norms of culture. Generally, diversity is seen as a positive within the Meta 2 Worldview. Because there are many social and cognitive biases and lived experiences around race and ethnicity, what people see is influenced by their expectations, assumptions, and biases about certain groups and one's worldview. We see that the Individuist narrative *extends to* and helps *inform* a more tolerant instinct that values diversity, but does not result in a knee jerk set of behaviors that are obvious. Certainly, there is more work to be done as we explore race, ethnicity, and our instincts.

For example, one of the most basic of cognitive biases is our tendency toward implicit bias. In an *American Educator* article titled "Understanding Implicit Bias," senior researcher for the Kirwan Institute Cheryl Staats writes, "Implicit bias refers to the automatic and unconscious stereotypes that drive people to behave and make decisions in certain ways."[3] A 2012 report from the American Psychological Association's Task Force on Preventing Discrimination and Promoting Diversity found that biases—including implicit biases—are pervasive across people and institutions.[4] Although the behaviors of children may impact adult decision-making processes, implicit biases about sex and race may influence how those behaviors are perceived and how they are addressed, creating a vicious cycle over time, exacerbating inequalities.[5] We are convinced that by adding the awareness of one's Instinctual Pattern, we will be able to map how children interpret this bias, along with how life experiences reinforce them in ways that are unique to each worldview. It will help us understand the interaction of this bias with one's foundational instincts in a real-world setting.

THE BEGINNING OF INTERSECTIONALITY

One thing to keep in mind when we mention Instinctual Patterns is that they are not fixed attributes to measure and account for in some quantitative score. These base markers don't help us understand our worldview by accounting for our age, gender, and ethnicity as one might check boxes on a census. Since birth, our base markers have been present, and they have been receiving feedback from our life experiences nonstop. Along with them, the unique pattern of instincts we have helps us make sense of the worldview we are constructing. At this point, to say that we can attribute a defined percentage to gender, or ethnicity, in how an individual arrived at their personal identity, is to not understand this concept.

In 1991, UCLA and Columbia law professor and civil rights advocate Kimberlé Williams Crenshaw wrote what some think constitutes the dawn of intersectionality: the article "Mapping the Margins: Intersectionality, Identity Politics, and Violence Against Women of Color."[6] In its introduction, she succinctly offers a framework for understanding race and gender:

"The embrace of identity politics, however, has been in tension with the dominant conception of social justice. Race, gender and other identity categories are most often treated in the mainstream liberal discourse as vestiges of bias or domination—that is, as intrinsically negative frameworks in which social power works to exclude or marginalize those who are different." According to this understanding, our liberating objective should be to empty such categories of any

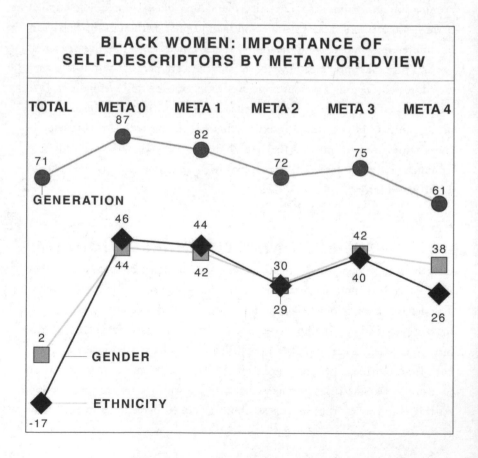

social significance. Yet, implicit in strands of feminist and racial liberation movements, for example, is the view that the social power in the delineating differences need not be the power of domination; it can instead be the source of social empowerment and reconstruction.

We can see that to understand how these influences bear on the identities of people is a very complex task and one that we are only beginning to tackle. We can shed some light on the topic by considering some basic realities. When we try to capture insights on many of these topics, we should acknowledge that not all data is equal. As we noted earlier, context is king. When we look at how these data points are to be interpreted, we must remember that most of the opinions are captured from the perspective of a population that 76.5 percent of them self-describe as Caucasian. We must give thought as to how to apportion and capture the degree of inspiration and empowerment coming from those who are "differ-

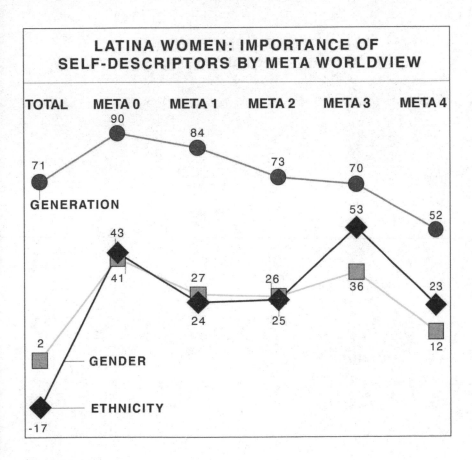

LATINA WOMEN: IMPORTANCE OF
SELF-DESCRIPTORS BY META WORLDVIEW

TOTAL	META 0	META 1	META 2	META 3	META 4

GENERATION: 71, 90, 84, 73, 70, 52

GENDER: 2, 41, 24, 25, 36, 12

ETHNICITY: -17, 43, 27, 26, 53, 23

ent" from this plurality. Indeed, understanding one's Instinctual Pattern might further lead to different perceptions along the way. We need to tread lightly when making declarative assertions. Consider how we can begin to describe these traits.

In the following charts, we can see how the total U.S. population of women rate the importance of ethnicity, generation (age), and gender across all Instinctual Patterns. You will note that the total population (along the left boundary), including the 76.5 percent Caucasians, rated ethnicity at -17, gender as a 2, and age at 71. When we combine ethnicity (Black) and gender (female), we get a very different perspective. Look at the categories from left to right. We see that one's age or generation is pretty consistent across all of the worldviews and at a high level. This category does not appear to be overly influenced by other population variables. However, the categories of ethnicity and gender appear to be tightly

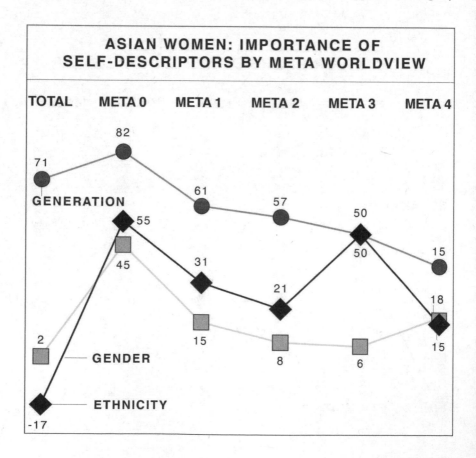

intertwined with Instinctual Pattern and at a much higher level than the total score would imply. The total score is -17 for ethnicity and 2 for gender, while they rated at 44 for both ethnicity and gender for the Meta 0. The lowest ratings were recorded by the Meta 4 Black Women, with an 26 for ethnicity and 38 for gender.

One might mistake this to be a condition exclusive to Black women. We also offer a look at how the impact of Latina and Asian women affect these categories. Again, age is pretty much unaffected by adding ethnicity and gender to the equation. There are some differences between the Latina and Asian women. Latinas were again tightly intertwined across the Instinctual Patterns for ethnicity and gender, but at a lower level than Black women. Asian women saw a Meta 3 rating of 50 for ethnicity, the same as for Black women. For gender, they were more muted than the other ethnicities across the various Meta Worldviews. I would suggest that some of the scores are very much expressions of their individual worldviews in concert with the these attributes that we are presenting now.

THE META 2 INDIVIDUIST'S PROFILE

Here are some of the Meta 2's most salient concerns:

- **INDIVIDUAL AUTONOMY:** An Individuist prioritizes the individual over allegiance to a group. They're inclined to frame issues of gender, age, and ethnicity from the perspective of valuing each person's individual identity. By and large, this group's profile and narrative likely show them tolerating a whole range of lifestyles, traditions, and behaviors—even if their own ultimate choice is to live a conventional life.

- **EQUALITY ABOVE ALL:** In general, Individuists desire justice and equal access for all people, no matter their age, gender, ethnicity, or abilities. The group examines issues and life situations through a careful filter of fairness and care, and they try to do so with as much equanimity as possible.

- ## RESISTING CONFORMITY: Meta 2
  Individuists are not especially inspired by authority, so they may buck traditional roles and rules about gender, age, and ethnicity. Their morality directs them to focus on diversity and inclusion, resisting those that limit choices for people. They actively battle conformity and remain dedicated advocates for individual rights and expression.

- ## BEING AN EARLY ADOPTER: This is a
  hallmark of the Individuist as well as a source of pride. They are the most likely meta group to achieve "influencer" status. This is also true for the causes they support. The movements they support or start often find their way into mass adoption.

Do you remember the movie *Norma Rae*, released forty years ago? Sally Field played Norma Rae, a factory worker at a textile mill who, after working long hours for little pay in lousy conditions for far too long, begins to fight for worker solidarity and unionization to create better conditions for all of the mill workers, not just herself. As Angela Allan writes in the *Atlantic*'s "40 Years Ago, *Norma Rae* Understood How Corporations Weaponized Race," the movie "not only insisted that racial solidarity could solve economic injustice, but it also suggested that worker solidarity could overcome social injustice."[7] Norma Rae, the main character—based on a real-life heroine—is a classic Meta 2, a nonconformist exhibiting high levels of the Care and Fairness instincts. Another example of a strong movie/real-life Individuist? Erin Brockovich!

Or consider the response to the COVID-19 pandemic. This tragedy has evoked every emotion possible. Not only has the pandemic affected us physically, it has also challenged our very culture and the way we live. For the United States, specifically, it has shined a light on just how polarized we've become as a nation—where even wearing a mask is a political act—and how much we've forsaken those citizens at the margins of society. If we step back and think about the way people have responded to the disease, we see that it follows the fork between the Individuist Meta 2 and the Social Binding Meta 3 patterns. As Eden's research suggests, Individuists "rely more on emotional concerns," and Social Binders "are more concerned about making judgements themselves."[8]

The Meta 2's immediate response to the virus was to provide for the safety of all people relative to the disease. Their first concern was how to prevent more people from getting the disease and how to best take care of those who get it. The research suggests that Meta 2s relied on an expansive set of criteria when considering how to proceed: the nature of the disease, its transmission rate, its severity, the impact of comorbidity, and who gets infected. All of this, within a context of heightened emotionality, is trademark Meta 2. To them, the idea of "shelter in place" was an arduous ask for all civilians, especially economically, but it made sense. The trade-off of economic hardship for safety, prevention, and care was made much more readily by Individuists than by Social Binders. In other words, Meta 2s consider the many impacts on individuals as they seek to make a moral judgment on how to react.

The Social Binders, on the other hand, simplified the decision, taking a pro forma, binary, reductionist approach. They asked: Are lockdowns and being fined for not wearing a mask right or wrong, according to my beliefs? Are they valid points of view or not? We believe that judgments of right and wrong are not relevant to the discussion of the validity of one's worldview. We will leave this to our discussion of the narrative of the Social Binding perspective in the next chapter. Relative to the motivational challenge of mask wearing, the Meta 3s are less likely to have a "relative risk" calculator when considering the trade-off of the economy versus the virus. This argument may get truncated, considering other related topics such as the right to demand obedience to the ordinance, objective accuracy of the tactic, and even the source of the information informing it. To them, it is more likely a yes-or-no decision. The Meta 2 and Meta 3 worldviews are fundamentally different—if you are an Individuist, you may understand the words that describe a Social Binder, but you probably will never truly understand what it means to process the world from that point of view—and vice versa. Even a pandemic is subject to our instinctual worldviews. This reductionist point of view of the social binding worldview takes place in a lot of different ways; people don't like being told how to manage their lives. Think about the way our conversations around guns, the environment, and abortion often are motivated by our instincts but get argued with tactics that seem to be detached from the emotions that were originally triggered. For example, when our authority instinct gets violated we might feel angry about vague and unproven recommendations, or we may not trust the source of the remedy, or doubt they have it all figured out. Eventually, all of these thoughts and feelings might result in a single unifying emotion such as "You can't tell me what to do." I often refer to this process as deploying proxies as a substitute for the original emotion. An emotion as strong as not wanting to be told what to do, unfortunately, is often a sign of an intractable stalement.

HOW A META 2'S INSTINCTS PLAYED OUT IN THE PANDEMIC

- **Universal care:** There was a growing crescendo of care, nurturing, and empathy for those people who were faced with the virus—not just in the Meta 2s' own community, and not just the patients, but also their families and the front-line EMT and healthcare workers. The Individuist feels that interventions must address everyone afflicted, not just those to whom one feels a kinship.

- **Public help was needed:** The Individuist feels that the blameless scourge of a virus should invalidate the timeless American credo of self-reliance, of avoiding public help. It should also provide the justification for universal healthcare, temporary wage supports, and if possible, some help for the environment as well. This is why when the meatpacking workers were forced to show up for work and risk infection because they were ironically classified as essential workers, their treatment was judged as unfair and unjust by many of those with Individuist leanings.

When the Meta 2 looks at the world, they see people as essentially equal, all deserving of safety, and, if possible, happiness. They ask: How do we treat each other? How do we care for each other? Do we all truly have equal access to opportunity and justice?

SUMMARY

If we delve deep we see not just the individual story elements of a person's life, but the blueprint, a map to the thoughts, ideas, beliefs, and worldview that shape the decisions they make. Below is how a Meta 2 might describe themselves in a few sentences, what they consider a life well lived, and a list of movies that embody the spirit of a Meta 2.

META WORLDVIEW 2 SUMMARY
NARRATIVE
If I think about life, my real focus is on people and how they are treated. We aspire to treat people as equals both in terms of opportunity and in terms of fairness in how we live our lives. How you start your life should not place you in a hole as to what is possible in your life.
IDEAL FOR A LIFE WELL LIVED
• Life is a balance between other people, nature, and within a government that **protects** everyone's life, liberty and pursuit of happiness. • I live my life in a way that fulfills my individual potential. • I live in a way that cares for others, supports their goals, and aspires to treat everyone fairly.
EXEMPLARS OF ENTERTAINMENT
• *Blade Runner* • *Moonlight* • *Brokeback Mountain* • *Avatar* • *To Kill a Mockingbird*

META WORLDVIEW 2

VALUES

Life is full of newness and opportunities to push the envelope.	Individual liberty is more important than conformity.	We need to give people the space to live their lives on their terms.
Accomplishments are self satisfying, keeping score is optional.	There are real benefits to embracing different points of view.	Humor that challenges authority is splendid.
Progressive politics of diversity and individuality.		Everyone has a right to human rights and a fair shake.

DESCRIPTORS

Variety	Diversity	Risk vs Reward	Causes that benefit people
Universal view of humanity (vs. Tribalism)	Social Movements	Compassion	Fairness

VOTING

10% Republican	59% Democratic	4% Libertarian	27% Independent

TRIGGERS*

Variety and Choice	Pain and suffering (especially of children)	Images of cheating or trust	Reciprocity within relationships

POSITIVE ASSOCIATIONS

Care	Peace	Compassion	Empathy
Sympathy	Protect	Defend	Guard
Preserve	Assist	Safety	Insure

NEGATIVE ASSOCIATIONS

Kill	Endanger	Cruel	Brutal
War	Damage	Ruin	Crush
Abandon	Spurn	Impair	Exploit
Wound	Abuse		

*The Righteous Mind

The chart above summarizes many of the Meta 2 Individuists' distinct characteristics, triggers, and positive and negative word associations. It's a handy reference as you begin to digest the four different Instinctual Patterns and how they are the same or differ. We also include some details on voting behavior.[9]

CHAPTER 5

BETTER TOGETHER: THE SOCIAL BINDER WORLDVIEW

The Meta 3 worldview is shared by those who reside at the opposite end of the Social Binding Spectrum from the Meta 2 Individuist, and as such, they have a completely different perspective on the world. This group takes a cross-sectional view of all five foundational instincts to shape its perspective, with a more even contribution from each instinct.

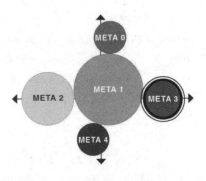

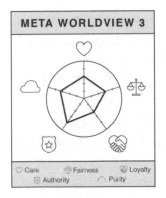

CHARACTERISTICS OF THE META 3 WORLDVIEW

The Meta 3 individual prioritizes the sanctity of the group and the community over the individual. To the Meta 3 Social Binder, authority and traditions define our roles and responsibilities. We all have a role to play in a hierarchy. This worldview acknowledges that power is distributed inequitably, but that it is natural for society to have leaders and followers, winners and losers. By this reasoning, if someone's life goes off the rails, it is up to that individual to fit in and take responsibility. The Meta 3 is less inclined to guarantee equality of access or to spread compassion around as freely as the Meta 2 Individuist does—fairness is often seen as proportional to an individual's contribution to society. In fact, by comparison, Meta 3s generally speaking have a muted sense of compassion for those outside their group of origin. If sacrifices must be made, it is not desirable, but those decisions must—and should—be made individually. Additionally, Meta 3s share a special sense of protecting their group from sabotage, as they loathe disloyalty. Social Binders hold in high esteem the institutions that strive to protect their cultural values. They can have fierce loyalty to their group of origin, however that is defined. To Meta 3s, the idea that rank has its privileges is quite apt. This means that earning an important rank within the group often comes with additional perks and privileges. This is part of the natural order of things. Essentially, membership in the group, or culture, accrues benefits to those who take on the responsibilities of maintaining the community. Likewise, Meta 3s abide by their codes of conduct to avoid social taboos that affect us all. Often, these codes involve the purity of cleanliness and invoke a higher spiritual power.

THE META 3'S STORY

Just as a Meta 2's Instinctual Pattern is represented by a narrative that reflects how their instincts may be triggered in daily life, so does a social binder enjoy a narrative that describes their specific profile. A Meta 3 might tell their story like this:

> In simple terms, this is how I see the world: There is a natural order, a right and a wrong way to do things, and if you adhere to this order, life tends to proceed smoothly. There are leaders and followers, team players and individuals, and winners and losers. It is not that hard. When I go to work and everyone does their part, things go well. But sometimes some folks think that they know best, and go out on their own, things grind to a halt. Like I said, it's not that hard. I do know that I get a lot of strength from my relationship with God. When I am unsure, I have a place to turn for guidance.
>
> In general, I lead a sensible life. I don't feel the need to rush out and get the latest fashion, electronics, or even music. I don't pay attention to trends. That way I don't waste time and money on things that won't last.

One thing that gets under my skin is when people ignore the great traditions of our culture. If we could just get everyone back on the same page, things would run more smoothly. When we see ourselves as one people, not splintered into special groups, we can accomplish anything we aspire to. It's when we put our personal interests ahead of the greater good that things start to fall apart. We have to recognize that there are existential threats out there, and that united we stand. Sometimes, I think there are too many people out for themselves. I understand that anyone can fall on hard times, but we are all responsible for how our own lives turn out.

If we pull apart the layers of this narrative, we begin to understand it more completely.

THERE IS A NATURAL ORDER

The natural order of life is a foundational belief for the Meta 3. They feel strongly that there is a right and wrong way to do things. Their mission, then, is to adhere to the rules, as reinforced by tradition. As their narrative says, "What could be so hard about that?" The authoritative instinct runs counter to the fairness doctrine so beloved by the Meta 2 Individuist, and Meta 3s believe that "if it doesn't impact you directly, you should keep your opinions to yourself." Under the right circumstances, however, just like the Individuists, the Social Binders do not hesitate to let their beliefs be known.

To be clear, this set of objective behaviors are learned and articulated over time, but the inclination to see the world as right versus wrong and natural versus unnatural comes from an instinctual preference for order and stability. As a result, there is no doubt or internal dissonance to quell. The natural order is one based on a hierarchy of power. Leaders have more power than followers, and that is natural. So, too, is the right to accumulate power by faithfully abiding by the roles and responsibilities of life. When you accumulate enough tokens for your achievements, you've earned your rewards.

A STRONG RELATIONSHIP TO GOD

The Purity instinct is a good fit for lovers of order and tradition. It is often linked to the notion of a higher order, handed down by a divine power. Meta 3s' goal is to avoid things that are culturally taboo entirely, rather than fight them off if they are infected by them. God defines certain things as sacred and in need of protection from desecration by things we find disgusting. For example, chastity might be considered sacred, and in need of protection from unnatural events like pedophilia, incest, and rape.

A PRETTY SENSIBLE LIFE

The urge to conform is complicated by other instincts. For example, the Meta 3 possesses a strong loyalty to his or her own group of origin, which can spill over into an "us and them" mindset. The rewards for conformity are often limited to the members of a particular group of origin, and not extended to others. Likewise, when the foundational elements of the group structure come under attack, whether jokingly or through actual harm, the Meta 3 Social Binder reacts strongly.

In terms of lifestyle, the Meta 3 describes him- or herself as sensible. This group sees chasing trends as a waste of time and resources. Typically, they are among the last to embrace a new trend or lifestyle. Rather, they define the "good life" as steady, marked by tradition and conformity. When this group does adopt a new way of doing things, it's likely for the long haul.

Because the Meta 3 values loyalty, they are hardwired to search for a point of differentiation between Us and Them. Naturally, this enables both divisiveness and unity—unity within the group, and divisiveness outside of it. But the Social Binder instinct is not specific to any group within a culture; there are Social Binders of all stripes. For example, Caucasian and Black American Social Binders both agree that the government cannot be trusted to tell us the truth about the COVID-19 virus—but for different reasons. One may think the virus isn't much more serious than the common flu and that the attention given to it is a "liberal hoax," a pretext for other government officials to harass President Trump and criticize his administration, while the other side simply believes the government has no credibility on healthcare, period.

If Meta 3s find themselves in hard times, they believe that the primary road to recovery is personal responsibility. They place little faith in compassionate government agencies or programs. While they would not wish for anyone to fall by the wayside, if they are forced to choose between that and putting the larger group at risk, the sanctity of the group will prevail.

THE ELEMENTS OF THE META 3'S IDENTITY

From this brief and basic narrative, we can glean an amazing amount of insight about the worldview of the Meta 3 Social Binder. Let's begin, as above, by using that narrative or story of the group as the lens through which to understand how the Social Binder instinct manifests itself in combination with the base markers of age, gender, and ethnicity.

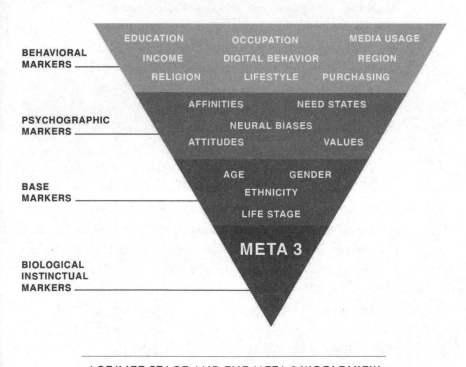

AGE/LIFE STAGE AND THE META 3 WORLDVIEW

As noted in our discussion of the Individuist group, the interaction between generation and age is complicated. The traits that inform the Meta 3 group are clear.

How those traits manifest at various life stages is variable. Here are some of the associations with age that we have learned from the base narrative:

- **AGE AS A GROUP IDENTIFIER:** Even more than those associated with most other Instinctual Patterns, a member of the Meta 3 group is very likely to identify as a member of their generation. The traditions and rules that characterize any particular generation will carry special meaning for the Social Binder. For Meta 3s who grew up in the 1970s, age-related cultural clashes may have been simplified as an us-versus-them division between hippies and a silent majority. In today's version, there are more than enough groups to find age-related disputes with. For example, think of the Millennials' dispute with the Boomers for leaving them with student debt, perpetual wars, a crumbling environment, and a fractured economic promise. There are many more ways to see differences with one another today—politics, lifestyle, gender, etc.—such that a simple age difference would probably not carry the weight that it did in the past.

- **AGE AS SIGNIFIER FOR RESPECT:** One of the hallmarks of the Meta 3 Social Binders is that elders have special status, demanding deference and respect. This is a corollary of the leaders and followers, winners and losers scenario. Stratifying respect through the prism of age is a value shared by Meta 3s cross-culturally, as well—a true hallmark of the IP.

- **GENERATIONAL LIFESTYLES:** The lifestyles of Social Binders tend to be anchored in the generational milestones of each era. They tend to honor chivalrous traditions and well-established norms and standards—the "good old days." Understanding that this group has a special regard for social norms and traditions, one could imagine that many of the younger generation, despite the general social convention of adults addressing one another by their first names, might use Mr. or Mrs. as an honorific for a respected elder in their midst.

GENDER AND THE META 3 WORLDVIEW

The Meta 3 Social Binder, with his or her sensitivity to the "natural order," is particularly aware of gender as a defining characteristic in our rapidly changing world.

- **GENDER ROLES:** Life is much simpler for this group when there are prescribed roles for everyone. The traditional roles of men and women are among the most rigidly ingrained of all time, an easy shorthand for the way things have always been done. This also elevates the Purity instinct as an inoculator for the taboos of society, reinforced by some forms of institutional religion. Defining what is and what is not "disgusting" in terms of gender mores is part of the Meta 3 instinctual worldview. As a group, Social Binders are likely to resist broad changes in how gender roles are interpreted.

  Consider the 2016 election of Donald Trump. The conventional wisdom assumed that women would be loath to support the candidate due to his history of misogyny and alleged sexual abuse. Yet when the ballots were counted, President Trump received a 47 percent plurality of Caucasian women voters, beating Hillary Clinton by two percentage points. Pundits were at a loss. But had they understood the Social Binder sensibility, it might not have been such a surprise. Trump's promise of a return to more defined gender roles, and an escape from the modern cultural trend of sexual fluidity, was key.

- **GENDER IDENTIFICATION:** The Meta 3 is definitely challenged by the evolution in our understanding of the gender spectrum. They may struggle with the need to accommodate people who are Lesbian, Gay, Bisexual, Transgender, and Queer/Questioning. This, too, is a cross-cultural instinct. Many Black American communities have been slow to accept gay marriage as a political reality. Given the variability in these Instinctual Patterns, the level of individual resistance to change varies as well, but some form of resistance is a hallmark of Social Binders. The longer a view is in the public square, the more likely the Social Binders will come to see it as part of a new tradition and have it conform with their worldview.

ETHNICITY AND THE META 3 WORLDVIEW

As noted above, ethnicity, as a trait used to describe oneself, is generally seen as something that must be considered with a high degree of sensitivity to understand its impact. It turns out that the impact depends very much on who does the describing. Ethnic communities in the U.S. are substantially more likely to rate their

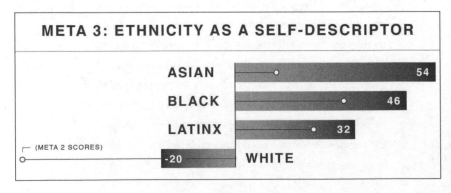

META 3: ETHNICITY AS A SELF-DESCRIPTOR

ASIAN	54
BLACK	46
LATINX	32
(META 2 SCORES) WHITE	-20

ethnicity as a virtue than the Caucasian majority. The actual numbers for the Social Binder group are displayed in the chart above. The majority, Caucasians, identify ethnicity as a negative trait, while the ethnic communities see it as a virtue.

It is important that we understand the role of the majority in these ratings. When they are asked about the importance of ethnicity from the position of white privilege and power, ethnicity appears as much less relevant to how they describe themselves. Since 76.5 percent of the country self-describes as Caucasian,[1] it is not a top-of-mind distinction for them, simply by virtue of their majority status.

Of course, ethnicity is a complex idea, and the orientation of the Social Binder group on this issue will reveal more about how they process these generalized traits. Simply put, when Meta 3s think of how to define their "in-group," race and ethnicity are often a starting point.

There is a lot of discussion today about implicit, or unconscious, bias. To be clear, implicit bias is a species-wide characteristic, but research suggests that just because someone harbors a bias does not mean that they will act on it. We think that creating awareness about implicit bias, along with the role of Instinctual Patterns in how we react to it, could be a fruitful exercise. Recently, several corporations, including Starbucks, have introduced implicit bias training as a way to discuss race and ethnicity. We think that these training programs should be expanded but might be more impactful if they included the role of instincts as well as learned behaviors.

- **INGROUP BIAS:** As you might guess, the Meta 3 is very tuned in to their in-group. The instincts of Loyalty and Authority compel them to define their group of origin and, likely, the traditions that apply to membership. As with gender and generation, these traditionalists will resist realignment of groups of origin. However, life experience and circumstance should never be ruled out. Personal experience with gender differences, more experience across the ethnic spectrum, and even rising rates of mixed-race marriage often overrule long-held traditions, at least in the private sphere. But in the worst case, they are also used to rationalize the dehumanizing treatment of others.

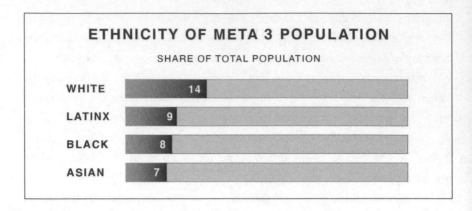

This chart shows the difference between Meta 3 Social Binder scores across the Caucasian, Black American, Asian, and Latinx populations. We estimate that 14 percent of the Caucasian population in the U.S. are Meta 3 Social Binders. This is compared to 7.3 percent of Black Americans, 7.5 percent of Asian Americans, and 9.1 percent of Latinx Americans. The real magic is when we consider how the Meta 3 Social Binder Instinctual Pattern will wrap up the biological, social, interpersonal, evolutionary, and personal experiences of a person into an integrated whole. As with each Instinctual Pattern of this model, this mission will have some similarities and some differences for which to account. Meta 3s come with a clear point of view, a near binary decision tree of for or against, in-group or outsider. Yet, as in other profiles, there is wide variety in how the instinct manifests. Factoring in age, gender, and ethnicity goes a long way toward helping define the motivations of the Meta 3s.

One of my favorite examples of a Social Binder is found in the film *Patton*, released in 1970, during the Vietnam War, interestingly. It won an Academy Award for Best Picture that year. It's a biopic about General S. Patton, a famous tank commander during World War II, and the role is played by George C. Scott as a classic Social Binder—clad in his uniform, decorated with badges and medals, a vision of authority, hierarchy, and social order. As the *New York Times* put it in a review of the movie in 1970, entitled "A Salute to a Rebel," Patton is "a man about whom only the Establishment could become genuinely sentimental."[2] Scott's opening monologue says it all: "Americans traditionally love to fight. All real Americans love the sting of battle. Americans love a winner and will not tolerate a loser. Americans play to win all the time."

So, what is the typical Meta 3 Social Binder response to a pandemic like COVID-19? Consider the instinctual starting point.

HOW A META 3'S INSTINCTS PLAYED OUT IN THE PANDEMIC

- **THEY'RE COMMUNITY-CENTRIC:** All dilemmas, however personal, are filtered through the lens of the larger community. Without overstating it, this point of view (POV) is often comfortable with a simple decision point: Is this good for the group or bad? There was a rush to adopt a narrative that the pandemic was being over "emotionalized" with predictions of death and destruction that could not be true. Eventually they decided that what was being proposed by the government was not appropriate and thus could be resisted.

- **THEY GRAVITATE TOWARD AUTHORITY:** The Social Binder group is quite comfortable with the hierarchical distribution of power. In the early stages of the pandemic, everyone was relatively compliant, but soon the Meta 3s balked in their support of social distancing and shutting down the economy. The idea of everyone being treated in the same way was likely chafing at their notion of hierarchical authority. They also shared a simple notion: The strength of the nation could handle a death rate that, at the time, was projected to be roughly equivalent to the seasonal flu, between thirty and sixty thousand. There was no reason to capitulate, putting the whole community (in some ways) at much greater risk. They believed the choice was between their economic health and their physical health, and they chose to bet on the economy.

- **LOYALTY IS KEY:** Depending on your in-group at the start of the pandemic, it was easy to think that it would mostly happen to *them*, not us. The divisions that evolved took on a haves and have-nots split. While the virus was an efficient and democratic distributor of doom, those without resources had a lifestyle that was decidedly at increased risk. Those with a high Loyalty instinct felt the question of risk was complicated by having to add economic well-being to the equation. This resulted in the haves being a primarily Caucasian majority. By virtue of the population distribution in the U.S., the have-nots were disproportionally people of color, of varied immigration status, poorer, and those with uncertain employment status. These variables, plus a Social Binder's already high Loyalty instinct, drove the belief that it was worth taking a risk in order to open the economy, especially since the have-nots were bearing the brunt of that risk. Remember the predicament of the meatpackers across America?

- **COMPLIANCE IS SEEN AS A BADGE OF DISHONOR:** Because of the snowball effect of these tendencies, the idea of displaying the badges of social distancing—wearing a mask, for example—became a bridge too far for many Social Binders, who were convinced that the risk was being shouldered primarily by others. Adhering to these guidelines would be the equivalent of identifying with the enemy. It would also mean capitulation to the will of others, and that is anathema to the Meta 3's worldview.

SUMMARY

For a quick glance, below is how a Meta 3 might describe themselves in a few sentences, what they consider a life well lived, and a list of movies with characters that embody the spirit of a Meta 3.

META WORLDVIEW 3 SUMMARY
NARRATIVE
When you appear on this earth, there are certain realities that you must face. There is a natural order to life. There are leaders and there are followers and a right way to do things. If you play by the rules, things should work out for the best.
IDEAL FOR A LIFE WELL LIVED
• I live life according to the idea that you get what you put into it, in a system that provides everyone with the **access** to life, liberty and the pursuit of happiness.   • I live my life in a way that allows me to work and pay my obligations and earn the just rewards for my contributions   • I live in a way that judges me on my own merit and how well I follow the rules and support our culture.
EXEMPLARS OF ENTERTAINMENT
• *Patton*   • *Braveheart*   • *The Chronicles of Narnia*   • *Gran Torino*   • *Dark Night*

As with the Individuists in the previous chapter, the following chart summarizes many of the Social Binders' distinct characteristics and triggers, along with positive and negative word associations. Use it as a guide to compare and contrast the five Instinctual Patterns we discuss in the book.

The Meta 2 in the previous chapter and the Meta 3 in this chapter represent the opposite ends of the Social Binding Spectrum, with the Meta 2 embodying an individualist approach and the Meta 3 reinforcing the clear-cut rules that benefit the community rather than individuals. Meta 2s are independent and autonomous; they prioritize the needs and rights of the individual and are competitive relative to their personal points of view. Meta 3s, on the other hand, are duty bound to live a life of deciding, doing, and acting on the principles of the culture. They value working toward a common goal, fitting in to the traditions of the group, and supporting others who accept and adapt to the responsibilities of the group. Both Worldviews believe in and fight for democratic principles—

META WORLDVIEW 3

VALUES

Social cohesion and order are foundational.	There is a right way and wrong way to do things.	There is a natural order to life, and something bigger than myself.
You are either with us or against us.	To those on the inside much accrues: Compassion & Respect.	Those on the outside engender little empathy.
Traditions are guides to how things should be.	Conservative Republicans predominate along with 20% Independents.	Group is not to be sacrificed for individual plights.

DESCRIPTORS

Patriotism	Order	Cohesion	Boundaries
Rules	Traditions	Security	Cleanliness

VOTING

54% Republican	21% Democratic	3% Libertarian	22% Independent

TRIGGERS*

Orderliness: Organizational Chart	Codes of life, values, rules of ethics	Symbols of status, rank & privilege	Sensitivity to Deceit and Treachery
Security & Traditions	Respect & Rules		

POSITIVE ASSOCIATIONS

Obey	Duty	Law	Venerate
Honor	Respect	Mother/Father	Pessimism
Hierarchy	Tradition	Rank	Conformity
Leader	Class		

NEGATIVE ASSOCIATIONS

Defiance	Disrespect	Dissent	Disobey
Insurgent	Unfaithful	Mutinous	Defector
Nonconformity	Protest	Refusal	Denouncements
Riot	Obstruct		

*The Righteous Mind

representative government, human rights, and economic opportunities in a free-market system—but each in their own way, with Atticus driven to defend Tom Robinson through his biological propensity toward fairness, justice, and care, and William Wallace driven to fight for liberty for his fellow Scots.

Now let's take a look at the last three Meta Worldviews, all considered Centrist, but all with varying degrees of Loyalty.

CHAPTER 6

A FINE BALANCE: THE THREE CENTRIST WORLDVIEWS

N ow we come to the final three of our Instinctual Patterns. I fondly call them the Centrist Stack, because they are all defined in some part by the centrist tendencies that make up the status quo. Residing between the polar extreme Meta 2s (the Individuists) and Meta 3s (the Social Binders), this group shares some traits with both, but seeks balance in all they do. Altogether, it is the largest group. But, as some lean more toward the Individuists, some hew more toward the Social Binders, and some are smack in the middle, there are enough distinctions among them to qualify for three separate titles.

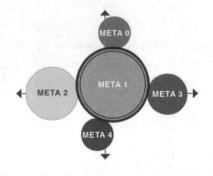

In our population model, the Meta 1s, or Centrists, are the largest pattern, residing exactly between the two polar extremes—the Meta 2 Individuists and the Meta 3 Social Binders—on the spectrum. This does not mean the Meta 1 worldview is complacent, or necessarily "centrist" in the political sense. Rather, this group takes a balanced instinctual approach, with each instinct contributing roughly equally to their choices and behavior.

CHARACTERISTICS OF THE META 1 WORLDVIEW

This group balances a sense of individuality with the traditions of social order and cohesion. As a result, they are often the voice of the status quo. They have genuine compassion for those who find themselves in a difficult situation, but they try to assist by working within the broader social order. Their votes are spread across parties and independent candidates at levels aligned with national averages and participation rates. They have a real respect for the underpinnings of the culture. They intuitively prefer entertainment that does not chip away at these foundations, and they value broad-based alternatives. A good summary of their philosophy might be: Work hard, play by the rules, and things will sort themselves out.

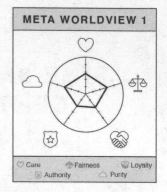

THE META 1'S STORY

In thinking about the world that we live in, there is a lot of noise and stress that disguises the fact that we have it pretty good. We all have a place in this world, and there are expectations and responsibilities to be met. Within the natural order of things, there is a lot of freedom for us all. The key is to balance these two things. Ideally, that should not be too hard. It is only when we get too selfish in our approach that we get into trouble. Some folks seem to enjoy poking holes into our traditions and history. I know it is not the end of the world, but when I hear it, it makes me feel somewhat out of sorts. I just don't like it, I guess. We can find the common ground, but when people insist on extreme positions, we get into trouble.

When we step back and survey things, it's important to protect what we have. Our history reflects our shared values and dreams, which have so far served us well. We need to take care of each other, but remember that no one person is more important than the group. We shouldn't just settle for the status quo, but invest in it, building on what we have and making it work for everyone. Progress is good, but being different just for the sake of being different doesn't make much sense to me.

WE HAVE IT PRETTY GOOD...
EXPECTATIONS AND RESPONSIBILITIES

This feeling that "we have it pretty good" extols the status quo as something aspirational. Centrists marry equal parts empathy for other people and respect for the traditions of society. The fairness doctrine, so dominant in the Individuist, is reined in for the Centrists, mainly by their devotion to tradition and group culture.

TRADITIONS AND HISTORY

When the Meta 1 Centrist refers to traditions and history, they're generally talking about normative behavior, the building blocks of the culture. They may become uneasy when people denigrate those norms, even as a joke, because they really value the cultural mainstream. But unlike the more dogmatic and territorial instincts of the Social Binder, the Centrist is defending what they perceive as the majority. They're suspicious of extreme positions (in either direction) and are rarely on the hunt for new trends or styles. They're pretty much satisfied with the current cultural memes and traditions. For example, when the ice bucket challenge hit Facebook on behalf of ALS, it was first promoted by Individuists as a new and different way to fundraise. When it reached the mainstream of public appeal, it was embraced by the Centrists.

SHARED VALUES

In this narrative, an understanding that life will deal both good and bad outcomes is paramount. Compassion and empathy are offered to those who find themselves in a bad situation, but with the caveat that we can't distort our values too much for the sake of rescuing people. The goal of the Meta 1 point of view is to balance our personal values with empathy for others.

THE ELEMENTS OF THE META 1 IDENTITY

From this brief and basic narrative, we can surmise an amazing amount about the Meta 1 Worldview. Let's filter this insight, as we've done before, through the other foundational traits of age, gender, and ethnicity.

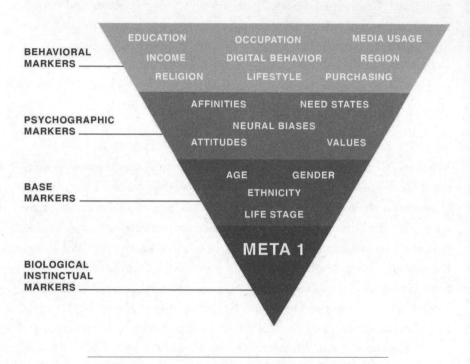

BEHAVIORAL MARKERS
EDUCATION   OCCUPATION   MEDIA USAGE
INCOME   DIGITAL BEHAVIOR   REGION
RELIGION   LIFESTYLE   PURCHASING

PSYCHOGRAPHIC MARKERS
AFFINITIES   NEED STATES
NEURAL BIASES
ATTITUDES   VALUES

BASE MARKERS
AGE   GENDER
ETHNICITY
LIFE STAGE

META 1

BIOLOGICAL INSTINCTUAL MARKERS

AGE/LIFE STAGE AND THE META 1 WORLDVIEW

The Meta 1 Centrists, more than any other group, will represent the *mainstream* reaction to age or generation—at every stage. Consider their taste in music, for example. If we take into account age-related preferences, there will be differences, for sure, as to what constitutes "mainstream." For example, the age-related appeal of hip-hop among Millennials versus Baby Boomers. The appeal for Millennials outstrips that for Baby Boomers by a factor of ten. What is more interesting is the role of the Centrists across generations.

If we take a look at the total twelve genres in our music study, we can see the relationship between the Meta 2, Meta 1, and Meta 3 worldviews.

The summary table below shows that Meta 2s have the highest percentage of "strongly liking" any genre and the lowest percentage of "strongly dislik-

AFFINITY TOWARD MUSICAL GENRES

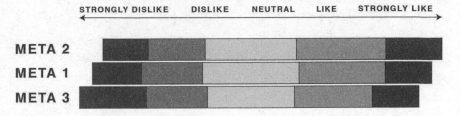

ing" any genre. The opposite is true for the Meta 3s. They show the lowest "strongly likes" and the most "strongly dislikes" of any group. As we might expect, the Meta 1 is in the middle. This is interesting, as it demonstrates each Meta worldview's musical tendency. What is more interesting, however, is the broader traits that the data shows, relative to how we think about each worldview. The Meta 2 is someone who is likely to seek out many new things across a wide variety of topics. This is the very behavior that we might expect from them as to music. They sample and tend to like a greater palate than the others. The Meta 3s are likely to know what they like and stick to it as they display the highest percentage of dislikes. The Meta 1 results show that they come by a moderating influence honestly.

GENDER AND THE META 1 CENTRIST

Gender is a cultural flashpoint today. The mainstream is struggling to come to grips with new knowledge and norms around gender expression and sexuality. As the largest of our IP groups, Meta 1 contains a wide range of reactions. Some will resist incorporating changes to traditional roles, while others are more open. As with most instinctual adaptations for this group, it will take time to accommodate change and accept new traditions.

Gender as a term of self-description at the population level is found to have

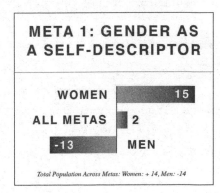

META 1: GENDER AS A SELF-DESCRIPTOR

WOMEN — 15

ALL METAS — 2

-13 — MEN

Total Population Across Metas: Women: + 14, Men: -14

a 2 rating. This could imply a level of apathy for this attribute in general. However, at the Instinctual Pattern level, the gender of the rater appears to be a significant variable. Male Meta 1s rated gender as a less significant trait (-13) when considered in a self-description. But female Meta 1 do not consider gender as less significant, as the population total score might imply. Within their self-description they rate gender as a 15. As we discussed when we introduced gender above, the idea that those in a relative position of power, men, may not think of gender as a valuable distinction to make.

ETHNICITY AND THE META 1 CENTRIST

Ethnicity, for the Centrist Meta 1 grouping, also tells a logical story. First, the population model shows a negative rating for this attribute (-17) meaning the population as a whole considers ethnicity as an unimportant element for a self-description). As in other Instinctual Patterns, the detail is enhanced by the sub-group analysis. White women report that ethnicity is very negative (-36), whereas black women rated it as very important (+44).

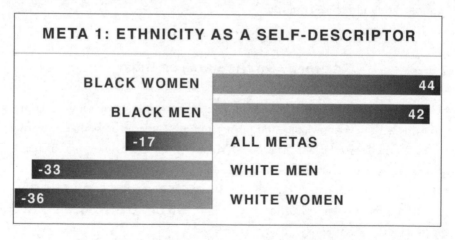

META 1: ETHNICITY AS A SELF-DESCRIPTOR

BLACK WOMEN	44
BLACK MEN	42
-17	ALL METAS
-33	WHITE MEN
-36	WHITE WOMEN

The difference among male Meta 1 Worldview is consistent to how women reacted. White men rated ethnicity as strongly negative (-33) while black men responded strong assertion of significance in the positive direction +42. Unlike other cultural shifts, there may be no mainstream resolution to this gulf. Rather,

THE SEARCH FOR WHY

it's a warning that even mainstream opinion remains deceptively divided along ethnic lines, and probably will be for a long time.

WHICH PRIMARY INSTINCTS DRIVE THE META 1?

As we noted, the Meta 1 Worldview draws on a broad range of instincts. These people tend to balance their instincts for fairness and authority, which often reaffirms their attachment to the status quo.

A cinematic interpretation of the Meta 1 sensibility would espouse a mainstream cultural point of view (at the time it was made). Think *Forrest Gump, Coming to America, The Breakfast Club* or even *Citizen Kane*. The key is to place it in history and figure out whose point of view it represents. Take, for example, *Forrest Gump*, a film that won Tom Hanks an Oscar, and a favorite of many film buffs. The movie debuted in 1994, taking America on a tour of many of the historical events of the last forty years of the twentieth century. It revisited the civil rights movement, John Lennon's death, the Vietnam War, Nixon's China opening, etc. Through it all, Forrest Gump never had a bad thing to say about America. In fact, in an interview with the *L.A. Daily News*, Joel Sill, the film's executive music producer, mentioned that all of the bands on the soundtrack were American. "All the material in there is American. Bob [Zemeckis, the director] felt strongly about it. He felt Forrest wouldn't buy anything not American." This is an example of full-throated appeal to the status quo.[1]

META WORLDVIEW 1 SUMMARY

NARRATIVE

In thinking about the world that we live in, there is a lot of noise and stress that disguises the fact that we have it pretty good. We all have a place in this world, and there are expectations and responsibilities to be met. Within the natural order of things, there is a lot of freedom for us all. We can find the common ground, but when people insist on extreme positions, we get into trouble.

IDEAL FOR A LIFE WELL LIVED

- I know that in that our system of government was set up to **ensure** everyone with life, liberty, and the pursuit of happiness.
- My life balances all that we want with all that we have.
- I live in a way that acknowledges our liberties while being cognitive of all that traditions that inspire them.

EXEMPLARS OF ENTERTAINMENT

- *Forrest Gump*
- *The Lion King*
- *The Lord of the Rings*
- *Batman Begins*
- *Citizen Kane*

META WORLDVIEW 1

VALUES

We have it pretty good.	Its just a question of balance.	There is a natural order to life.
A right and wrong way to do things.	Rank has its privileges.	Status is a sign of achievement.
Democratic, Republican and Independents.		Tension between fairness and hierarchical authority.

DESCRIPTORS			
Patriotism	Safety	Security	Conformity
Traditions	Social Cohesion	Compassion	Fairness
VOTING			
32% Republican	39% Democratic	1% Libertarian	28% Independent
TRIGGERS			
Images of Status	Social Order	Personal Safety	
POSITIVE ASSOCIATIONS			
Care	Shield	Protect	Fair
Rights	Equity	Together	Family
Collective	Join	Insider	Tradition
Permission			
NEGATIVE ASSOCIATIONS			
Expose	Wound	Betray	Exclude
Disrespect	Defector	Non-conformist	Protest
Refuse	Denounce	Riot	Obstruct

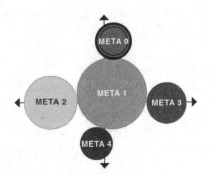

THE META 0 WORLDVIEW

In the schematic of the Instinctual Patterns, the Meta 0 Worldview, the Balanced individual, resides above the Centrist, with a particular focus on the instinct of loyalty. As with Centrists, Meta 0s also draw from a full array of influences across our five foundational instincts.

CHARACTERISTICS OF
THE META 0 WORLDVIEW

The Meta 0 pattern is characterized by a particular sensitivity to individual differences. This sensitivity is spawned by the Loyalty instinct, and is originally

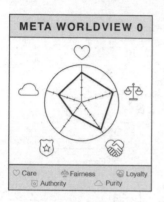

tied to one's group of origin. However, for the Meta 0 individual, it applies to a wide array of categories—race, ethnicity, and gender, of course, as well as political, economic, and other qualitative concerns. In many ways, the Meta 0 Balanced individual shares the Centrist views, but shows a much greater capacity to bridge the new with the old. For example, new trends discovered by the Individuist community are often disseminated by the Meta 0 group on their way to the mainstream.

THE META 0'S STORY

When I see the world, I feel exhilarated. There are so many exciting developments in areas like technology and entertainment in our increasingly connected world. But I am also very aware of all the ways that we can be pulled in different directions and grow apart from one another. So, while it is an exciting time to be alive, we also have to be aware of our traditions and history and the role they play in what we do. We are all responsible for ourselves, and we need to stay on the right path as we embrace the world.

For me, it is important to acknowledge that there are powers larger than us. It keeps me grounded. Even if you aren't religious, some things are still bigger than you. We have to protect what we value, and it is not necessary to always push the envelope. I take great comfort in thinking about our traditions and feel safe and secure when things seem to be running smoothly. In short, we should enjoy the robust world we have before us. I try to remember this is only possible when we keep things running smoothly and cohesively for the greater good. That is just another way we keep growing. New music, new food, new ideas about wellness and happiness are most successful when we integrate them into how we already do things. Our life is pretty sweet. Let's just keep it between the rails.

PULLED IN DIFFERENT DIRECTIONS

Given their high sensitivity to individual differences—social concerns, family, status, race, gender, age, you name it—Meta 0s are very aware of how even seemingly small differences can create big chasms between people.

POWERS LARGER THAN MYSELF

The Meta 0 individual likely has some kind of relationship to a power larger than themselves and feels that life requires an explanation that is beyond any single point of view. This can be either religious or more broadly spiritual, but it always connotes reliance on others for support.

SAFE AND SECURE

As with most in the Centrist Stack groups, the Meta 0 typically feels secure when life is running smoothly. The balance of compassion and order is the goal of this group. As they might say, you don't have to push the envelope to find peace.

A BRIDGE BETWEEN THE OLD AND NEW

The idea that we are better off integrating the new with the old is certainly a bedrock trait for this group. Synthesis of ideas is a way of encouraging incremental progress, while still "keeping it between the rails."

THE ELEMENTS OF THE META 0'S IDENTITY

From this brief and basic narrative, we can surmise quite a bit about the worldview of the Meta 0 Balanced individual. As always, we'll filter it through the base markers of age, gender, and ethnicity. Since the Balanced pattern is closely related

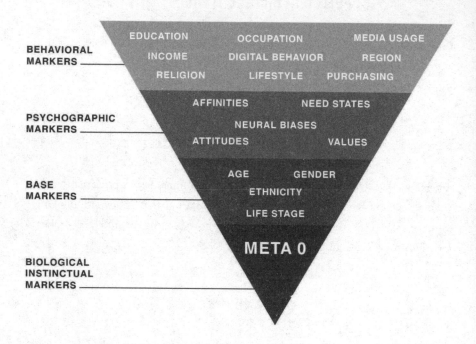

BEHAVIORAL MARKERS — EDUCATION OCCUPATION MEDIA USAGE INCOME DIGITAL BEHAVIOR REGION RELIGION LIFESTYLE PURCHASING

PSYCHOGRAPHIC MARKERS — AFFINITIES NEED STATES NEURAL BIASES ATTITUDES VALUES

BASE MARKERS — AGE GENDER ETHNICITY LIFE STAGE

META 0

BIOLOGICAL INSTINCTUAL MARKERS —

to the Centrist, mainstream outcomes generally apply to both groups. These centrist tendencies inform the base insights as to age, gender, and ethnicity. Now let's look at the additional unique considerations of the Balanced pattern to Age/ Generation, Gender and Ethnicity.

AGE/LIFE STAGE AND THE META 0 WORLDVIEW

As we discussed elsewhere, age is often a highly significant factor when describing oneself to others. In fact, it was the highest-rated trait that we studied. Not surprisingly, those in the Meta 0 community rated age as substantially more important than the general population does. This is likely

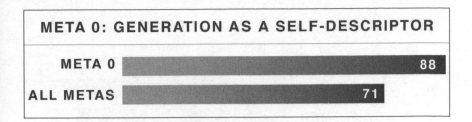

META 0: GENERATION AS A SELF-DESCRIPTOR

META 0	88
ALL METAS	71

because they recognize that generational differences can be true drivers of conflict or inclusion.

GENDER AND THE MEGA 0 WORLDVIEW

At the population level, remember, we saw a deep divide between how male and female Meta 0s rated the importance of gender. The total population rated it as relatively unimportant (+2). Similarly, male Meta 0 rated it (+3). Female Meta 0 offered a counter opinion by rating it a (+22). As a point of reference, this chart also shows how different this rating in from the Meta 1 ratings. Both Meta men and women consider this trait as more significant that their Meta 1 counterparts.

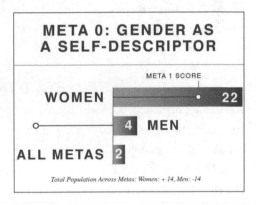

META 0: GENDER AS A SELF-DESCRIPTOR

META 1 SCORE

WOMEN ——————● 22

○———— 4 MEN

ALL METAS 2

Total Population Across Metas: Women: + 14, Men: -14

ETHNICITY AND THE MEGA 0 WORLDVIEW

Ethnicity follows a similar path to age for this Instinctual Pattern. At the general population level, with the outsized influence of white people, ethnicity is consistently rated as a negative influence within their self-descriptions. But when we asked the Meta 0s to rate ethnicity, we got some interesting results. The strong negative ratings of the white subset disappeared and were replaced by essentially neutral ratings. Given the volatility of race and ethnicity in America, this is a significant and even encouraging finding. (Black Meta 0s continued to rate eth-

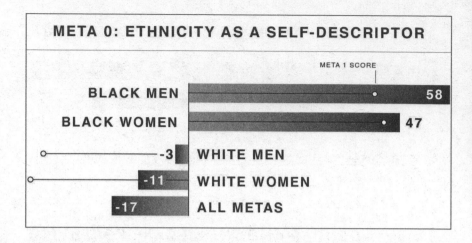

nicity as a strongly positive influence.) In America, starting off with a Caucasian point of view that is neutral is encouraging. At least this group, who are so aware of our differences, seem to acknowledge its significance, especially as compared to the larger Meta 1 group.

THE META 0 INDIVIDUAL'S PROFILE

As we have discussed, the Individuists spearhead most new trends and lifestyles, but often the Meta 0 folks are the next adopters. A former NFL player once subconsciously related to me a perfect example of the Meta 0 skill set. He said that the most successful NFL teams have a unique chemistry in the locker room. "By nature, pro athletes are pretty much rules guys," he said. "But on the really successful teams, there are usually a few guys that have the knack of being able to explain how things work to others." He then explained himself that some key players are known as "me/I" guys—that is, they have trouble putting the team ahead of their own accomplishments. A few "me/I" guys can be managed, especially if they come with superstar talent. But at a team level, it is important "having a person that keeps everyone on the same page and knowing what is acceptable and what is not is a real difference maker," he said. This is the role of the Meta 0.

SUMMARY

META WORLDVIEW 0			
VALUES			
Eyes on the Horizon.	If we are keeping score I might as well win.		Its up to me to make things happen.
Push forward but keep it in between the rails.	I like my chances.		There are powers larger than me.
We is made of you AND me.		Democratic, Republican & Independent.	
DESCRIPTORS			
Newness	Forward-Looking	Connected	Compassion
Expansive	Traditions	Wellness & Spirituality	Responsible
VOTING			
36% Republican	38% Democratic	1% Libertarian	25% Independent
TRIGGERS			
Nurturing	Boundaries	Collaboration	Traditions
Optimism	Responsibility	Conformity	
POSITIVE ASSOCIATIONS			
Compassion	Empathy	Homeland	Love
Care	Guard	Family	Order
Equal	Justice	Member	Ally
Lawful	Nation		
NEGATIVE ASSOCIATIONS			
Harm	Unjust	Deceive	Apathy
Abandon	Dishonest	Preferential favor	Cheat
Unscrupulous			

IDEAL FOR A LIFE WELL LIVED

Our government ensures access to liberty and pursuit of happiness, within reason.

I live my life in a way that understands that with every liberty we have, there is a responsibility attached to it.

I live in a way that understands that our culture is what makes us different, and membership is prized.

EXEMPLARS OF ENTERTAINMENT

Captain America: The Winter Soldier
Catch Me If You Can
Sully
The Breakfast Club
Jaws

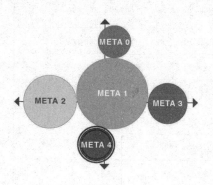

THE META 4 WORLDVIEW

In the schematic of the Instinctual Patterns, the Meta 4 Worldview resides below the Centrist, but with a lower Loyalty instinct. This worldview, also closely related to the Centrist, draws from a full array of influences across our five foundational instincts. These people's impulses toward both social binding and individuation ensure a balanced approach to life.

CHARACTERISTICS OF THE META 4 WORLDVIEW

The Meta 4 Worldview shares many instincts with the Centrist. The key difference is a consistently low Loyalty instinct. The Meta 4 defines their group of origin as mostly involving family and others with whom they have a direct personal connection. Yet it's not exclusivity that drives this trait for the Meta 4 individual. In fact, they tend to approach everyone with the same open hand. Their assumption is that everyone is eligible to the benefits of life. Many of the often significant barriers between people—like ethnicity, race, income, age, and religion—are rated less important to this group than to the other Instinctual Patterns.

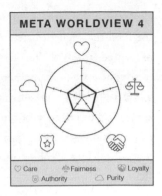

THE META 4'S STORY

If I were to describe myself, I would say that I think that most people are doing the best they can. While I think that life is pretty good and I am confident that I can make things happen, I also think there are lots of things we don't have control over, like our health. In fact, I sometimes don't even want to get the results of my medical tests, just in case they're bad.

I know there is a lot of injustice out there, but I don't know what can be done about it. I don't wish bad luck on anyone, but I don't feel compelled to do anything about it when it shows up. In fact, one of the real virtues of the modern age is that we have so many new ways to explore and do things. Technology opens up all sorts of new avenues, so there's no reason for anyone to stay locked into the same old way of doing things. I want to do what I want to do without a lot of interference from anyone, and I would offer the same courtesy to everyone else.

My main focus is on making sure my family is taken care of before anything else. I really try to give my loved ones as much knowledge as possible so that they don't make the same mistakes I did. I think everyone should be treated fairly, as long as they play by the rules.

WE DON'T HAVE A LOT OF CONTROL

The relationship between the Meta 1 Centrist point of view that "life is pretty good" and a belief that "we don't have a lot of control over life events" is a perfect example of the Meta 4 pattern. The sentiment that "life is good" is derived from the Centrists' full-throated support of the status quo. But the acknowledgment of limited control is their signature worldview. It almost borders on apathy or detachment, even to the point of fatalism. To wit, Meta 4 often have a markedly different response to questions that other profiles—even opposing ones—generally agree on. For instance: "I think that education is a key to a good life." This question typically gets more than 80 percent agreement from all respondents. In contrast, the Meta 4 cohort routinely answers this question with more ambiguity. Even a presumed common good—education—is suspect with this group.

DON'T GET INVOLVED

As with others in the Centrist Stack, Meta 4s seek to balance compassion for individuals and the sanctity of the group. Their compassion for individuals does not extend to wanting to get involved. They have empathy for the person in the predicament, but do not feel responsible for doing anything about it. This kind of approach-avoidance strategy is one way that the Meta 4s maintain the hallmark equilibrium of the Centrist Stack.

One unique trait of this Instinctual Pattern seems to be an embrace of technological solutions. This group does over-index on affinity toward technology, perhaps because of its promise to solve big problems without their personal participation.

MY FAMILY, MY PROBLEM

When it does get personal for Meta 4s, it's through family and close friends. They will gladly give loved ones advice so that they don't make the same mistakes as they did, hoping to see them through life's trials, but they would not feel any inherent motivation to share that wisdom more broadly with the wider world. The strong sense of sharing with loved ones is a key attribute of the Meta 4, although they are seemingly detached from the wider world.

AGE, GENDER, ETHNICITY, AND THE META 4

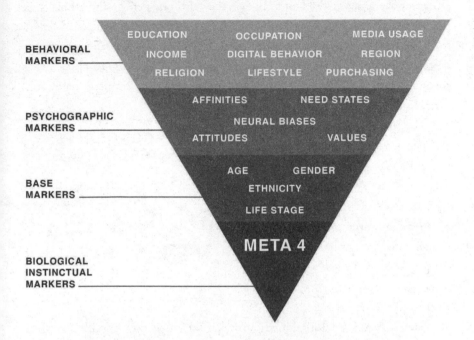

| BEHAVIORAL MARKERS | EDUCATION INCOME RELIGION | OCCUPATION DIGITAL BEHAVIOR LIFESTYLE | MEDIA USAGE REGION PURCHASING |

PSYCHOGRAPHIC MARKERS — AFFINITIES NEED STATES / NEURAL BIASES / ATTITUDES VALUES

BASE MARKERS — AGE GENDER / ETHNICITY / LIFE STAGE

META 4

BIOLOGICAL INSTINCTUAL MARKERS —

As with others in the Centrist Stack, Meta 4s espouse broad-based opinions in the areas of age/life stage, gender, and ethnicity. A full-throated endorsement of the status quo is the instinctual preference of this group, but that doesn't mean there aren't quirks in their approach.

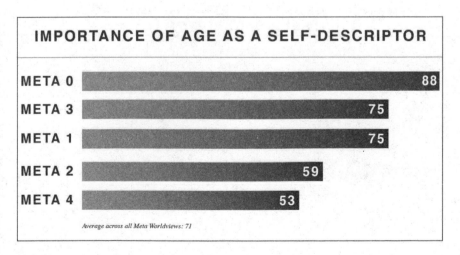

IMPORTANCE OF AGE AS A SELF-DESCRIPTOR

META 0	88
META 3	75
META 1	75
META 2	59
META 4	53

Average across all Meta Worldviews: 71

For instance, of all of the Instinctual Patterns, the Meta 4 has the lowest rating for age as a self-descriptor. In fact, they also rate gender and ethnicity as the lowest level of any of our Instinctual Patterns. Unlike the Balanced Meta 0, the pattern *most* aware of individual differences, the Meta 4 pattern pushes these descriptors into the background, embracing instead a broad approach to membership. Their definition of their group of origin has a distinctly permeable membrane.

The Meta 4 also has an unusual perspective on gender. Their total rating for gender is modestly negative. Meta 4 men, especially, tend to rate this trait as highly negative. But even the Meta 4 women rate gender as barely positive—an extremely low score in comparison to women with other Instinctual Patterns.

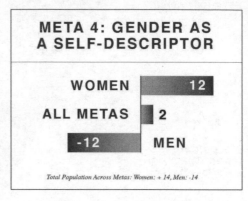

META 4: GENDER AS A SELF-DESCRIPTOR

WOMEN 12
ALL METAS 2
-12 MEN

Total Population Across Metas: Women: + 14, Men: -14

Meta 4s engage with ethnicity in much the same way. Specifically, white Meta 4s are very negative in their rating of ethnicity. Black Americans, Asian Americans, and Latinx Americans all rate ethnicity as a somewhat positive trait. Again, consistent with their Instinctual Pattern, the rating here from Meta 4 minority populations is subdued as compared to other IPs.

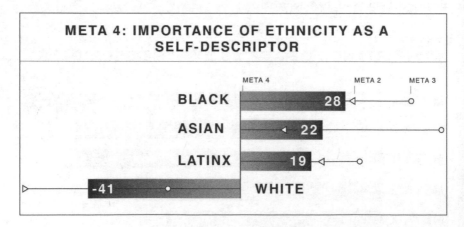

META 4: IMPORTANCE OF ETHNICITY AS A SELF-DESCRIPTOR

META 4   META 2   META 3

BLACK 28
ASIAN 22
LATINX 19
-41 WHITE

THE META 4 PROFILE

To fully grasp the Meta 4 point of view, consider the story arc of the series *The Big Bang Theory*. It focuses on a foursome of friends approaching adulthood in their own unique ways, clearly valuing one another while also dealing with new friends, marriages, and careers. Each sees the world in his own terms, yet they base their desires and expectations on the status quo of mainstream life. The producer, Chuck Lorre, described the characters' evolutions this way: "When the show began, Sheldon couldn't touch people, but now he is married. Howard was an obnoxious, delusional playboy, but he ends up a devoted husband and father."[2]

FATALIST

I would say that I think that most people are doing the best they can. While I think that life is pretty good and I am confident that I can make things happen, I also think there are lots of things we don't have control over, like our health. I think everyone should be treated fairly, as long as they play by the rules.

IDEAL FOR A LIFE WELL LIVED

We are lucky to have a government that protects everyone's life, liberty, and pursuit of happiness.

I live my life in a way that fulfills my individual potential.

I live in a way that allows me to fulfill my individual potential, but I don't feel any responsibility to expand the status quo. We all have to do the best we can.

EXEMPLARS OF ENTERTAINMENT

Arrival
Planet of the Apes
Gravity
X-Men United
Guardians of the Galaxy

SUMMARY

META WORLDVIEW 4			
VALUES			
Not very optimistic.	I feel like I need to find my own way with that order.		Democratic skew, and lots of Independents.
No real confidence that things work out in the end.	There are very few easy answers.		Tension between fairness and hierarchical authority.
There is a natural order to life.		Curiosity drives my interests.	
DESCRIPTORS			
Introvert	Early adopter	Detached	Nonjudgmental
Nerdy	Private		
VOTING			
27% Republican	40% Democratic	4% Libertarian	29% Independent
TRIGGERS			
Defile	Obstruct	Attack	Exploit
Deceive	Abandon	Wound	Solitary
Inequality	Newness	Harm	Diffuse
POSITIVE ASSOCIATIONS			
Guard	Justness	Reciprocity	Fair
Tolerant	Duty	Law	Permit
Comply	Ambivalence	Solitary	Diverse
New			
NEGATIVE ASSOCIATIONS			
Defile	Obstruct	Deceive	Attack
Wound	Intrude	Inequality	

CHAPTER 7

BREAKING IT DOWN: THE FIVE INSTINCTUAL PATTERNS, DECONSTRUCTED

S o now we have a baseline understanding of what makes each of the Instinctual Patterns tick. The five Meta Worldviews give us a common language for understanding why people do what they do. And the Model of Why offers a functional way of organizing those insights. As we explored the worldviews, we also looked at how each pattern might manifest itself alongside the base markers of age/life stage, gender, and ethnicity. In this chapter, we'll consider not just how those base markers but

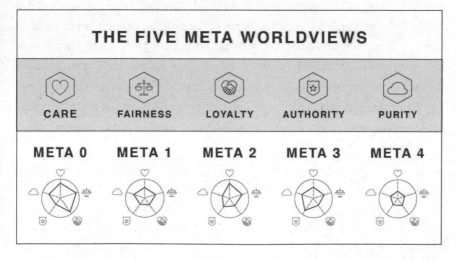

also how other data points that are psychographic and behavioral can layer and blend to create a more complete and powerful picture of who a person is—and why they do what they do. Some represent isolated attributes; others are related theories that can advance our knowledge.

The value of collecting any data at all is to the degree to which it provides insight into why people do what they do. Any bit of data must improve our ability to act on that insight, and how much it helps depends on the type and amount we're able to secure. This is the filter we use to decide what data to collect. This keeps us from clogging the pipeline with data that might be interesting but doesn't add to our mission of figuring out why people do what they do and then making constructive use of that information.

Here's an example: In many segmentation models, the data is used to sort people into buckets based on their differences. Certainly the criteria for sorting usually reflects some bias on the part of those doing the sorting, but even if they aren't biased, the data itself would not be very helpful in providing direction on how best to communicate with customers—to help change their lifetime value to a company, for example. For us, a grouping has little value if it doesn't help us answer the question of *why* and provide guidance on how we can act upon that insight. A collection of public data about someone, readily available and easy to acquire—where they shop, how educated they are, how often they go to Starbucks—is a highly unreliable guide as to *why* they do what they do. Though it's worth noting that these days we all have many identities that collect and fall like waves, based on our age/life stage, gender, and ethnicity, and we also have an evolving mix of tastes and preferences. Some are more important than others—some we'd die for, others we could easily abandon. To state the obvious, the more identities we address, the more effective our communications can be. But when we can't target more than one, it's important to determine *which* will surface *when*, especially at decision-making time—when endorsing or purchasing a product, watching a TV program, voting for a candidate, or deciding which charity to support.

Our data sorting gives us a filter to use when assessing what is important. This is a critical step. It's not surprising that we typically don't have access to all types of data, or if we do, we only have a sample set of each type. Limited resources are something we all understand, so when we start a project, we're very clear on our objective first. We're aligned on the problem we're trying to solve. Then we determine which data and which methods are best suited to the problem at hand.

As we seek to make data work harder, it might help to, again, keep in mind our purpose. People organize their sense of self in a running story that we hope to tap into so we can better understand their motivations. These stories are personal and come in two versions—one public, one private. That is, the story I share with my public, perhaps work colleagues, may be sanitized a bit. It probably also filters answers to questions in a way that captures how we hope others will see us. This version might be loaded with a bit of the "aspirational" you. (Sociologist Erving Goffman in his book *The Presentation of Self in Everyday Life*[1] discussed his belief that all people present themselves to others like actors on a stage, playing a character who guides others' perception of them, all with the goal of increasing their social status. Goffman believed this self-presentation was a natural part of everyday social exchanges and mostly an honest representation, though I wonder if social media these days would skew his thinking.) The second one, the private version, the one you keep in your head ("backstage" as Goffman says[2]), is the one that we hope to get closer to with the data we collect. In our model, getting to know someone's Instinctual Pattern is a key to letting us bypass the aspirational person and get closer to understanding the building blocks of their worldview. From that point of view, as we add data relative to these other layers, we can increase the accuracy of our understanding of a person's story and can do a better job of engaging with someone.

I like to think of the PathSight Model of Why as the art and science of triangulating demographic, psychographic, behavioral, and attitudinal segmentation with biological instincts plus advanced analytics and machine learning to understand why people do what they do. This is very similar to how data scientists think about the different types of data and analytical disciplines available to them. Each type of data provides some level of information, but as your data system becomes more sophisticated (remember the difference between complicated and complex back in Chapter 1?), it's harder to mine, but more valuable to the enterprise, moving from information to optimization. In data science, the four types/levels of data are as follows:

1. **DESCRIPTIVE DETAILS:** *What* **happened.**
   This is the literal description of what happened. For example, this book rose two spots on the *New York Times* bestseller list, this stock price fell by X, or I chose to buy a Tesla rather than a Chevrolet Bolt. In the Model of Why, we use conventional data to describe what happens, too. The outcomes of our model always map back to the conventional descriptions of what happened.

This makes using the Model of Why convenient as it doesn't require us to use other factors to understand what is happening.

2. **DIAGNOSTIC: Explains *why* this happened.** This takes an event, such as a book falling in the Amazon rankings, and uncovers the trends and root causes of why it happened. This is where the Model of Why provides a new way of figuring out the reason for what has changed. By introducing the Instinctual Patterns, we can see the different causes and effects beyond our conventional clues. For example, we can review how our book is selling by analyzing each Meta population to diagnose which is one is underperforming. Perhaps, we might change the words, images, or themes on the marking messages that target the underperforming Meta. This brings us back to knowing why people do what they do and leads us away from guessing.

3. **PREDICTIVE: Foresees What *might/will* happen.** Here, we look at probability of outcomes, and this is where some of the advances in data science can really power the Model of Why. An example: We might expect a book to appeal to certain types of readers (i.e., science-fiction aficionados, people looking for parenting advice) and will sell X number of copies based on an author's social following or the number and type of reviews it gets. Using data to make predictions helps us tailor marketing campaigns and messaging for different Meta groups.

4. **PRESCRIPTIVE: Informs *how we can make* something happen.** This is the final stage and where we pull all of these data together to end up with a better result. An example: Building on the descriptive, diagnostic, and predictive data we've already acquired in our book example above, we will know such details as who will buy the book, how many of each Meta Worldview would do so, and if they're likely to purchase online or in stores. The first step is to prepare our marketing

campaigns to align with the preferences of each Meta Worldview. We can design our messages, plan how to distribute them and measure the outcomes. We also have the opportunity to adjust each campaign on the fly. For example, if our Meta 3 sales are lagging, we might realize that Facebook is a high-demand platform for Meta 3 worldviews. Realizing that we are lagging in the Meta 3 sales, we would have the capability to increase our ad spend on Facebook in response to this data. This kind of integrated planning based on analyzing, speaking to, and measuring the outcome of our Meta Worldview is the perfect prescription for today's market.

The chart below—the PathSight Engagement Planning Tool we use when we engage clients—represents how we organize our work when it comes to crafting narratives and stories that focus on influencing others. Stories help people make sense of the world, so they're a powerful tool for articulating an influential point of view. This tool and process is meant to help clients be better able to tell great stories that move hearts and minds. Our model is intended to serve a variety of needs: a demonstrator fighting for a cause, an employee asking for resources, a brand touting the benefits of their product, for example. Once you start listening for stories—each of us presenting a worldview that's a blend of our biology, demographics, and psychographics—you begin to recognize that ideas such as liberalism—with its tenets of individual rights, democracy, free-market capitalism, and growth—socialism, collectivism, nationalism, authoritarianism, colonialism, imperialism, Progress Is Good, the American Dream, the Melting Pot, the Frontier Myth, and the Promised Land are just stories someone created that match people's intuitive sense of what is good and right. You realize that for each story that's told that makes sense to you, there are other stories that make sense to other tribes. Successful brands, activists, political commentators, and entertainment producers know this and are good at telling stories that inspire us to action—stories that grab us and hold on to our attention because they've explained how the world works to you. The goal is for all of us to become better at understanding what drives our points of view, but also to be more discerning about the stories we hear from others.

The first column in our Engagement Planning Tool references the relevant Meta Worldview. Depending on our goal, we may need to account for one or multiple worldviews. The next column references the available data that we have to use as a resource to help us to develop formal narratives that reflect any particular worldview. You will see that we can access available data across all markers: public, psychometric, base markers, and finally, instinctual markers. We have referenced this throughout this book in our inverse pyramid chart. The column "Story Tactics" is a list to guide our investigation of the available data for a specific campaign or strategy. In this next section, we will discuss the types of information and tactics that we may have access to for any single engagement.

Specifically, we will cover:

- How we summarize the Meta Worldview
- For the purpose of this story, what is the age/life stage, gender, and/or ethnicity impact.
- Are there cognitive biases to consider?
- Do we have any insights into the values of the target?
- What tactics are suggested by the lifestyles, affinities, or attitudes of the target?
- Can we build a story arc that accounts for these?
- What means of implementing this campaign will be considered?

It is important to understand that we may never have all the data that we would like, but the cascading effect of each of these data sets allows more confidence than relying on traditional segmentation systems. Likewise, we typically don't use all the tactics on our list for any one engagement. The chart below is meant to represent an array of options from which we can pick and choose, and it is not exhaustive.

MAKING DATA WORK HARDER

To parse the many layers of data we might use, we've mapped out a process for planning each of our engagements. We will start at the bottom and work our way up.

THE PATHSIGHT ENGAGEMENT PLANNING TOOL		
META WORLDVIEW	**NARRATIVE DATA SOURCE**	**STORY TACTICS**
Meta Worldview 0	Behavioral (Public) Markers	Publishing Platforms
Meta Worldview 1	Psychographic Markers	Story Arcs
Meta Worldview 2	Base Markers	Lifestyle, Affinities, Attitudes
Meta Worldview 3	Biologic Instinctual Markers	Values
Meta Worldview 4		Cognitive Biases
		Life Stage, Gender, Ethnicity
		Summary of Worldview

FOUNDATIONAL INSTINCTS

At the base of every one of our analyses are the Instinctual Patterns. The Instinctual Patterns can be obtained by surveying any population or subset thereof. If you are interested in finding out your IP, you can take a survey at www.TheModelofWhy.com. Other methods include using data markers to look at how Instinctual Patterns are distributed across various populations. PathSight has begun to build data sets that reveal how these IPs relate to individual brands, content, media platforms, messaging copy, themes, and images. One simple example is in how we develop our preferences for automobiles. In our research, we have found that Meta 3 Social Binders prefer Mercedes-Benz because of how the brand describes their value proposition for each Meta Worldview. Specifically, this value proposition defines what a classic luxury car means to the Meta 3 consumer, Mercedes-Benz has several assets at their disposal. First, they have had a long, staid run at the top of the luxury market. They emphasize their attention to precision engineering, and the resultant price tag is one that connotes a reward for achieving life's goals. All of these are important to the Meta 3 Worldview.

Tesla, on the other hand, is a new entry into the luxury auto marketplace. The brand constructed a value proposition that began by appealing to a different Meta Worldview. Tesla began with a different conceptualization of a luxury car, beginning with its engineering. It conceived a battery-powered electric vehicle with a dramatic reliance on technology, a unique sales strategy, sleek design, and an eco-friendly footprint. All of these benefits align with those of the Meta 2 Worldview who, not coincidentally, made up the early adopters of the Tesla.

In most cases, our goal is to generate content or messaging that will appeal to and answer the needs of specific slices of people, but PathSight is always pursuing new ways to use these Instinctual Patterns. For example, we are currently collaborating with MEE Productions, a Philadelphia-based research company specializing in urban populations, to study Gen Z low-income minority populations of color. MEE's goal is to better understand who the influencers are in this population, and how they are managing unique generational challenges. As their website says:

> MEE Productions Inc. is a research and health communications company that specializes in low-income Black American and Latinx groups. Since 1992, MEE has researched the lives and lifestyles of generations of young people who have been at the heart of seismic cultural changes. Today, this cohort is the Urban Generation Z (Zoomers, Plurals, Deltas or simply Post-Millennials). We know that this generation includes millions of lower-income urban youth of color who should be recognized as cultural influencers in line with the legacies of their historical peers.[3]
>
> Our past research has documented how urban youth have led the emergence of the Hip-Hop Generation, revolutionized expressions of sexuality and adopted unique ways of thriving within systems where failure is built in and their environments are filled with stress and trauma. We have discovered over time that these emerging young adults often have an outsized impact on how things turn out. As social justice and activism become more prominent in today's society, it is more important than ever to understand what motivates the be-

havior of the trendsetting urban cohort of Generation Z. Now, we are investigating how today's generation will define their approach to resilience, justice and fairness in this time of upheaval.[4]

It's worth noting again, that the nature of one's Instinctual Pattern is not hardwired to deliver a particular behavior. As we've said, the IPs comingle with other core traits that together present a unique behavior profile.

AGE/LIFE STAGE, GENDER, AND ETHNICITY

As we discussed earlier, a person's age/life stage, gender, and ethnicity are very important base markers that can result in a new concept of their identity. When we add them to the mix with our Instinctual Pattern, we envision a sort of feedback loop for a person's life experiences to weigh in on what is happening. When we are infants, the feedback is typically limited to our parents and our childcare milieu. Then, when we get to school, we expand our field of feedback to teachers, peers, and the broad sentiments of others. So, in a very direct sense, how we think about how the world is reacting to us is a very powerful and intimate source that can shape how we think about everything. As we mature, this can be the source for our individual and social identities.

For this exercise of planning how to engage someone with a narrative, we might ask how a twenty-two-year-old Black American woman living in New York City sees her world from the point of view of her Meta 2 Individuist pattern. What if she has a Meta 3 Social Binder point of view instead? What if we're talking about a Black American woman who is fifty-two years old? How would that make a difference? Essentially, what would this comingling of age/life stage, gender, and ethnicity with Instinctual Pattern reveal about someone's personality and decision making?

More broadly, how will one's Instinctual Pattern likely affect how they see the shifting sands of our modern world? What do the range of Instinctual Patterns think about the gig economy, for example? What about capitalism? How about racism? Economic opportunity? The range of Instinctual Patterns/ Meta Worldviews ensures that there is no single "voice of a generation," regardless of how history may write it.

As we dive deeper into the demographic and psychographic descriptions of people, more and more layers of experience come into focus, allowing us to consider attributes, attitudes, and affinities—key areas of a person's psychographic markers. Let's look at three of the most ubiquitous data points: religion, family, and accomplishments.

LIFESTYLE, ATTRIBUTES, AND ATTITUDES

Religion

For some people, religion is as important to their identity as age/life life stage, gender, or ethnicity. For others, it's an afterthought at best. Throughout history, there have always been groups who deemed religion the source of all things good, and those who saw it as a major source of conflict.

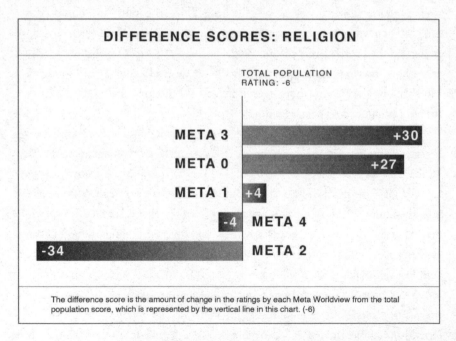

DIFFERENCE SCORES: RELIGION

TOTAL POPULATION
RATING: -6

META 3   +30
META 0   +27
META 1   +4
-4   META 4
-34   META 2

The difference score is the amount of change in the ratings by each Meta Worldview from the total population score, which is represented by the vertical line in this chart. (-6)

As the Western world has become more secular, these tensions have persisted. In the United States' secular West, religion as a self-descriptor has suffered in popular opinion over time, especially with Meta 2s and Meta 4s. In fact, this is one of those factors that differentiates Individuists from Social Binders. The Meta 0, with their emphasis on how we are different, rate religion as important to them. In fact they rated religion a full 27 points above the average rating. Meta 1s are more than 4 points higher than the population norm. Because Meta 3s believe in many of the articles of faith of many religions (e.g., the golden rule) and take an all-or-nothing approach to life, they rated religion at 30 points more that average.

Not surprisingly, the other end of the spectrum has a different point of view. Meta 2 and Meta 4 both have a negative view of religion as a characteristic to be identified in an introduction. Meta 4 rates it a -4 from the average while Meta 2 rated it as -34. This is seen as a trait that they do not want to be identified with when describing themselves.

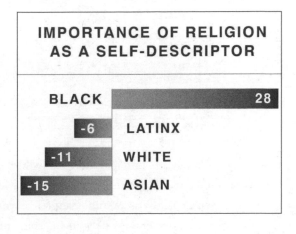

You may notice that these scores fit very neatly within the narratives of each group. Simply put, Individuists often describe themselves as having an aversion to the conformity of labels and group membership. Social Binders embrace group identity, conformity, authority, and hierarchy, and have a particular affinity for the Purity instinct, which is a strong indicator of many of the traditional beliefs and behaviors.

For the record, these descriptions do not depict any specific religion. This is how each pattern defines the *importance* of religion to their identity. As with other attributes, how each Instinctual Pattern relates to their particular religion is a study that's currently underway. We do, however, have a general rating as to how individual ethnicities rate the importance of religion. For instance, you can see that Black Americans have reported a significant positive net-affinity for religion. These variations should be factored into our analysis.

Family

In the United States, family is a modest component of how Americans describe themselves when compared to other factors. As with ethnicity, the Meta 0 is the

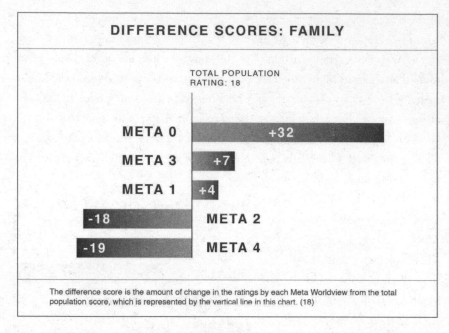

The difference score is the amount of change in the ratings by each Meta Worldview from the total population score, which is represented by the vertical line in this chart. (18)

most aware of family as a differentiator—fully thirty-two points higher than the total population score. Opposite that score is the Meta 4 pattern revealing a reluctance to identify family as an important reference point. This may be because that pattern tends to shun all labels, in the spirit of universalism. The Meta 2 Individuist feels similarly, given their general aversion for grouping people. The Meta 1 modestly adds to the total score (+4), and the Social Binder Meta 3 is seven points beyond the total score.

As with most attributes, introducing other variables also heightens the complexity of this one's expression. For instance, if we add ethnicity to the picture, the importance of family varies dramatically.

The total U.S. score as to the importance of Family is nearly an eighteen point rating. Total ratings of females are only slightly more sensitive to the total ratings as they add +2 points. White and Asian women have a slightly similar rating to this variable as they hover around this total rating. Black women added fifteen points to the rating, with Latina women adding seven points over the total score. Once you can dissect variables at this level of detail, you can see why earlier attempts at segmentation often felt so clumsy and inaccurate.

DIFFERENCE SCORES FOR WOMEN: FAMILY

TOTAL POPULATION
RATING: 18

BLACK +15

LATINA +7

WOMEN +2

ASIAN +1

WHITE -2

The difference score is the amount of change in the ratings by each Meta Worldview from the total population score, which is represented by the vertical line in this chart. (18)

DIFFERENCE SCORES: ACCOMPLISHMENTS

TOTAL POPULATION
RATING: 24

META 0 +6

META 1 +1

META 3 +/-0

-3 **META 2**

-8 **META 4**

The difference score is the amount of change in the ratings by each Meta Worldview from the total population score, which is represented by the vertical line in this chart. (24)

Accomplishments

The accomplishments that people use to describe themselves reside, of course, in the behavioral layer of data. Think of them as the low-hanging fruit of personal knowledge. They might include your grades in school, the sports you play, the awards you've won, your professional success. These are easily accessible, and usually a low-risk way of learning more about someone. However, the downside is that they don't reveal much about a person's worldview. As a variable, they seem to lack the stability of a core trait like generational age markers, perhaps because people's generation brings them together by identifying a common thread, whereas accomplishments are more individual in nature. As a point of reference, accomplishments have a total score of +24. This is a rather middling score considering that scores range from the +70s for age to -17 for ethnicity. Maybe for this same reason, there's only a modest disparity between the lowest score of (-8) for the Meta 4 and a (+6) for the Meta 3 regarding accomplishments.

We can conclude that how people regard and describe their accomplishments provides a glimpse into the instincts for each group. Meta 4 may feel that accomplishments are, in general, in keeping with their avoidance of belong to any group. At the other end of the spectrum, Social Binders are more discerning. They tend to have a code that judges the merit of accomplishments deserving attention. In other words, the achievements must rise to the occasion of having been earned. Social Binders reserve special pride for feats that require character and loyalty in order to accomplish them. That distinction is not likely to be attained by the mere mention of an accomplishment, but if something is really earned, it is cause for celebration. Participation trophies not included.

For our Model of Why, just as these foundational instincts and key markers generate crucial methods for understanding people, we build on that with a range of other psychographic data, which we highlight over the next few sections.

COGNITIVE BIAS

We briefly touched on cognitive biases earlier in this book, and I want to reiterate that it's important to consider them in our search for why. They reveal how we often act contrary to our best interest because it's just easier to take a shortcut (there are genuine benefits to cognitive bias, too—we'd never take a risk or make quick decisions without them!). These biases can be thought of as our brain's natural blind spots in critical thinking, and they range from a tendency to focus on information that confirms our preconceptions (confirmation bias), to agreeing with the group instead of evaluating options (groupthink or bandwagon effect), to making a decision based only on the information that's immediately available to us rather than adjusting our opinion as new information becomes available (anchoring). We'd prefer to keep the status quo (yes, there's a bias for that, too!) and stick with what we already think we know. Very few people are fine living with uncertainty.

One of my objectives, as you know, was to look for a foundational theory that would be broad enough to answer questions that might arise in the search for why. The work of Daniel Kahneman and Amos Tversky inspired a market unto itself built on a different, but related, scientific inquiry into rational choice. While Moral Foundations Theory offers insights on how we construct meaningful worldviews, the work of Kahneman and Tversky challenges those worldviews with their universal model that explores the theory of rational choice.

Kahneman and Tversky catalogued the heuristics, or shortcuts, that the brain provides us, in order to make decisions—absolutely necessary when we're typically making hundreds of decisions a day, in a wide array of settings. In their 1981 article "The Framing of Decisions and the Psychology of Choice,"[5] Kahneman and Tversky detailed how framing affects decision making; preferences change when "the same problem is framed in a different way."[6]

Later, going one step further, Dr. Richard Thaler, professor of Behavioral Science at the University of Chicago and author of the bestselling *Nudge: Improving Decisions About Health, Wealth and Happiness*, earned a Nobel Prize in 2017 for his work showing how Kahneman's and Tversky's methods could improve public policy and personal health outcomes.[7]

In the 1970s, Kahneman and Tversky fundamentally changed how people thought about thinking. In a 2016 *New Yorker* article, "The Two Friends Who Changed How We Think About How We Think," Richard Thaler and Cass Sunstein explained the duo's lasting effect: "In the period between 1971 and 1979, they published the work that would eventually win Kahneman the Nobel Prize in Economics. (The prize would certainly have been shared with Tversky had he still been alive. Nobel Prizes are not awarded posthumously.) There were two distinct themes: judgment and decision-making."[8] With findings near universal, but narrow in functionality, their work has influenced the fields of psychology, economics, medicine, law, business, and public policy.

Here is an example from their classic treatise in which we can see the effects of framing. It is interesting to keep in mind that they wrote this forty years ago; the issue they use as an example—a dangerous Asian disease—has proved prescient. Today, as I write this book the whole world is in the midst of a pandemic. Because we're dealing with the health risks of COVID-19, let's consider these framing tactics and how we, as U.S. citizens, might respond:

PROBLEM 1: Imagine that the U.S. is preparing for the outbreak of an unusual Asian disease, which is expected to kill 600 people. Two alternative programs to combat the disease have been proposed. Assume that the exact scientific estimate of the consequences of the programs are as follows:

If Program A is adopted, 200 people will be saved. (72 percent)

If Program B is adopted, there is ⅓ probability that 600 people will be saved, and ⅔ probability that no people will be saved. (28 percent)

Which of the two programs would you favor?

The majority choice in this problem is risk averse: The prospect of certainly saving 200 lives is more attractive than a risky prospect of equal expected value: that is, a one-in-three chance of saving 600 lives.

A second group of respondents was given the cover story of problem 1 with a different formulation of the alternative programs, as follows:

PROBLEM 2:

If Program C is adopted 400 people will die. (22 percent)

If Program D is adopted there is ⅓ probability that nobody will die, and ⅔ probability that **600** people will die. (78 percent)

Which of the two programs would you favor?

The majority choice in problem 2 is risk taking: The certain death of 400 people is less acceptable than the two-in-three chance that 600 will die. The preferences in problems 1 and 2 illustrate a common pattern: Choices involving gains are often risk averse and choices involving losses are often risk taking. However, it is easy to see that the two problems are effectively identical. The only difference between them is that the outcomes are described in problem 1 by the number of lives saved and in problem 2 by the number of lives lost. The change is accompanied by a pronounced shift from risk aversion to risk taking. We have observed this reversal in several groups of respondents, including university faculty and physicians. Inconsistent responses to problems 1 and 2 arise from the conjunction of a framing effect with contradictory attitudes toward risks involving gains and losses."[9]

Tversky and Kahneman knew their results challenged the commonly accepted theory that people, when faced with a decision to make, acted rationally.

Their groundbreaking research has impacted businesses across a variety of industries, and within a variety of disciplines—marketing, communications, user experience (UX), and product design. This work has been particularly useful to us when we think about marketing and communication strategies for our clients. Marketing is all about architecting robust relationships with customers, and that starts with identifying, anticipating, and satisfying their needs and wants—the Model of Why gets us there. So, knowing how loss aversion works, we'll suggest our clients use language that speaks to this loss aversion in such marketing tactics as discounts, coupons, reward programs, urgency, and free trials (e.g., the offer should be framed as a reward, not a risk). Free trials are a popular tactic, especially in technology—free month of Showtime or Netflix or Disney+. In a free trial, once the trial is over people will likely stick with you because they don't want to "lose" the product or service they already have. Urgency is another popular tactic. The name says it all—"Buy now and save 25 percent, offer ends Friday." Think "Limited Quantity Available." Loss aversion is even linked to designing for behavior change.

When we apply tactics designed to influence someone, it's helpful to take into account their confirmation bias. Depending on someone's Meta Worldview, we can personalize a message and a promise that aligns with their strongly held beliefs. For example, an anti-smoking public service announcement (PSA) that tells us a good person is one who is responsible for meeting their obligations to family and dependents speaks directly to the Meta 3's deeply held belief that family comes first. A message that might supply some extra motivation would be: "Do your duty for your family by making a plan to quit smoking now. It is, after all, the right thing to do because they depend on you to be there for them." This message would not work for a Meta 2, who's ultimately concerned with fulfilling his or her personal dreams about the future. For them the perfect message might be something like: "Your future can only fulfill your dreams when you make a decision to stop smoking." To match a message to strongly held beliefs, you just might tap into a person's confirmation bias.

The chart below is an example of how widespread and accessible the concept of neurologic mapping has become today. This informatic is useful to have on hand when wanting to know how people think and how to incentivize behavior change. Please note the labels that are listed in each quadrant of the chart. These represent the content areas that are relevant to that cognitive bias.

THE COGNITIVE BIAS CODEX

We store memories differently based on how they were experienced

We reduce events and lists to their key elements

What Should We Remember?

We discard specifics to form generalities

We edit and reinforce some memories after the fact

We favor simple–looking options and complete information over complex, ambiguous options

To avoid mistakes, we aim to preserve autonomy and group status, and avoid irreversible decisions

To get things done, we tend to complete things we've invested time and energy in

To stay focused, we favor the immediate, relatable thing in front of us

To act, we must be confident we can make an impact and feel what we do is important

Need To

Act Fast

The Cognitive Bias Codex—180+ biases, designed by John Manoogian III (jm3)

We project our current mindset and assumptions onto the past and future

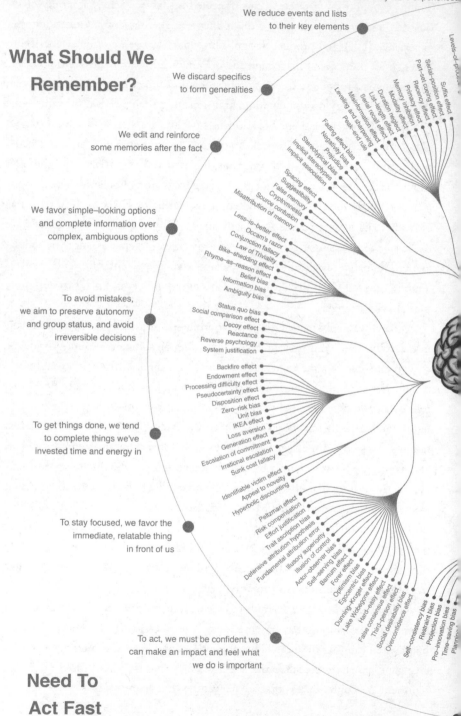

Levels-of-process

Suffix effect
Serial-position effect
Part-set cueing effect
Recency effect
Primacy effect
Memory inhibition
Modality effect
Duration neglect
List-length effect
Serial recall effect
Misinformation effect
Leveling and sharpening
Peak-end rule
Fading affect bias
Negativity bias
Prejudice
Stereotypical bias
Implicit stereotypes
Implicit association

Spacing effect
Suggestibility
False memory
Cryptomnesia
Source confusion
Misattribution of memory

Less-is-better effect
Occam's razor
Conjunction fallacy
Law of Triviality
Bike-shedding effect
Rhyme-as-reason effect
Belief bias
Information bias
Ambiguity bias

Status quo bias
Social comparison effect
Decoy effect
Reactance
Reverse psychology
System justification

Backfire effect
Endowment effect
Processing difficulty effect
Pseudocertainty effect
Disposition effect
Zero-risk bias
Unit bias
IKEA effect
Loss aversion
Generation effect
Escalation of commitment
Irrational escalation
Sunk cost fallacy

Identifiable victim effect
Appeal to novelty
Hyperbolic discounting

Peltzman effect
Risk compensation
Effort justification
Trait ascription bias
Defensive attribution hypothesis
Fundamental attribution error
Illusory superiority
Illusion of control
Actor-observer bias
Self-serving bias
Barnum effect
Forer effect
Optimism bias
Egocentric bias
Dunning-Kruger effect
Lake Wobegone effect
Hard-easy effect
False consensus effect
Third-person effect
Social desirability bias
Overconfidence bias

Self-consistency bias
Restraint bias
Projection bias
Pro-innovation bias
Time-saving bias
Planning

Too Much Information

We notice things already primed in memory or repeated often

Bizarre, funny, visually striking, or anthropomorphic things stick out more than non-bizarre/unfunny things

We notice when something has changed

We are drawn to details that confirm our own existing beliefs

We notice flaws in others more easily than we notice flaws in ourselves

We tend to find stories and patterns even when looking at sparse data

We fill in characteristics from stereotypes, generalities, and prior histories

We imagine things and people we're familiar with or fond of as better

We simplify probabilities and numbers to make them easier to think about

We think we know what other people are thinking

Not Enough Meaning

Mood-congruent memory bias
Frequency illusion
Baader-Meinhof Phenomenon
Empathy gap
Omission bias
Base rate fallacy
Bizarreness effect
Humor effect
Von Restorff effect
Picture superiority effect
Self-relevance effect
Negativity bias
Anchoring
Conservatism
Contrast effect
Distinction bias
Focusing effect
Framing effect
Money illusion
Weber-Fechner law
Confirmation bias
Congruence bias
Post-purchase rationalization
Choice-supportive bias
Selective perception
Observer-expectancy effect
Experimenter's bias
Observer effect
Expectation bias
Ostrich effect
Subjective validation
Continued influence effect
Semmelweis reflex
Bias blind spot
Naïve cynicism
Naïve realism
Confabulation
Clustering illusion
Insensitivity to sample size
Neglect of probability
Anecdotal fallacy
Illusion of validity
Masked-man fallacy
Recency illusion
Gambler's fallacy
Hot-hand fallacy
Illusory correlation
Pareidolia
Anthropomorphism
Group attribution error
Ultimate attribution error
Stereotyping
Essentialism
Functional fixedness
Moral credential effect
Just-world hypothesis
Argument from fallacy
Authority bias
Automation bias
Bandwagon effect
Placebo effect
Out-group homogeneity bias
Cross-race effect
In-group favoritism
Halo effect
Cheerleader effect
Positivity effect
Reactive devaluation
Well-traveled road effect
Mental accounting
Appeal to probability fallacy
Normalcy bias
Murphy's Law
Zero sum bias
Survivorship bias
Subadditivity effect
Denomination effect
The magical number 7 ± 2
Illusion of transparency
Curse of knowledge
Spotlight effect

SCHWARTZ VALUES

When the time comes to look beyond observable behaviors, there are several psychometric tools with long histories. They fall into three general categories: aptitude, personality, and skills tests. Each provides a different slice of insight to layer onto any personal profile. At the outset, the hope was that these instruments could unlock the predictive capabilities of behavioral science. These hopes have not yet been realized.

Still, this hasn't dampened the use of such high-profile instruments as the Myers-Briggs Type Indicator, the Big Five Traits, the Minnesota Multiphasic Personality Index (MMPI), and countless other surveys and questionnaires. Each has its professional supporters and detractors, and many have already over-promised results to a marketplace hungry for guidance. Our goal is to integrate as many of these observations and tools as possible into a dynamic model.

For example, the corporate world is still eager to train around concepts like empathy or emotional intelligence—for sales, marketing, human resources training, and policy. The Model of Why can provide a basis for this work, as well as related training challenges like implicit bias and decision-making skills. It is a complex mission, one that must avoid false promises of neatly wrapped answers. We think that every data point can add useful dimension to the picture, but as we have stressed, we resist simple cause-and-effect solutions.

Any of these instruments or programs can be a source of information that can add to our insights as we seek to develop the most relevant story for each engagement. For an example of how we use values in our campaigns, we will review the Schwartz Model of Basic Values. There has been much scholarly work done on how this system relates to the premise of the Moral Foundations Theory explored earlier in the book. Let's take a deeper look.

Values have been an important focus of research and discussion across all fields in the social sciences for more than a hundred years. Popular culture also shapes—and is shaped by—the values of its time, whether promulgated by a superhero movie or a pundit on a talk show. Fictional heroes inspire us to reflect on our own lives and what we might change, while politicians, teachers, CEOs, and journalists urge us to embrace certain timeless values—community, loyalty, service—and replace outdated ones. In a 2019 op-ed in the *New York Times*, David Brooks described the lies our culture tells us—that you can make yourself happy if you drop fifteen pounds. That life is an individual journey so it's best to keep your options open, or that rich and successful people are worth more than poor and less successful people.[10] We tend to assume that strong values don't arise spontaneously, but are the result of good parenting or healthy cultural habits.

In today's hyper-connected, hyper-polarized world, values have become a flashpoint. Whether you're on the right or the left or somewhere in between, we're all wondering where our culture went so wrong and why so much bad behavior is now condoned. In terms of the Model of Why, we think of values as an underlying cause for the decisions people make, a factor that shapes one's perception of the world.

Values have also become a cultural shorthand—a way to quickly judge whether someone is good, bad, or neutral. What makes matters fraught is that both ends of the Social Binding Spectrum, the Individuist and the Social Binder, claim to live according to deeply held beliefs and values. As a result, when evaluating one another's behaviors, we are sometimes more likely to seek a sense of moral superiority than a true understanding.

All values share certain characteristics, and the Schwartz Value Theory defines six of them, as follows:[11]

1. **Values are beliefs linked inextricably to affect. When values are activated, they become infused with feeling.** For instance, people for whom independence is an important value become aroused if their independence is threatened, despair when they are helpless to protect it, and are happy when they can enjoy it. If we think of the classic wanderlust in literature, we might find an obvious example. It may seem trite, but how many stories turn on a protagonist's need to move on, to find themselves (*this town is too small for someone with big dreams*)? It's especially exaggerated when someone has their right to independence thwarted. Remember the Incredible Hulk superhero? When he was feeling constrained, how did he handle his rage? As I recall, there was a pretty direct linkage to his affect!

2. **Values refer to desirable goals that motivate action.** People for whom social order, justice, and helpfulness are important values are motivated to pursue these goals. Motivations are

often attributed to one's values. What we believe in is commonly cited as reason or impetus for action. Continuing with our superhero metaphor, can you guess at how many heroic actions were motivated by believing in "Truth, Justice and the American Way"?[12]

3. **Values transcend specific actions and situations.** Obedience and honesty values, for example, are relevant in the workplace or school. Children are now being taught kindness in some classrooms, right along with their other studies. These values are also important in business or politics, with friends or strangers. This feature distinguishes values from norms and attitudes, which can shift among situations. Often the weight of our values takes on an aura of its own. There are those that think a violation of a value is serious regardless of whether the value was violated by an inch or a mile. However, if you witness any values-inspired critique of the difference between a treasonous untruth and a white lie, you may see some differences of opinion.

4. **Values serve as standards guiding the selection or evaluation of actions, policies, people, and events.** People decide what is good or bad, justified or illegitimate, worth doing or avoiding, based on how it lines up with their values. But the impact is rarely conscious. Values only enter our awareness when we're considering a course of action with conflicting implications for two deeply held values. What's interesting about this defining characteristic is that values are not typically at the heart of our everyday decision-making. Our values are more likely to be used when we are called to make a judgment about whether things are fair or just, or a person is moral or evil, or if a person violated a particular value that is important to us. When we are asked to consider making these judgments of character, we invoke this criterion. For example, do you think the Joker in the 2019 movie of the same name is a sympathetic character, even given his heinous behavior?

5. **Values are ordered by relative importance.** Do you attribute more importance to achievement or justice, to novelty or tradition? This hierarchical feature is another way that values are distinct from norms and attitudes. This defining characteristic allows us to make judgments about others, based on how we rank their values. This judgment may be positive or negative depending on those rankings.

6. **The relative importance of multiple values guides action.** Any attitude or behavior typically has implications for more than one value. For example, attending church might express and promote tradition and conformity values at the expense of hedonism and stimulation values. The trade-off among relevant, competing values guides attitudes and behaviors. Values influence action when they are relevant in the context (hence likely to be activated) and important to the actor. Ranking the order of values is certainly aligned with the movement inspired by the study of intersectionality. In this case, we may want to inquire, would a Black Female Millennial share the values of White Female Millennial. The level of inquiry is possible as we apply this layer of scrutiny.

As noted, there is a growing body of research that looks at how the Schwartz model may be related to the Moral Foundations Theory posited by Haidt and Joseph. The first question was whether these two frameworks were simply measuring different aspects of the same thing. Some recent analytic research seems to settle this question by declaring that "Values and Foundations are distinct."[13]

The Schwartz Theory of Basic Values presents a circular model of ten discrete values. The circle is broken into four quadrants presuming that the opposing quadrants reflect conflicting values.

Rather than just listing these values, the model proposes the likely motivations behind each. This prompted researchers to investigate what, exactly, this model was measuring. Schwartz states, "These values are likely to be universal because they are grounded in one or more of three universal re-

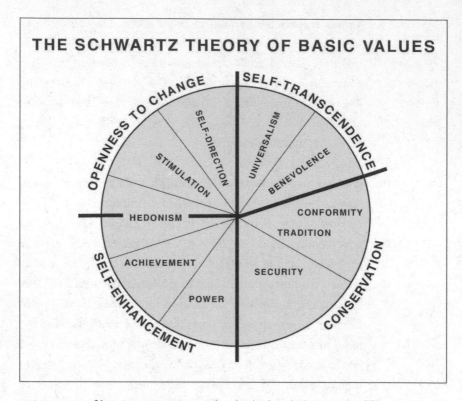

quirements of human existence with which they help to cope. These requirements are: the needs of individuals as biological organisms, the requisites of coordinated social interaction, and the survival and welfare needs of groups. Individuals cannot cope successfully with these requirements of human existence on their own. Rather, people must articulate appropriate goals to cope with them, communicate with others about them, and gain cooperation in their pursuit."[14]

Although the theory defines ten values, it also postulates that, at a more basic level, values form a continuum of related motivations (hence the circular structure). To clarify the nature of the continuum, I note the shared motivational emphases of adjacent values.

1. **Power and achievement:** social superiority and esteem
2. **Achievement and hedonism:** self-centered satisfaction
3. **Hedonism and stimulation:** a desire for affectively pleasant arousal

4. **Stimulation and self-direction:** intrinsic interest in novelty and mastery

5. **Self-direction and universalism:** reliance upon one's own judgment and comfort with the diversity of existence

6. **Universalism and benevolence:** enhancement of others and transcendence of selfish interests

7. **Benevolence and tradition:** devotion to one's in-group

8. **Benevolence and conformity:** normative behavior that promotes close relationships

9. **Conformity and tradition:** subordination of self in favor of socially imposed expectations[15]

The theory posits that self-transcendence sits in opposition to self-enhancement, just as openness to change does for conservation. In principle, self-transcendence and openness to change should be motivated by the care and fairness foundations of the Individuist Perspective, while conservation and self-enhancement seem motivated by the Social Binding perspective, relying on the foundations of authority, loyalty, and purity. This is supported by the recently available research of Feldman:

> "Our findings show that when combined, the two (Values and Foundations) may serve to better predict value-laden and morality-relevant cognition, decisions, and behaviors. Both literatures have much to benefit from joining forces in the prediction of human psyche and behavior, as both constructs have been shown to hold important implications for cognition, decision making, and everyday life behaviors."[16]

We have found the Schwartz system very helpful to consider as an input to our engagement planning process. If we have access to the results of an actual Schwartz survey, all the better. However, if we know the Instinctual Pattern of the person or group of people we're examining, we can make a good guess on where they'd fall in the Schwartz Model.

A CULTURAL DIVIDE

In her book *Rule Makers, Rule Breakers*, psychologist Michele Gelfand talks about how behavior "largely depends on whether we live in a tight or loose culture. The side of the divide that a culture exists on reflects the strength of its social norms and the strictness with which it enforces them." A tight society, then, has strict norms and "little tolerance for deviance," opting for stability and tradition. A loose society is "highly permissive" and welcomes rule-breaking and innovation. Gelfand goes on to say that "Social norms are the glue that holds groups together; they give us our identity, and they help us coordinate in unprecedented ways. Yet cultures vary in the strength of their social glue, with profound consequences for our worldviews, our environments, and our brains." This classification system works equally well when describing nations, social classes, companies, and families.

This research conducted by Gelfand and her colleagues studied the behaviors of 7,000 people across thirty countries, and classified each country along a tightness-looseness continuum. The United States, though not the loosest, leaned in that direction. Singapore, India, and Malaysia were classified as tight.

Nations that have been constantly threatened by invaders or ecological challenges, Gelfand notes, tend to go tighter. They also lean toward authority and loyalty. The same goes for families. The lower classes may feel under constant threat, so security is paramount, and they enforce strict adherence to rules to ensure survival. Upper-class families, on the other hand, may feel rules are made to be broken. They encourage their kids to explore.

It's easy to see, then, how both national and local cultures can align with the foundations found in the Moral Foundations Theory.

To see how Instinctual Patterns are adjusted at the population level, witness the difference between the U.S. and Canada. Despite sharing a border, a continent, and a good chunk of history, the distribution of the Instinctual Patterns shows *why* a different culture has evolved in each country.

DISTRIBUTION OF META WORLDVIEWS

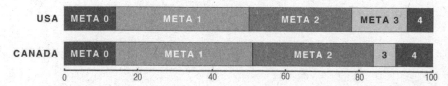

The cultural similarities between the countries show lots of ways in which they are the same. For example, the Meta 0 and Meta 1 distribution is virtually the same in both countries. This is the concentration that has full-throated support of the status quo, so it is not surprising that the centrist portion of the cultures are stable and plentiful. However, at the poles of the Social Binding Spectrum, there are substantial differences. Canadians have a 5 percent advantage among the Meta 2 Individuists in relation to the U.S. Consequently, they are much less represented on the Social Binder end of the continuum, 6 percent vs. 15 percent for the U.S., and have more Meta 4, at a rate of 10 percent vs. 7 percent in the U.S.

As we have done elsewhere, we surveyed Canadians on the perceived importance of age/life stage, gender, ethnicity, religion, family, and accomplishments. The results are as follows.

The most obvious difference between the two cultures is that the U.S., as discussed, regards age/life stage as far and away the most significant of the six attributes. Canadians galvanize around family rating it as a 64 for their total population. In the U.S., family rated a 16 for the total population. Canada, rated age a 0 for the total population while the U.S. rated it at 71. Ethnicity was -15 total score in the U.S., and only -6 total score for Canada. Religion was a much bigger factor for Canadians (-32) versus (-6) for the Americans. Gender polled at 1 for Canada and 2 for the U.S.

Does the Meta 2 Individuists and Meta 3 Social Binders contribute to the difference between the U.S. and Canada, one of which identifies most strongly with family, and the other with age/life stage? Possibly. What is most surprising is that two countries with a shared common history, and many cultural commonalities, can differ in such fundamental ways. By sorting via Meta Worldview, we can imagine a set of narratives to explain these differences.

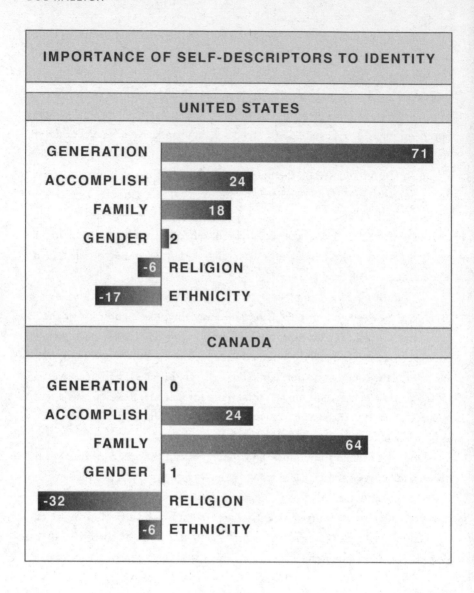

IMPORTANCE OF SELF-DESCRIPTORS TO IDENTITY

UNITED STATES

GENERATION 71
ACCOMPLISH 24
FAMILY 18
GENDER 2
-6 RELIGION
-17 ETHNICITY

CANADA

GENERATION 0
ACCOMPLISH 24
FAMILY 64
GENDER 1
-32 RELIGION
-6 ETHNICITY

CONSUMER 1	CONSUMER 2
VALUES	
· Fairness · Care · Impact on Individuals · Tends to be open to new things · Resists conformity to tradition · Great tolerance for differences	· The community is sacrosanct · Loyalty · Authority · Purity · Traditions, process and security are key · Muted sense of personal empathy
LIKELY TO KNOW	
· Democrat (or leaning Democrat) · The environment is in crisis · Drives a Tesla · Loves Sailing and Skiing · Art and Music are passions · Donate to Save the Rainforest · Last Vacation: Agritourism in Peru	· Republican (or leaning Republican) · Environment is just in a cycle and OK · Drives a Mercedes · Likes the NFL and Golf · Likes Country Music · Donates to Wounded Warrior · Last Vacation: Family to Disney World
KEY VOCABULARY DERIVATIVES	
· Care · Compassion · Peace · Justice · Insure	· Order · Patriotism · Traditions · Cohesion · Loyalty

SKILLS TRAINING AND CODE SHIFTING

SKILLS TRAINING

As sentient beings, we humans are capable of changing our behavior. It depends on the person, the behavior, and the intervention. There are generally two types of training available for making such changes—behavior-training programs and verbal persuasion approaches. Which program works best depends on someone's Instinctual Pattern. William Schofield of the University of Minnesota coined the acronym "YAVIS"—Young, Attractive, Verbal, Intelligent, Successful—to describe people who are typically open to verbal persuasion, such as talk therapy. Non-YAVIS people usually prefer a definitive reward structure, more characteristic of behavior-training programs. If you recall our discussion about accomplishments, you may remember that Meta 2 Individuists are easily persuaded to develop a new skill because it might make them *feel* or *seem* unique. A Social Binder Meta 3 individual is more likely to embark on a challenge that could *earn* them a reward or point of distinction. Tailoring the training to your audience's needs helps them digest new information in a way most compatible to how they process information. It's also important to understand the requirements of a specific job and to approach training with that lens. For example, in our client engagements, if we need to train a cohort for sales and the role demands a general curiosity about the world, a high degree of empathy for others, flexibility, and a general instinct for problem-solving, we might lean toward an Individuist approach. If, on the other hand, the job requires a person who is comfortable with processes that encourage doing it "our" way, who is rules-based and prefers to work in teams, we would take a Social Binding approach.

CODE-SWITCHING

Many of us inhabit different spaces in our lives, and often those spaces are culturally and linguistically different. We code-switch, then, so we can communicate with others unlike ourselves as seamlessly as possible. Specifically, code switching involves identifying specific details of a particular population and using them to change the way you present yourself to fit in or to demonstrate allegiance to that particular population or group. It's a complex and usually delicate practice that refers to switching or shifting language, minimizing an accent, or altering one's appearance, behavior, or other cultural behaviors. With friends or family we may talk in a tone that's specifically suited to them, other times we don't, such as putting on a game face or acting deferentially at the office. Once you're aware of code switching you start to see how ethnicity, race, gender, socio-economic level, and religion play out in different situations. This is especially seen in women, people of color, and other underrepresented groups who often need to navigate social situations, such as the workplace or school, to avoid or prepare themselves for potential judgment, mistreatment, or discrimination, and to advance professionally. The use of this tactic can be influenced by one's Instinctual Pattern as well. Social Binders are instinctually driven to loyalty, authority—there's a natural hierarchy—and to conform, but here the urge to conform is complicated by the fierce loyalty to their group of origin. Surprisingly, Individuists are more likely to code shift than Social Binders, out of instinctual flexibility, openness, and the desire to find common ground. Code switching can negatively affect people in several ways—constantly needing to downplay their race, ethnicity, sexual orientation, gender, ability, or religion can be exhausting, and at the same time they may face ridicule, or even anger, from their own group for changing their identity to fit in.

As an example of how powerful code shifting can be, remember how President Obama could effortlessly identify and signal to a Black audience that they shared a special intimacy. One particularly pointed example is when he went to visit basketball's Team USA in the locker room before their game against Brazil in the 2012 Olympics. As you can see in the video online, he goes down the line greeting the players and staff, and just after a standard handshake with a white Team USA staffer, he gives star player Kevin Durant a "dap," complete with back pat.

This is not a practice that can be utilized without careful evaluation. If it is used carelessly, the intimacy it presumes will not be reciprocated by the intended audience. For an example of this kind of inauthenticity, consider the mess that Vice President Biden generated by taking the liberty of challenging a radio personality on "blackness" when it came to his voting preferences. It can come at a cost—being accused of acting like those in power instead of embracing your own gender, race, or ethnicity, or feeling like you can't fully express who you are, genuinely and authentically.

LIFESTYLE, ATTRIBUTES, ATTITUDES

We have studied lifestyles, attributes, and attitudes around topics such as gambling, travel, food, entertainment, and music preferences. Needless to say, there is still much work to be done in this broad topic area. Often businesses rely on segmentation models that separate populations into hundreds of functional groups. The challenge is that relying on these segments, one often has trouble figuring out why they do what they do. This is where the PathSight Model of Why makes a profound difference.

Here is a simple example to consider: When marketers craft campaigns for products, they usually decide what segments to approach with their value proposition. For example, they might develop a segmentation strategy that targets high-income, general-market, middle-aged, married men. In doing so, they could end up with two people with very similar demographic profiles. Their profiles might look like this:

- Both forty-five years old
- Both Male
- Both Caucasian
- Both in the top 1 percent income bracket (affluent)
- One went to Harvard, the other attended Stanford
- Both married
- One lives in Greenwich, Connecticut, one in San Jose, California

At first glance, these men don't seem wildly different, right? By most lifestyle, attribute, and affinity segmentation systems, they would be nearly identical, especially since they even align on age/life stage, gender, and ethnicity. But there's a good chance these two men are fundamentally different. Those differences lie in *why* they do what they do.

With the Model of Why, we would begin by identifying their Instinctual Patterns. We might know that one of these men achieved these lofty milestones by relying on an Individuist Instinctual Pattern and the other did so by relying on a Social Binding Pattern. By starting with these foundational patterns, we add to our understanding of these target customers. Here's what we might learn:

CONSUMER 1

Values

• Fairness
• Care
• Impact on Individuals
• Tends to be open to new things
• Resists conformity to tradition
• Great tolerance for differences

Likely to Know

• Democrat (or leaning)
• The environment is in crisis
• Drives a Tesla
• Loves sailing and skiing
• Art and music are passions
• Donates to Save the Rainforest
• Last vacation: agritourism in Peru

Influential Words

• Care
• Compassion
• Peace
• Justice
• Benefit

CONSUMER 2

Values

• The community is sacrosanct
• Loyalty
• Authority
• Purity
• Traditions, process, and security are key
• Muted sense of personal empathy

Likely to Know

• Republican (or leaning)
• Environment is just in a cycle and okay
• Drives a Mercedes
• Likes the NFL and golf
• Likes country music
• Donates to Wounded Warrior
• Last Vacation: family went to Disney World

Influential Words

• Order
• Patriotism
• Traditions
• Compliant
• Loyalty

If we were to design a narrative for both of these people, we would do well to use the Model of Why. Even if we chose to consider them in the same grouping, using the model would inform us enough so we would know to avoid the words, images, and themes that might inadvertently offend either of them. Taking the trouble to try to avoid such an unforced error, or foolish mistake, in communication is certainly worth the effort.

WHAT DOES YOUR TASTE IN MUSIC SAY ABOUT YOU?

When we refer to a "lifestyle," it can mean several things—a keen interest in sports, a proclivity for music, a love of technology or gardening or travel. When we are sculpting a story in the hopes of engaging someone, we might look for signs of these interests in their purchasing habits or social media posts. Or we may have access to data from a questionnaire, a formal assessment, or a data set on a particular topic. Whatever the source, these lifestyle preferences are invaluable to rounding out our profile of a given individual. At PathSight, for instance, we have original research on music as it correlates to worldviews. So how might music function as a potential element of our evolving story?

We have tracked the appeal of each of fifteen genres of music across our Meta Worldviews. For simplicity's sake, we'll limit our analysis here to three of our worldviews: Meta 1, Meta 2, and Meta 3.

We start by looking for patterns. We note that of the fifteen genres, the Meta 2 Worldview shows the most positive affinity rating for twelve of them. The Meta 3 Worldview shows more affinity for two of them (classical and country), while the Meta 1 Worldview shows more affinity for 1 (pop). This is not surprising, when you consider the characteristics of these three worldviews.

The Meta 2 Worldview enjoys a wide range of interests, even within a particular vertical. Hence, the large number of high affinity scores. They also take pride in their ability to discover new trends and themes, so sampling from a wide array of choices is clearly consistent with their orientation. Even the specific genres attest to this fact. Indie, EDM, punk, reggae, and world music—the genres that Meta 2s express the most affinity for—are generally considered alternatives to conventional genres like pop, not their antithesis.

Also consistent with the Meta 2 orientation are the categories they did *not* register the highest affinity for: Christian, country, and pop. As you'll recall, Meta 2s are also less likely to consider a traditional religion as a major part of their identity. In this chart we can see that, in addition to a low affinity score, they actually have a very high *negative affinity* score for Christian music.

The other genres that they did not have the highest affinity for were country and pop music. Country music historically has built a following that appeals to broad-based stories that evoke the instincts of social binding, including traditional family values, patriotism, and heroism. Pop music is, by definition, a tribute to the mainstream, with appeals to mainstream values. This genre still elicits a relatively high rating from the Meta 2s, but perhaps with its mainstream themes, it does not resonate with their desire to be perceived as on the cutting edge.

So if we are using music as a theme in our story to connect with the Meta 2, we should not be bashful about sampling new and alternative styles that celebrate the nontraditional. For example, even if patriotism is a theme of the story, we might use personal and individual stories that evoke the outcome of the patriotic acts on the people and let the music narrate these.

AFFINITY TOWARDS MUSIC GENRES

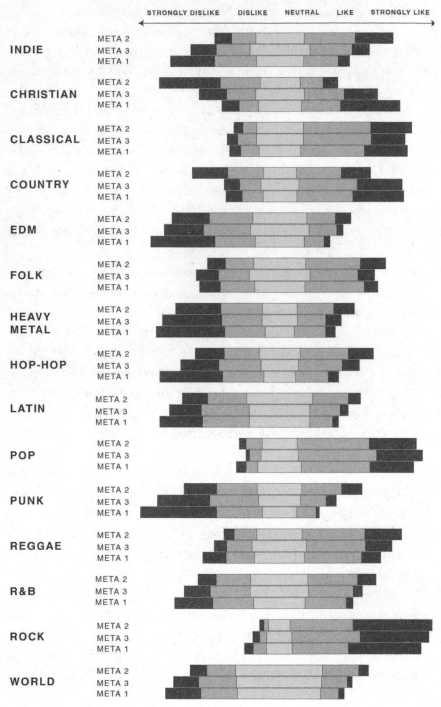

STRONGLY DISLIKE   DISLIKE   NEUTRAL   LIKE   STRONGLY LIKE

INDIE
META 2
META 3
META 1

CHRISTIAN
META 2
META 3
META 1

CLASSICAL
META 2
META 3
META 1

COUNTRY
META 2
META 3
META 1

EDM
META 2
META 3
META 1

FOLK
META 2
META 3
META 1

HEAVY METAL
META 2
META 3
META 1

HOP-HOP
META 2
META 3
META 1

LATIN
META 2
META 3
META 1

POP
META 2
META 3
META 1

PUNK
META 2
META 3
META 1

REGGAE
META 2
META 3
META 1

R&B
META 2
META 3
META 1

ROCK
META 2
META 3
META 1

WORLD
META 2
META 3
META 1

This summary table shows that generally Meta 2s have the highest percentage of "strongly liking" any genre and the lowest percentage of "strongly disliking" any genre. The opposite is true for the Meta 3. That worldview shows the lowest "strongly likes" and the most "strongly dislikes" of any group. Clearly, they know what they like and stick to it. As we might expect, the Meta 1 is in the middle, coming by their moderating influence honestly.

Within this lifestyle, there's plenty of room to move—it doesn't demand an all-or-nothing approach to affinity. For example, despite the aversion among most Meta 2s for Christian music, there are still those who find it appealing—after all, 13 percent of the Meta 2s rated it likable and 8 percent rated it as a strong like. This is important to our larger understanding of the Model of Why. Generally, you can find a pathway that appeals to each worldview on any subject; you just have to decide if it is worth the effort to construct a story that might not resonate as effectively with others.

Considering pop music, Meta 1 is the worldview that edges out the others for the highest affinity rating. By definition, this is a tribute to the mainstream, a bedrock principle for this worldview. In fact, pop is the *only* genre for which Meta 1 has the highest affinity. In constructing a story around music for the Meta 1, we might feature pop music as a leading thematic attribute to accentuate a product, good, or service that has mainstream virtues. Beyond that, we should not be afraid to use different genres to highlight special moments in the story— music as a support, not the dominant aspect of the message.

As we know, the Meta 3 is driven by the sanctity of the community, believing in a natural order in life and the role of family values and tradition. Clearly their ardor for Christian music is in line with these tendencies. Country music also underscores their affinity for traditional family values, patriotism, and heroism. The Meta 3s also have an appetite that is clear and distinct, not tied to novelty or trends. As we can see, the Meta 3 is the least likely to express a strong affinity for alternative genres like indie, world, reggae, punk, and Latin. But again, it's not black-and-white. You can see from the chart above that the plurality of Meta 3 has a negative affinity for indie music, for instance. Yet 19 percent reported liking it, and 6 percent voted for "strongly like." There is a pathway to find Meta 3s who like indie music—just not your typical Meta 3 pathway.

If we look at classical music, we see a genre that has all three worldviews virtually tied in their affinities. This is a case where the genre has such a broad-based appeal that it can mean different things to different people. The Meta 3 might see classical composition as a legacy, a source of inspiration for all music. The Meta 1 might see it as the ultimate mainstream genre, simply because everybody likes it (or, at least, everybody likes *The Nutcracker*). The Meta 2 might see it as the ultimate homage to sampling because of its limitless complexity and reach.

This is just one simple analysis of one accessible lifestyle, sorted by one variable: affinity. Can you imagine if we also sorted by age/life stage, gender, and ethnicity? Think of the intersectional robustness that would add to our story.

PUTTING THE PIECES TOGETHER

After we have collected all this data in our Model of Why, the last two stages of our client engagements include using what we've learned to craft messages through words, images, and themes that speak to people based on how they see the world and make decisions about it.

CAMPAIGN STORY

Our primary purpose in aggregating these data points is to construct a story that will galvanize all the salient points that will appeal to a person or group of people. We do so by highlighting the instincts that are important to their worldview. This will include the words, images, and themes that we think will resonate. If appropriate, we will incorporate an individual or group's likely values, lifestyles, and affinities that are relevant to the mission. The structure and detail of the story will depend on the purpose of the engagement and the amount of data available for the project. When constructing any story for this purpose, we have found success by organizing the information in these categories of a Story Outline.

Purpose of the Engagement: A description of the use of the story and the issues it is meant to address— Is there a conflict to be resolved? How are we to understand the target audience and how do they want the world to work? It can be as simple as these examples: Will this product, service, or movement fulfill my need to belong? Will it right an injustice? Will it guarantee that my family stays safe? Or allow me to express my creativity? Or help me reduce my carbon footprint? Alleviate my stress or even bring me joy?

Instinctual Pattern: A brief write-up of how the IP is understood, plus how it comingles with the following factors—the traits and circumstances of the "hero" in the story.

- Age/Life Stage
- Gender
- Ethnicity

Words, Imagery, Themes: A sample of these categories that are relevant and recommended to capture the purpose. If any particular cognitive biases are relevant, they are included here—the "themes" of the story.

Values, Lifestyle, Affinities: These contextual variables are often used to add personalization elements when needed—the "moral" of the story and the traits your hero will come to embody.

Observations and Other Inputs: This is a general category that captures any other observable idiosyncrasies.

As we look to examples of stories that are developed to engage people in a way that is meaningful to them, every bit of data that we have access to is eligible for scrutiny. For instance, let's look at the work of the Ad Council, a nonprofit organization that produces public service announcements (PSAs), very often when the U.S. experiences a major national crisis. The Ad Council partners with a sponsor—usually a government agency or a nonprofit—that champions a specific message. Some of their best-known campaigns include working with the National Institutes of Health on the anti-drug "Just Say No" campaign, with the United Negro College Fund on "A Mind Is a Terrible Thing to Waste," with Forest Fire Prevention on "Only You Can Prevent Forest Fires" (just recently changed to "Wildfires"), the U.S. Department of Transportation on "Friends Don't Let Friends Drive Drunk," and with the National Crime Prevention Council on "Take a Bite Out of Crime." The resulting PSAs might be informational, transactional, or even express a distinct opinion.

In the summer of 2020, the Ad Council crafted and released a PSA after George Floyd was killed while in police custody, using his last words: "I can't breathe." His death and the killings of other Black Americans ignited global protests against police brutality as an outcome of systemic racism within the police force. The PSA, "Fight for Freedom," opens with an image of the American flag and children watching fireworks, and a voice-over saying freedom is at the core of America, including everyday acts of freedom—driving across the fifty states, jogging wherever you please, sleeping safely in your bed, bird-watching in the park, wearing a hoodie, and breathing. The specific freedoms in the PSA were chosen to illustrate a point: These are the very same freedoms most Americans take for granted *if* they're not Black Americans, and the very same freedoms that resulted in the murder or harassment of innocent Black men and women. For them, the story is not the same.

This highlights the complexity of assuming that everyone would see and hear this PSA and automatically have the same reaction. As a PSA, this does a good job focusing on the broad-based concept of fairness in our culture. Ultimately, positing that Black and brown people do not have the same access to these simple moments of life that most Caucasians take for granted asks the viewer to make a judgment about fairness. In this context, most people would understand the point of view of the campaign. We might also predict that there is enough emotionality in the spot that it could be a gateway to a stronger reaction, depending on one's worldview.

This being the case, one should not assume that this story will end there, especially at the time of its airing, which was close to the actual event. To understand how this might be received across America, we would have to employ the concept of intersectionality to anticipate its impact. We would begin by considering the appeal of the message relative to our Social Binding Spectrum. How would we anticipate someone with a Meta 2 Worldview reacting? Certainly, the idea of cultural fairness could trigger a strong reaction as to how many Meta 2s might feel about withholding these freedoms. We could project that the nurturing instinct of their Care/Harm sensitivity would be triggered, even leading to an emotional reaction that could blame the actions of the institutions, like the police, for this unfairness. At the other end of the spectrum is the Meta 3 Worldview. These people might acknowledge it's unfair to deny these same freedoms to Black and brown citizens, but they'd likely interpret and act upon the messaging differently. We might expect that they wouldn't dwell on the individual loss, but rather believe that as a culture, we need to do a better job making sure that these freedoms are more widely available. And so it's possible that as a result of the messaging Meta 3s might not draw a connection between denying these freedoms and the need for reforming institutions like the police.

This is a relatively clear-cut analysis so far. However, to be accurate in our assessment, we need to account for the differences that Americans have around the concepts of ethnicity, age/life stage, and gender. Before we adopt a communication strategy like this PSA for use in one of our stories, we would like to be able to project how, for example, a GenX Caucasian male living in an urban environment might react to these messages as opposed to a Millennial Black woman living in a suburb. One might not need to go to this level of detail for every single story, but we should at least understand and account for the impact any variable could have on the final narrative, a boon to users of the Model of Why, because our model provides access to many different variables.

PLATFORM DISTRIBUTION

Selecting a media platform to deliver messages or campaigns is not merely a choice of convenience. Each platform has a sweet spot—the nexus of the Instinctual Pattern that it appeals to naturally and the appropriate content for that audience, including addressing its chief concerns. As an example, a generic Social Binder is likely to seek platforms that reinforce his or her cultural traditions, do not flaunt socially provocative points of view through their choice of content, and likely will reinforce the memes of mainstream culture. There is no need to pursue those choices that foist conflict and nonconformity on their consumers. Facebook is a great case—once the home of innovators, it is now considered a bedrock of Meta 3 Social Binders.

Now you have seen the way we propose integrating these layers of data into a cohesive and comprehensive picture. For us, it's crucial to treat the data and the strategic decisions that need to be made at each stage as interrelated, each building upon the others—fundamentally connected and all understood through the filters of Instinctual Patterns and base markers. You can use this planning system at a personal level to gain insights into your worldview and its construc-

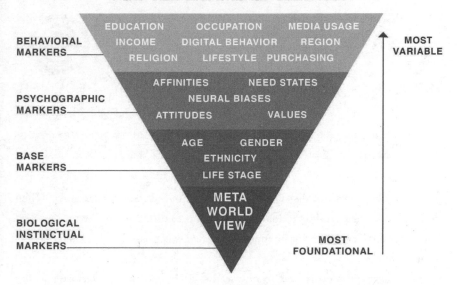

THE CUSTOMER JOURNEY ACCOUNTS FOR THE LAYERS OF IDENTITY

tion. You can also apply it to understanding life's ecosystem and how to operate within the layers of instinctual challenges you might face. Most important, it can be used to influence others through communications, marketing, or behavior change programs.

ENGAGEMENT PLANNING

It might be helpful to demonstrate how our Engagement Planning Tool can be used. In most situations, we will only have access to a limited number of considerations. If we were working with a large data source, we would likely have access to many more layers of inputs to consider. The chart below characterizes how we traditionally prepare for a communications campaign. This chart shows how we can transform layers of data points into a functional point of view. Let's explore the difference between a traditional approach and one informed by the Model of Why.

Notice the first thing the sender of the message does is figure out the value proposition. In a traditional workflow, this consists of how to present the message to the intended target of the communication. It could be either services or

VALUE PROPOSITION » WHAT TO SAY » WHERE TO PUBLISH » WHO WILL GET IT?

SENDER   MESSAGE   CHANNEL   RECEIVER

*OUR **NEW** APPROACH

"THEY JUST GET ME" « WHAT MUST BE CONFIRMED « WHAT MEDIA « WHO? WHY? HOW?

products that we seek to distribute in the course of business, for example. When we want to bring a product to market, our goal is to differentiate the product and share that differentiation in the most distinctive way possible, to as many people as possible.

The next question is how to phrase the pitch, and which platforms to use for the campaign. Depending on the communication, this can include television content or ads for television or radio, banner ads on particular websites, blogs, newsletters, and social media promos. In the end, these campaigns will be packaged up and delivered to a desired audience. Often cost, bias, and convenience will determine how these judgments are made.

When using the Model of Why, we instead start with the receiver of the message. What do we know from our layers of data about this person? What is their Instinctual Pattern? What are the relevant base markers?

From there, we generate insights about *why* a person might be interested in our offer and craft a message that focuses on the wisdom of their Instinctual Pattern. We can then mindfully select an array of channel partners to deliver this message. This way, the target comes away feeling validated and believing that "they get me!"

We can add other relevant data and observations from the psychometric and behavioral layers, revealing a more complete picture of the target.

PUTTING THE MODEL OF WHY TO WORK

Imagine we are interested in helping a foundation that is raising money for low-income families displaced by the COVID-19 pandemic. The layers of data and observations would first be centered on our key foundations in the Model of Why:

Foundational Instincts: This spirit of the cause is tailor-made for Meta 2 Individuists. One can easily imagine an appeal—for the "less fortunate families," "struggling with high costs," fearing "economic devastation" through "no fault of their own"—that would activate the Care/Harm and Fairness/Reciprocity instinct. And to broaden the appeal to include the Centrist Stack, we might address the message to "our community," ensuring that the victims are not considered "others." We might also seek additional insights by surveying potential donors to see how the different Instinctual Patterns feel about housing support.

Base Markers: How do we think that age/life stage will affect this value proposition? By focusing in on the Individuist side of the Social Binding Spectrum, we will reach a broad range of ages, genders, and ethnicities, due to the relative stability of our Instinctual Patterns. It would be fruitful to discuss how the themes of the appeal are structured in terms of imagery and words. We do know that women and many ethnic minorities are particularly sensitive to whether this appeal will include references to them and doesn't explicitly exclude them.

Psychographic Markers: This broad set of data points could help us personalize our work. Let's assume that we have data that allows us to make inferences about cognitive bias, attitudes, and values. We know from the Schwartz Model of Basic Values that some likely motivators from the Care/Harm and Fairness/Reciprocity instincts are empathy, benevolence, and universalism, so these should be communicated in the copy and imagery of the campaign. There may also be a motivation from the "Openness to Change" quadrant that would influence the media of choice. This recognizes another trait of Individuists—interest in new things—which may factor into selecting a platform where Meta 2s over-index. In that milieu, the urge to find new ways of doing things means resisting societal pressure to conform. Thus, by selecting a platform where Meta 2s over-index, they might feel the freedom to explore these differences. Finally, when we phrase the "ask," we might want to structure it in a way that requests only a three-month commitment secured with a credit card. This will be likely to generate larger donations and requires an action to stop the donation that many will never perform. Also, the copy would benefit from describing the donor's motivations and decisions as forthright and honorable.

Narrative: When we design a narrative, it is important to understand both the goals and the target. Since this topic has some urgency, the campaign should try to attract the most potential donors, in a way that will appeal to "True Believers" and to a broader "Committed but Distracted" sector. The first thing that we would consider is how to make a judgment about the value proposition that the foundation is organized around. For this exercise, let's say the narrative is structured this way: "This foundation is supporting those less fortunate families that are struggling with the high cost of living in the economic devastation wreaked upon them, through no fault of their own, by the COVID-19 pandemic. We are hoping to raise $1 million dollars to keep families in their homes in our community for the next three months." This is reasonable and empathic, without the highly emotional descriptions that might cause some of the less zealous supporters to pass on the value proposition.

Media Platform: One of the hallmarks of this planning system is that the requirements of any platform can be accommodated. It is important to keep in mind the desirability of the platform for the audience we are pursuing. For this exercise, we would probably launch one of the GoFundMe-style platforms, with support from other general market platforms, as well.

When all is said and done, what we are suggesting here is a model that promotes a different starting point, driven by the Instinctual Patterns we have identified. From there, we have demonstrated how the model can layer on a range of other types of data to provide a vivid look into the ways in which people see the world. What follows now are more real-world examples of how to use the Model of Why for planning communication engagements.

CHAPTER 8

THE LANGUAGE OF WHY

T he analysis and synthesis of new information can be challeng-ing, especially if it goes against decades of thought. We all have our natural defaults for explaining the world. For example, when you see a well-behaved young adult, you might immedi-ately think, "He must have been raised by parents who taught him right from wrong." Or maybe you think that this kind of good behavior is common for people like "that." Or you might assume that this particular boy's instincts and life experiences have combined to reveal a positive result.

The Model of Why is built on the logic that such defaults are not necessar-ily primarily the province of a person's age/life stage, gender, or ethnicity, but of something deeper. It may be hard to adjust to at first, but once we learn to put this new thinking to use, it can help us understand our own motivations, as well as refine and improve how we communicate in our relationships—both personal and professional. It can also help us comprehend and manage larger, more global issues beyond our control.

If we think of the Model of Why as a new language, we suddenly see how the data points we have been discussing can have myriad meanings. Let's look at some examples that may expand the ways we approach and engage with one another.

PLAYING THE INSTINCTUAL PATTERNS GAME

In this section, we expect some reader participation. Instead of me giving you a collection of didactic stories revealing the principles of our Model of Why, let's try a mental exercise, one that I find myself using often. You can play this game anywhere, with anyone. When you pay close attention, you can easily determine the Instinctual Patterns of the people around you.

I'll show you how it's done.

I frequently commute to New York City for work, and the train is a perfect laboratory for observation. People display their worldviews very openly, yet unwittingly. One day, I witnessed a conversation between two female passengers on the train whom I sat opposite, nearly knee to knee, for well over an hour. The women did not know each other. They both appeared to be traveling to the city for work. Both were white, and somewhere between forty-five and fifty years old. But there were differences between them, too.

The first woman was dressed stylishly. She carried the *New York Times* with her and a diorama of a structure that she said was for a client who planned to convert a balcony into an organic garden. The second woman wore a blue pinstripe suit. She carried a briefcase and a *Wall Street Journal*.

Since we were seated so close together, I couldn't help but overhear. Passenger One wanted to talk to Passenger Two. Again and again, One advanced entreaties, offering an explanation of her diorama and explaining that she was a designer with her own practice. Two nodded politely but did not reciprocate with personal information of her own. At this point, according to my knowledge of Instinctual Patterns, Passenger One trended for the Meta 2 Individuist pattern, from her choice of the *New York Times* to her interest in design and her style-conscious wardrobe. Passenger Two, by the way she appeared to rebuff One's probing, as well as her traditional dress and the *Wall Street Journal* that she carried, trended toward the opposite Meta 3 Social Binding side of the scale.

(In case it's not obvious, you are permitted to make excessive leaps of faith in this game!)

The next few minutes of conversation added to my certainty. Passenger One began talking about a column she'd read in the *Times* by the opinion writer Nicholas Kristof, about a friend of his who had tragically died of cancer, bankrupt and uninsured. Passenger Two listened, and then flatly offered the rebuttal, "He should've bought insurance."

There was silence between the two women for quite a while, until we arrived in the tunnel to Grand Central Terminal, when, true to her apparent Meta 2 pattern, Passenger One broke the ice yet again. One asked Two if she had ever heard of the Susan G. Komen Foundation, a nonprofit organization dedicated to fighting breast cancer and saving lives. Yes, Passenger Two replied. She knew the organization well. The women discovered an element of comity between them— they had both run in a Susan G. Komen 5k race in New York City. When our train arrived at the station, the interlude ended on that note—a common bond.

In this case, clues such as dress, reading materials, and speaking habits, more so than the typical demographics of age/life stage, gender, and ethnicity, gave a pretty clear indication of each person's Instinctual Pattern. These two women shared demographic similarities, but their attributes and affinities were very different. Yet they did share an interest in a particular cause, suggesting there's always a way to build common ground. In earlier models, these two women would have been considered essentially the same: same age, same location, and judging from their wardrobes, same socioeconomic bracket. Yet after my brief thought experiment on the train, I am pretty sure that they would have different motivations for just about everything.

As you become steeped in the Model of Why, you may find yourself playing this game, conjuring fantasies about others based on their bumper stickers, laptop decals, car choices, and television preferences. Professionally, this can actually be an advantage, as you learn to "read a room" more efficiently and accurately. Early on in my work, I found that I misread a roomful of marketers when I gave a presentation to a financial services company. My talk seemed to be well received. Since they were marketing professionals and creatives, who tend to fall more in line with one side of the spectrum, I thought that they were most likely a roomful of Individuists. At one point, they asked me to talk about how we select candidates to vote for, and my response was that our Instinctual Patterns likely have a lot to do with it. Can you guess what happened?

Well, to my surprise, the boss revealed himself to be a Meta 3 Social Binder, by his refusal to believe that instincts could do all that I promised. His stature in the group silenced the others. He was sure that his opinion was the result of a reasoned review of the facts, and he aggressively shut down any discussion. It was a lesson I learned: Don't get too far ahead of yourself. If you pay attention to the person receiving your message, your odds of successful engagement greatly improve.

This is true in many areas of life. Whether you're looking for a date, a job, or just a new opportunity, the more you can gauge the person sitting across from you, the better. I once worked with a twenty-eight-year-old woman named

Monica, who was conducting a job search in her chosen field of Library Science. Monica believed that she was underemployed, so she set out to reposition herself professionally. Her Instinctual Pattern was Individuist. She had a robust set of scores on four out of the five instincts, but she scored low for Authority.

Monica easily got interviews for positions that she felt were appropriate to her level and skill set. Yet she failed to get any job offers. All of the interviews followed the same line of questioning about her qualifications, experience, and vision. And each typically included an ad lib problem-solving exercise.

Library Science, naturally, places a premium on process, reliability, and thoroughness. According to Monica, problem-solving was an area where she could shine. She had a lot of ideas about how to solve common issues within library services and a zeal for detailing them.

She was particularly proud of her willingness to go beyond the conventional. When she recounted these interviews, it became clear that her proposals likely sounded unrealistic to her interviewers. In effect, all of her exemplary qualifications were undone by her overzealous, outside-the-box approach.

We surmised that her low Authority score was causing her to overestimate the wisdom of sharing her whole vision in the first meeting. With that as background, we did some role-playing to reorient her interview strategy. Shortly thereafter, she was offered a job.

The Model of Why, once we gain fluency, can open up a new layer of insight into the world. Let's see how this plays out in some other real-life scenarios.

Q. HOW CAN THE MODEL OF WHY SHAPE OUR PROFESSIONAL LIVES?

The business world is a wonderfully rich laboratory for human behavior, as well as the locus for many divisive issues, like income inequality, technology, globalization, and education. There the Model of Why has proven particularly interesting to human resources departments, given their responsibility for recruitment, hiring, training, and managing the organizational culture. PathSight once worked with a financial services company that was trying to design a program to fill vacancies as they arose. The goal was to make sure that hiring decisions would be made not solely based on an applicant's virtues, but also on the team's particular needs at the time. How do you think the Model of Why came into play?

The culture of any organization can be discerned through its people, systems, and tasks. Large companies will likely have several subcultures as well. The accounting division may have a different culture than the design department, or the sales and marketing divisions. The same process that helps define a corporation's overall culture can also be applied to each distinct department within a corporation.

Because companies are made up of people, we can start with how the worldviews of the employees are distributed over the organization. If we look, for example, at a human resources department, we can see that the distribution vacillates across the entire spectrum, with high or low collective Loyalty, for example, depending on the distribution. Because this department is typically responsible for enforcing employee conduct policies, but also tasked with cultural transformation and training and development, both entailing forward thinking and growth, a complex set of instincts and skill sets is needed.

Once we know the distribution of the Instinctual Patterns across the team, we can determine whether it's well prepared for the future. Do they have the right collection of resources to oversee the processes of the company? Do they have enough natural leaders to keep the company moving forward? This assessment can help define whether the ideal new hire would possess a new skill set for the growth of the department, or simply execute well on the same tasks the team is already doing. And, of course, we can assess their cultural match with the department.

Q. HOW CAN THE MODEL OF WHY AFFECT COMMUNICATIONS—AND OUR RELATIONSHIPS?

Communication is at the heart of all relationships. We've all witnessed—or experienced—relationships that never quite made it off the starting block, simply because someone said the wrong thing. Likewise, I hope you've experienced the opposite. In those lucky cases, you meet someone and you instantly click. Why does this happen? There are lots of variables, but one is instinctual synchronicity. If you think and communicate similarly about important topics, you are way ahead of the game.

Let us suppose that you have a Meta 2 Individuist orientation. The predominant instincts that you rely on are Care/Harm and Fairness/Reciprocity. During the course of your day, you engage with a friend or colleague about something significant. Let's assume that person has a Meta 3 Social Binding intuition. Remember, their Instinctual Pattern has a muted Care/Harm and Fairness/Reciprocity instinct, as well as a higher sensitivity to Loyalty, Authority, and Purity. How might this affect the trajectory of the conversation?

Say you were talking about healthcare, and you made the following statement to your acquaintance: "I don't believe how expensive my insurance is. I'm feeling like Medicare for all is the answer. There are just too many people who are left unprotected."

This remark reveals the effects of your active Care/Harm and Fairness/Reciprocity core. It shows that you reject the value proposition of private insurance. You feel that a government, single-payer alternative would be better able to do the job. You add the additional motivator of wanting to protect those not able to be covered by private insurance. This one comment hits all the high notes of your narrative.

How do you think your friend or colleague will hear this comment?

Remember her community orientation on the Social Binding Spectrum. She probably heard a willingness to let the government take care of responsibilities that should be taken care of by the individual. Furthermore, Meta 3 Social Binders have little sympathy for an ill-defined population of "others" who can't afford insurance. Depending on your level of intimacy or politeness, the conversation might be short and sweet, or extend into a futile debate trying change each other's instinctual point of view. If you are fluent in the Model of Why, forewarned is forearmed. If you know, or have a hunch, as to the Instinctual Pattern of your acquaintance, you'll likely be able to anticipate her response. If you don't know, these kinds of conversational lobs can work well as scouting missions. Just be prepared to disagree! On the other hand, if this conversation took place between two Individuists or two Social Binders, it could lead to a lasting bond between them.

So how can we pivot on this insight? The most expedient way is word choice. The right one can soften your colleague's point of view, while the wrong one can put her on the defensive. In this example, you might have chosen to avoid code words that could trigger an intuitive emotional reaction. For instance, "My insurance is very expensive. A single-payer system might be more affordable and provide more coverage for everyone." As you see, the code words—"responsibility for cost," "Medicare/government," and "unprotected people"—were avoided. This could neutralize the interaction, or at least prevent an unnecessary showdown, and works well for our casual interactions. We'd use the same process for our more intimate relationships, where the specific words used might carry more emotional impact. Here, each person in the relationship would likely feel a more heightened sense of awareness. At least, you'd hope so!

Q. HOW DO OUR INSTINCTS INFLUENCE OUR INTERESTS?

You will recall, from PathSight's work in the music industry, that Instinctual Patterns influence which musical genres a person is attracted to (and how many). Meta 3 Social Binders show interest in fewer total genres but have a strong affinity for country and Christian music. The same holds true for interests more generally. Your Instinctual Pattern metaphorically sets the table for a way to think about life, and your life experiences adjust the details.

Think about career choice. There are very few jobs suited to only one particular type of person, and you can imagine almost anyone succeeding at any job. But some jobs would appeal to you more *because* of your instincts. The same goes with interests. There are only a few interests that your Instinctual Pattern would *not* consider, but certain interests are specifically aligned with your instinct.

Most companies that go beyond niche appeal consider more than one Instinctual Pattern when marketing their products. Typically, one Instinctual Pattern may take the lead as the so-called superfans. They define who may be most interested, and in what order the other IPs will join.

Recently, PathSight worked with a group launching a comic book franchise. This project was not a typical data analysis, but it was a fascinating look at how to marshal the power of people in pursuit of an interest. The initial concept was a specialty product—a comic—to be distributed to a defined and notoriously exacting market, in such a way that would build on the assets of its content.

The group needed a defined value proposition, to ensure that a potentially fickle community would embrace and support the product distribution strategy. Beyond the bona fides of the creative team, we had to ask, Why might anyone care about this new offering? How could the creators demonstrate that they had something worthy of attention?

As you might guess, the first step was to identify a core audience who might act as authentic first supporters. Who were the people who would pride themselves on the discovery, on being there right from the beginning? In this case, the most likely core audience would be a hybrid of the Meta 2 and Meta 4. Together, as a group, they are driven by an instinct toward fairness. Primarily, they are interested in how the world impacts the individual, and they do not like to be "sold." They fancy their world as an extension of their own imaginations, as opposed to something they confront each day.

For this project, it was crucial that the founders spend a lot of time cultivating these relationships. If they expanded too rapidly, they might find short-term success, but ultimately end as a fad—a footnote in comic history.

We recommended a strategy similar to community organizing. The goal was to follow the characteristics of the core audience, as it grew. The product should pay off on what their core customer envisioned, regardless of who else came along later.

Once the core audience proved satisfied, we suggested moving beyond the Meta 2 and Meta 4 groups. We would target the Centrist audience next, then the Balanced Meta 0. The idea was to emulate the way people build friendships. The goal and tactical point of difference was to create a better-than-average product that knew its audience so well that the delivery of that product never disappointed—and even surprised and delighted—new friends.

Obviously, the launch of any product is complex—as is any corporate culture. The Model of Why can't give us all the answers, but it does help us strategize in a way more consistent with what people are actually like—not just what a prefabricated ad campaign or org chart expects to see. These insights not only help you personally—in creating the life, career, and relationships you want—but could, if implemented, help all organizations have a more honest and fruitful relationship with their customers, employees, and donors. In Chapter 10, we'll take a deeper dive into those possibilities.

CHAPTER 9

THE REACH OF WHY

S o now we understand how Instinctual Patterns affect our worldviews and motivate us to act. The foundation of these IPs provides our basic biological instincts, with unique demographic and psychographic data layered on top; with them, we get a fuller picture of who we are and why we do what we do. Our Instinctual Patterns can influence how we formulate impressions about age/life stage, gender, and ethnicity, not to mention the attitudes and behaviors of the people we encounter every day.

GROUP DYNAMICS

We also know that group dynamics are one of the oldest fields of study. Sociologists and psychologists have both investigated the role of groups in terms of personal development, socialization, attributes, and the power of influence. In this chapter, we'll explore how Meta Worldviews, with their potential for expanding our view of one another, can enhance group interactions.

Biologists such as Stephen Jay Gould have helped us understand that back when humans first moved in from the plains, they formed clans that contributed to their evolutionary growth and stability. Clans made rules to govern behavior and help manage the challenges of group living. Some were more successful than others. Those that endured refined the lessons learned from that success as their civilization evolved.

Of course, our individual Instinctual Patterns can contribute to our group success, too. Consider the following characteristics of successful groups[1] and the Instinctual Patterns that likely serve them.

1. **Hierarchical Structure.** Defining who is responsible for how the successful group will operate. Primary IP source: Meta 3 Social Binder.

2. **Group Defense.** The loyalty that is the core motivator for a group's self-defense is fueled by the Meta 3 Social Binder and Meta 0 Balanced patterns.

3. **Care for Offspring.** The instinct for Care is a characteristic that is close to a universal trait in the model. Care is ubiquitous, but the Meta 2 Worldview Individuist Pattern is most identified with these sentiments.

4. **Codifying the Culture.** Capturing the codes of culture and sharing them is primarily the function of Purity found to varying degrees in Centrist Meta 1s and Social Binder Meta 3s. These instincts are often seen as attempting to keep people away from the major taboos of a culture.

5. **Forward Thinking.** This tracks with uncovering new trends, trying different lifestyles, and a genuine interest in experimenting with variety and stimulation. This ensures that the group will have access to new developments and is a trait of the Individuist.

6. **Culture of Fairness.** When a culture establishes a sense of fairness, there is a strong instinct to consider other people's points of view as an operating principle. This give-and-take embeds a sense of fairness and reciprocity in the culture, which is a hallmark of the Individuist Meta 2 and Fatalist Meta 4 patterns.

The most consistently successful groups draw their strength from an amalgam of all these Instinctual Profiles. The most helpful characteristics we lean on are not static, or stand-alone; rather they are dynamic and evolving. As such, they influence and change the attributes they support. But how do they do that? Successful cultures are a balancing act. As we've said, they progress, or move forward, through periods of stability and upheaval, given the variety of life and the urge we all have to staunchly defend what we know. There are many ways to explain this process. But I believe that the way trends, values, affinities, and ideas move across our populations is dependent on the natural functionality of groups.

The graph below shows the standard evolution of a successful idea[2] and how different types of groups help to spread new ideas in society.

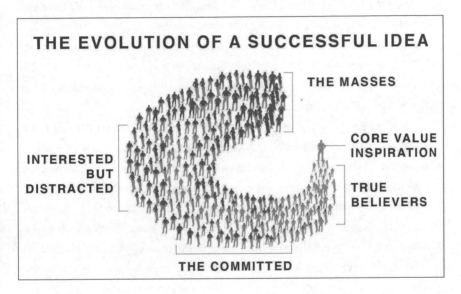

THE EVOLUTION OF A SUCCESSFUL IDEA

THE MASSES

CORE VALUE INSPIRATION

INTERESTED BUT DISTRACTED

TRUE BELIEVERS

THE COMMITTED

It can be a style trend, a political philosophy, or even a new musical innovation. At first, the core value inspiration is discovered by a small group of people who are somehow aligned with its organizing principle (most likely because of their Instinctual Pattern). This group might be interested in new things in general, or just interested in the specific topic of inspiration. We'll call this group the True Believers. They just *get it*. Sometimes these interests gain a certain degree of momentum, signaling it may be worthwhile for others to take note. This is where the next tier, the Committed, enters the picture.

Notice that the graphic shows that there is very little variation in Instinctual Pattern between the True Believers and the Committed. These two tiers can exist as a self-contained pod if the idea is narrow or exist as separate stages each with its own time table. Sometimes very avant-garde or specialty interests plateau at this level of appeal, which makes sense. However, those with broader potential can continue down the path if certified by these early adopters as authentic and worthy of attention.

The next tier in this group dynamic is the Interested but Distracted. They have a sizable degree of variability in their midst, but enough overlap with the True Believers and the Committed to see the significance of the core inspiration. If they adopt the trend, it's unlikely to wane. As the value proposition spreads, the Interested but Distracted may check in with the early adopters to ensure that the idea is still regarded as authentic. (At this point, the idea may even have morphed into a version that the originators hardly recognize.)

The final stage is Mass Appeal, where the newness recedes, and some of the true believers may in fact have defected. This is the stage where the trend finally achieves enough familiarity to be adopted by the traditionalists, generally the last group to sign on to new things.

There are myriad examples of this progression playing out in the real world, some massive and others modest. One massive shift was the arrival of hip-hop, which began in the music world but quickly influenced culture, fashion, technology, and more. Without getting too detailed, consider its basic chronology.

In the early eighties, there was a long-simmering trend among certain populations of Black Americans and other people of color toward the genre of "spoken word" poetry. The True Believers, who had been proponents of this form for some time, started to see it break through in particular cities, along with deejaying, graffiti, and breakdancing. These True Believers nurtured these trends for well over a decade in communities virtually shut off from white culture and politics.

As the Committed found this scene, it began to spread beyond the places of cultural origin for the new artistic movement, like the Bronx, to early media adopters. Many of the landmark trends of fashion, music, and culture in the past forty years were created not by the rich, but by these cultural opinion leaders. When they endorse a new element of music, fashion, or culture, the risk they take on is one of social capital. Long before there were internet influencers, these opinion leaders endorsed trends and gave them a springboard. This is how the early iterations of hip-hop reached suburban teens, the first outliers to embrace the new culture. In *The Tanning of America: How Hip-Hop Created a Culture That Rewrote the Rules of the New Economy*, ad executive Steve Stoute chronicles the turning point when hip-hop reached the suburbs and morphed into mainstream. Writing about the Sugarhill Gang's "Rapper's Delight," in 1979 the first rap song to ever chart on the Billboard Hot 100, Stoute says: "Before long, the dog whistle effect had permeated barriers of color and geography and transformed one of the first ever rap records from a word-of-mouth success to certified gold. . . . Soon folks of all backgrounds in the cities and suburbs of America were on the move like never before, rocking their own parties and heading into the uncharted waters of the 1980s." Stoute coined a term for hip-hop's transcendence of boundaries, calling it a "tanning spark."[3]

With the help of early influencers like DJ Kool Herc and Fab 5 Freddy, who blurred the lines and connected "rap to the artsy disco/punk rock scene and convinced gallery owners to open their doors to graffiti writers," the Interested but Distracted became avid fans and social conduits to a broader world through the contemporaneous innovation of MTV. Eventually the genre reached the masses, where it easily rivaled long-established genres like rock, pop, and country.

The science of marketing and branding has long depended on seeing consumers as groups with defined roles, rather than an ambiguous assortment of people sharing a common interest in a product or service. And in reality, these groups tend to have a life cycle: a beginning, a middle, and an end. Not surprisingly, our Instinctual Patterns influence where along this line we are likely to fall. Consider the hip-hop example above.

If we start at the beginning, the source of inspiration may be an idea, person, trend, or theme. The most likely people to discover it are those who are always on the lookout for new things—a typical trait for the Meta 2 Individuist. This group generally stands in opposition to the status quo and is instinctively motivated to detect deviations from it. The Individuists are also the most likely to be motivated by stimulation and variety. As new iterations of culture percolate, they likely act as True Believers.

When the time is right, the Committed join the movement. The Balanced Meta 0s have processes that allow them to filter innovations with their own unique skill sets. They naturally possess an awareness of the differences between people as one of their organizing characteristics. This group often interprets new trends for the broader mainstream audience. Meta 0s make sense of a trend and provide a moderating influence as they pass it along to the Interested but Distracted tier. This Interested but Distracted tier can make or break a trend's appeal to the masses. Consequently, they need help placing trends into the context of the status quo. Sometimes this is as simple as providing exposure, so that familiarity breeds comfort with newness. Other times, they need more overt instruction, in terms of marketing or engagement, to help them understand why a trend is authentic.

Meta 1 Centrists and Meta 4 are those with a full-throated appeal to the status quo. This is the place where trends and/or brands spend the most time with their audience. In successful campaigns, these trends meet the status quo and the masses are given a signal that lets them know that it is safe to engage. This is the phase when hip-hop took its place among the other musical symbols of the mainstream, like rock, country, and pop.

The final stage of a new trend's journey is when it is welcomed by the tradition-laden Social Binder. This suggests it may be with us for good. By this time, the Individuists have moved on, likely in search of something new. Smart brands or genres try to anticipate this moment and reintroduce themselves to Individuists with something new or unique at just the right time to start the discovery process all over again.

This process makes launching a brand or trend seem simple, but it is not. The smooth handoff between the Instinctual Patterns is not a given. There are substantive differences between the Instinctual Patterns that may hamper this evolution. And some brands refuse to acknowledge the process. They bypass the early stages and try to use a media blitz to replace the natural evolutionary process. What they usually end up creating is a fad, instead of a trend. Do you remember Pogs, Fidgit Spinners, Pet Rocks, the Macarena, Garbage Pail Kids, Razor Scooters, MySpace, or Pokémon GO? Don't worry if you don't; after all, they were only fads.

CULTURAL DYNAMISM OR FRICTION?

Now that we understand how groups form and function, let's explore how cultural dynamism can turn to cultural friction. One of the most obvious examples of group behavior today are our political tribes. In the United States, there are two remarkably stable points of view that have dominated since the founding of the country.

Simply put, one organizing principle has favored a strong central government with a central banking system. The other source of inspiration has favored states' rights, limited government, and individual liberty. This original argument between Alexander Hamilton and James Madison is still raging today, 233 years later.

Consider this graph as a visual representation of how today's voter distribution evolved.

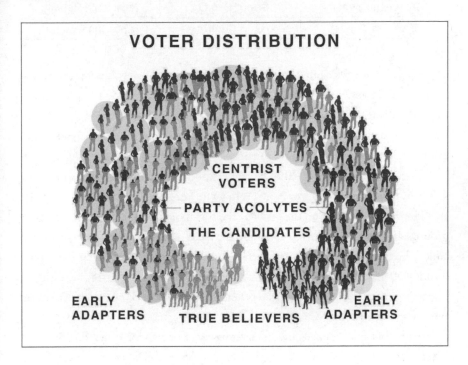

Here we see an array of potential profiles extending from, on one end, an Individuist perspective to, on the opposite end, a set of Social Binder profiles. Starting with the Individuists on the left-hand margin, the graph passes through the Centrist Stack in the middle and ends up at the right-hand margin with the Social Binders. The competing philosophies represent two immovable objects anchoring the continuum. The arguments from the Founding Fathers are still going on today, between purified versions like the Democratic Socialists and the Make America Great Again crowd.

META 2	TOPIC	META 3
Women's Right to Decide	Abortion	Pro-Life
Pro-Marriage Equality	Gay Marriage	"Traditional" Marriage
Anti-Death Penalty	Death Penalty	Pro-Death Penalty
Pro-Gun Control	Gun Control	Anti-Gun Control

We know that, broadly, these philosophical points of view bracket the Democratic and Republican Parties. We typically add the Libertarian Party and Independent categories to complete any inquiry about voting behavior. As we have stated, these clusters do not negate the influence of age/life stage, gender, and ethnicity, but rather provide a more complete picture of how they evolved.

These points of view need to be understood as extremely complex behavior sets, yet, from the chart above, we see that they are reliably associated with the two Instinctual Patterns on the poles of the social binding spectrum. The Meta 2 group self-identifies with the Democratic Party philosophy 58 percent of the time. The Meta 3 group, likewise, self-identifies with the Republican Party philosophy 60 percent of the time. Because Independent voters are typically expressing a preference for one party or the other, just without declaring a label, the true percentages are probably higher.

How this split happens has been the subject of much inquiry, but typically it has been conducted in piecemeal fashion within individual disciplines. This makes it hard to propose a clear cause-and-effect mechanism. Remember the philosopher Herbert Marcuse's adage that we mentioned earlier in the book—our first draft is written in neural ink, but edits are made from life experience? Instincts are inarguably influential, but political affiliations are not hardwired. Rather, there is a conspiracy of influences afoot.

One 2016 study[4] explored the dynamics of how and why people change their opinions. They categorized people's beliefs as political or nonpolitical. In this study, strongly held beliefs about any *political* topics—for instance, the death penalty—were nearly impossible to shake. This was the case for both the pro- and anti- sides.

The willingness to change one's opinion is represented by the height of the chart.

In this chart, the political topics are represented by the light gray graphs and

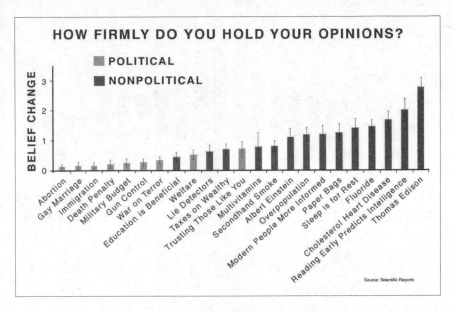

HOW FIRMLY DO YOU HOLD YOUR OPINIONS?

the nonpolitical are represented by the darker gray graphs. As you can see, the level of emotionality is markedly different when you're asking about Thomas Edison or paper bags than it is when the questions are on abortion, gay marriage, or immigration. We have found that strong opinions on these political issues are likely to be linked to specific Instinctual Patterns.

Below is a snapshot of how the Individuists and Social Binders tend to react to these topics.

This list of topics represents a continuum of opinions that stretch across our Social

META 2	PARTY	META 3
59	Democratic	21
10	Republican	54
27	Independent	22
4	Libertarian	3

Binding Spectrum, helping to visualize the relationship between the two extremes.

Those with Meta 2 and Meta 3 instincts tend to have strongly held beliefs on all these topics. The Centrist Stack of Meta 0, Meta 1, and Meta 4 tend to gravitate to less extreme positions. Hence the motivations are the most palpable for Individuist and Social Binding immovable forces. But curiously, the frequency of respondents is the lowest at the poles, and highest where the opinions take on a less emotional, more ambivalent meaning.

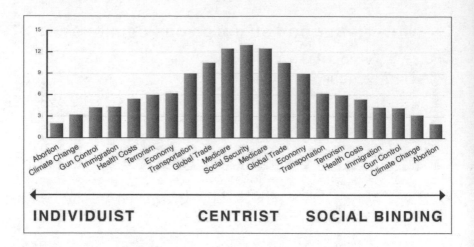

The urgency of many of these questions has brought those with "strongly held" opinions to the forefront of the public square. But while their voices may be the loudest, the public square has plenty of fluidity. I think of the square as being occupied by those with cognitive flexibility.

DENY, DEFLECT, OR DISTORT

One factor that drives people into tribes is the different ways that we process information. Each Instinctual Pattern tends to judge information by the degree to which it conforms with their narrative. For example, if you have a strong instinctual belief in cultural traditions, information that challenges those beliefs will feel discordant. Depending on how central that information is to your Instinctual Pattern and narrative, you will likely deploy one of three defenses: *deny* the accuracy of that information, *deflect* its relevance to the topic, or flat out *distort* it.[5]

How often has it been remarked that people seem to be living in separate realities these days? Each side believes that if only they could find the right words, they could make the opposition see the error of their ways. But armed with the Model of Why, we know that is a fool's errand. It is not our words that matter; it's the instinctual filter they travel through. This natural defense against contrarian information is a particular challenge in today's connected world, where the spread of peer-to-peer social media platforms and customized news feeds makes it easy for us to deny, deflect, and distort.

THE TRUMP EXPERIMENT

If we follow the model, we can explain how 2016 became the year of Donald Trump, without even referencing the standard explanations, like the disenfranchisement of the white working class or the low Black turnout.

To begin with, let's recall how generic Republican, Democrat, and Independent voters are described within the model. As noted, the Republican profile appeals to the Social Binder and the Democrat to the Individuist. The Independents are fairly evenly spread across all clusters. Profiles for each voter group are an amalgam, pulling from the dominant IP and the words, images, and themes that shape its narrative. These triggers stimulate the instincts that confirm when a party is aligned with a voter.

George Lakoff, a well-regarded cognitive scientist and linguist, has explained how the language of Republicans and Democrats makes sense from their origins. In some of his writings he uses a metaphor of a family to explain this. "The conservative and progressive worldviews dividing our country can most readily be understood in terms of moral worldviews that are encapsulated in two very different common forms of family life: The Nurturant Parent family (progressive) and the Strict Father family (conservative)."[6]

From this point of view, you can see why each party supports the platform it does, as Lakoff explains that it all stems from the parenting party members received. How we are "governed" by our parents extends to how we envision proper governance of our institutions. Here is his version of the president's appeal to Republican voters.

In the strict father family, father knows best. He knows right from wrong and has the ultimate authority to make sure his children and his spouse do what he says, which is taken to be what is right. Many conservative spouses accept this worldview, uphold the father's authority, and are strict in those realms of family life that they are in charge of. When his children disobey, it is his moral duty to punish them painfully enough so that, to avoid punishment, they will obey him (do what is right) and not just do what feels good. Through physical discipline they are supposed to become disciplined, internally strong, and able to prosper in the external world. What if they don't prosper? That means they are not disciplined, and therefore cannot be moral, and so deserve their poverty. This reasoning shows up in conservative politics in which the poor are seen as lazy and undeserving, and the rich as deserving their wealth. Responsibility is thus taken to be *personal responsibility* not social responsibility. What you become is only up to you; society has nothing to do with it. You are responsible for yourself, not for others—who are responsible for themselves.[7]

VOTING PATTERNS AND PREFERENCES

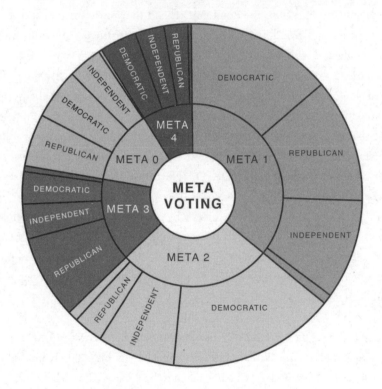

Instinctively, Republicans have a high regard for hierarchical order and tradition, and a strong sensitivity toward external threats to their defined group. Democrats tend to organize around the individual as the unit of concern. They also seek out variety and novelty and resist social conformity. As expected, Independents span the continuum. Let's remember that the emotional engines for these groups are at the poles, but the ballast of the culture comes from the middle. The chart Voting Patterns and Preferences shows how the population of Meta Worldviews translates to voting. The inner circle denotes the Meta Worldviews where the proportion of the population that it represents is shown by the size of each sector. For example, the Meta 3 represents 15 percent of the population. The percentage of them that opt in to support Republicans is 60 percent of that sector. Each sector is created the same way.

So it's worth asking, How was Trump's support organized? Was there a distinctive pattern? Did it cross demographic lines? We concluded that his primary support came from three Instinctual Patterns: the Meta 0s, who represent roughly 14 percent of the population; the Meta 1s (36 percent), and the Meta 3 Social Binders (15 percent). All of these groups share a reliance on the instincts of hierarchical authority, strong between-group boundaries, and a sensitivity to external threats. Trump's strategy from the very beginning has been to position the United States as under attack—from

- Immigrants
- Black Americans
- Poor urban dwellers
- Muslims
- Non-English-speakers

For the most part, this strategy has worked for President Trump because people in his coalition tend to hold a strong definition of what it means to be American. For them, one or more of the above bullet points misses what it means to be *authentically* American. And, to them, that is threatening. Consider the Trump voter pattern below.

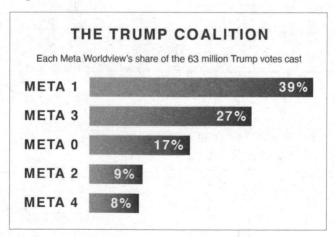

THE TRUMP COALITION

Each Meta Worldview's share of the 63 million Trump votes cast

META 1	39%
META 3	27%
META 0	17%
META 2	9%
META 4	8%

The Instinctual Patterns of the general population show this support was spread across Meta 0s, Meta 1s, and Meta 3s, with much lower support from the Meta 2 and Meta 4 groups. This pattern was the same across age/life stage, gender, income, and ethnicity. Consider the following representation of Trump's appeal among women voters across different ethnicities. The amplitudes varied, but the pattern of appeal did not.

WOMEN TRUMP VOTERS

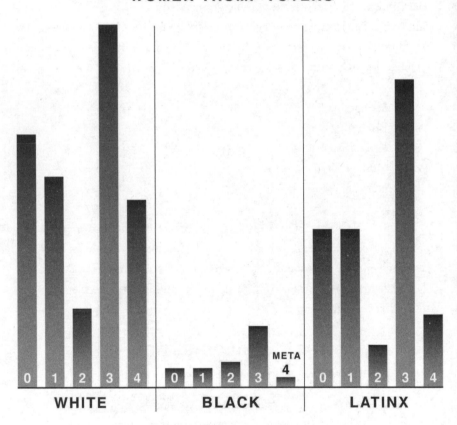

The bulk of the female Trump vote came from Meta 0s, Meta 1s, and Social Binder Meta 3s, regardless of ethnicity.

THE COMMUNITY OF TRUMP

As we have noted, the development of any group follows predictable patterns. It is important to understand where the support is initially generated. In short, the True Believers will attest to the authenticity of the movement as the community grows, but its representation among the Centrist Stack will be a measure of its long-term resilience.

Regarding the Trump Effect, the order of intensity goes from Social Binder to Balanced to Centrist. The largest number of votes came from Centrists, but the highest percentage of any pattern was in the Social Binders—in this case, the True Believers.

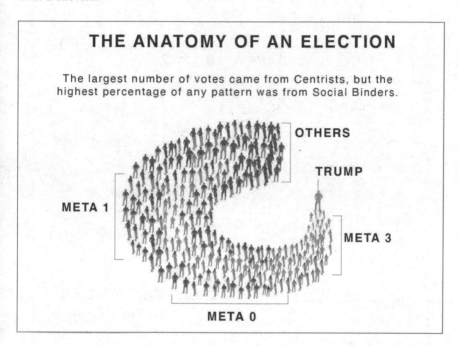

THE ANATOMY OF AN ELECTION

The largest number of votes came from Centrists, but the highest percentage of any pattern was from Social Binders.

OTHERS

TRUMP

META 1

META 3

META 0

Trump's campaign was a master class in instinctive triggering. It almost completely ignored actual policy, regulations, and laws (with the exception of immigration policy). Nor did he exhibit the kind of general empathy some centrist candidates do. Rather, he demonstrated specific empathy for *his kind* of voters. His provocative statements and flouting of norms proved to his followers that he understood them, because he echoed all that they longed to say to the Washington power brokers who had ignored them for decades.

By demonstrating his alignment with these voters, he secured the benefit of not having to gain their approval for specific policies, initiatives, or laws. When one is engaged at the instinctive level, inconvenient inconsistencies are easily forgiven—or handled by the defenses of denial, deflection, and distortion. (President Obama had a similar relationship with a different set of IP-inspired voters, who were likewise tolerant of his occasional misstatement.) Mr. Trump's instinctive connection motivated his followers to provide an authentic base of support. They prioritized boundaries between Americans and others (Loyalty) and the preservation of the traditions (Authority) of an idealized country.

Because he demonstrated that he really understood this point of view, there was no need for him to say, "I feel your pain." He channeled it in a very powerful manner; he acted on his supporters' behalf in the face of the "swamp."

A CAMPAIGN THAT DEMONSTRATED THESE INSTINCTS		
META 3	META 0	META 1
• Orderliness • Code of Living • Strong us vs them • Rank has its privilege • Sensitive to Deceit and Treachery • Security & Traditions • Respect for Rules • Generation, Religion, Family	• Awareness of the world boundaries • Differences defined • Families, Generation, Religion • Open to new things • Optimism • Fairness & Order	• Social Cohesion • Safety • Protecting Our Way of Life • Achievements • Generation, Family, Accomplishments • It's a question of balance

The narratives of these voters represent a commitment to a strong Social Binding instinct fueled by a clear-eyed sense of us versus them and anger at people who don't "play by the rules," as interpreted by this group. This is why the

Clinton campaign's belief that Mr. Trump would disqualify himself was short-sighted. All the things about Trump that liberals found offensive, his followers loved. In a nutshell, he was not afraid to be perceived as favoring whites, police, and evangelicals versus people of color, immigrants, and those who challenged law and order.

THE CHALLENGE OF GOVERNING

As General Washington informs Alexander Hamilton in the Broadway musical *Hamilton*, "Winning was easy. Governing is harder." Mr. Trump appears to have met his challenge. Given that he lost the popular vote, it's questionable whether he can really claim a mandate for his agenda.

For context, in the 2016 election, both candidates secured vote totals nearing 50 percent of the participating electorate. However, American participation rates are only about 56 percent of the voting-eligible population (VEP). That makes each vote total actually closer to 25 percent of the VEP. When we convert the Trump community to a proportion of the total eligible voting population, it looks like this:

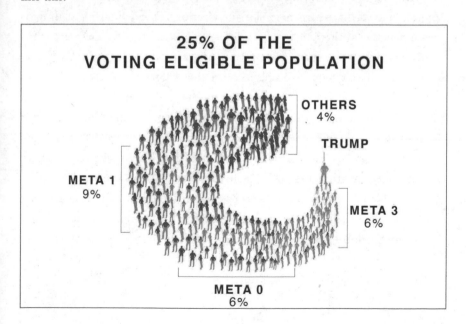

25% OF THE VOTING ELIGIBLE POPULATION

OTHERS
4%

TRUMP

META 1
9%

META 3
6%

META 0
6%

This means Mr. Trump's ardent supporters total about 25 percent of the VEP. The other 75 percent of voters did not cast votes for Mr. Trump. Of course, for pundits predicting and commenting on the election process, it is more useful to reference the behavior of "likely voters," even if a significant percentage will not actually go to the polls. But if America was a company selling a product called Participatory Democracy, we might reasonably expect the unsold market potential to be 75 percent.

What might be the impact if we could reverse the decline in voter participation? What if more voters were required to sign on to a candidate before he or she could claim a mandate? Would governance be more moderate if candidates had to win a true majority of voters? The extremes certainly benefit when participation rates are low. And in turn, we become ever more estranged from one another.

This is where the model offers hope. If we can learn how we are wired to see things differently, we might be able to create a system where voting is both more meaningful and more consequential. Can we make that sale? If we were to accept this challenge, we would need to marshal the forces of our model to understand why nearly 50 percent of the voting-eligible population does not vote. This affects the total range of Instinctual Patterns. My hunch is that the country, as a whole, is ambivalent to participation in our elections. People fundamentally disagree on whether voting is a benefit of living in a democracy, where every effort should be made to drive participation rates, or is a perk of being a member in the democracy club that requires people to prove they belong in the club before they can vote. This conversation appears to have been hijacked by the perception that one party has an advantage over the other, in the voting booth or in the electoral college. Clearly there are ways to increase voting if the country was serious about it. After all, Australia has near universal adult exercise of suffrage since it is the law of the land. To attack this challenge in the United States, a nonpartisan entity should be able to persuade the whole spectrum of Individuist and Social Binders, and those in between, to endorse that the principle of voting as a shared value of the entire country. It would certainly be rewarding to move in that direction.

CHAPTER 10

HOW TO USE THE MODEL

S ometimes we experience moments of clarity when we realize that we might have been wrong about a friend or acquaintance. They suddenly do or say something that doesn't fit into our narrative of them. For instance, you tell a friend that you've been receiving a lot of mail lately from charities. It's Giving Tuesday and you're mulling over all of the worthy causes: Wounded Warrior, American Heart Association, Sierra Club. "Who's the lucky recipient going to be?" you ask, hoping for suggestions. But your friend replies: "I vote for none of the above. I work too hard for my money." You weren't expecting such a response—it strikes you as hard-hearted and makes you look at your friend in a different light. In fact, you were having trouble deciding which charity to give to since you're such a "soft touch" on the giving front. So you file that comment away. Over time, you might find that it was just an off-the-cuff reply. Or it may be confirmed as a major difference between you and your friend, about an issue that is very meaningful to you.

By now, I'm sure you probably suspect that these differences are found in our particular Instinctual Patterns. It is a useful exercise to reflect on the kinds of messaging that you tend to react to, either positively or negatively. Are there messages that you have a visceral negative reaction to when you hear or see them? A commercial that you immediately change channels in order to avoid? How about a commercial that makes you happy or excited? Do you thrill to the syncopated rhythms of an Apple commercial, or perhaps the Hallmark tones of a Mother's Day promotion? The answer tells us something about the instincts that the ad campaigns are meant to trigger.

Marketing—whether of brands, consumer products, or causes—struggles mightily to strike the right note when seeking to reach and engage new audiences.

As we've seen, when an ad focuses only on demographics, the result is often a muddled mess of cause and effect. It's hard to sort out. And since the advent of big data modeling, many companies have simplified their quest to the most efficient method of generating responses—any responses—from a target. When fully implemented, this strategy includes fancy and complicated tactics like A/B testing, multivariate statistical analysis, and artificially intelligent algorithms—not the most simple research tools. More important, the *why* gets stripped out, and as a result, wonderfully rich brands and causes are stripped of their complexity, texture, and emotionality. But why do we have to make that trade-off?

Perhaps surprisingly, cause marketing communications and positioning relies on the same tools as product marketing—they both start with a rich understanding of their customers. Look at the next piece of mail you get from a charity or volunteer organization. They're virtually all reduced to a single appeal. On average, these campaigns generate less than a 5 percent response rate. It is numbing to think that our most intractable problems—hunger, cancer, homelessness, deforestation, refugees, population control, poverty, racism, and climate change—can move so few. What about the other 95 percent of the population who might respond in other ways? If people aren't motivated by the instinct to nurture victims, what about appealing to traditions of giving? Could we build a case for economic sanity or good old-fashioned altruism to inspire a little more action?

The Model of Why explains why most causes rely on the Care/Harm instinct for their marketing outreach. It's the closest of any instinct to a universal trait, present to some degree across all of the IPs. Most people have some capacity to care for and nurture children. This instinct may be stronger for one's own children, of course, but it has been socialized to include the children of others, the toys associated with children, their possessions, and even animals (think baby seals and the like). However, it's not evenly distributed across the IPs. See the continuum below.

The Individuists are loaded with Care; it dominates their view of the world. At the other extreme, the Social Binders have a much more muted sense of care and empathy. Other instincts may be stronger triggers for them, including self-preservation, allegiance to a group, or even authority and hierarchy.

Most charitable campaigns are designed with the assumption that our motivations are universal. For example, Care is often the single strand that charities

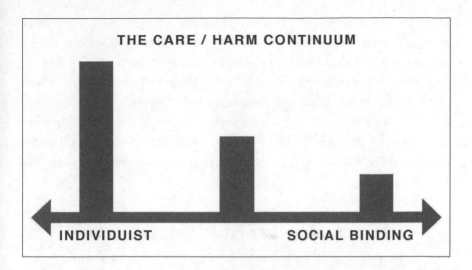

use to attract donors. However, the appeal of these campaigns is typically more complicated than that. A 2012 study, "How Political Identity and Charity Positioning Increase Donations,"[1] by Winterich, Zhang, and Mitteral, demonstrates how single-strand outreach programs may be missing the boat. In simple terms, there may be more than one way to the heart of potential donors. In this particular study, researchers created a fictitious charity and then set out to better understand the relationship between the charity's moral foundation and a donor's political identity, segmented between liberals and conservatives. The descriptions of the identities were generally in line with how we describe the Individuist and Social Binder patterns from our Social Binding Spectrum. The moral foundation of the made-up charity was made clear in a written description of the organization and its message. Descriptions varied by just thirteen words in a seventy-five-word message. Consider message A compared to message B below:

A. Save the Children creates lasting change for children in need, in the United States and around the world, through private intervention. Save the Children helps provide food, clothing, and medical aid to all children in poverty through privately funded support. The funds that Save the Children raises are managed and administered to children in need through private organizations, especially local citizens and religious organizations. These private agencies will use the funds to help children who are in need of food, clothing, and medical care.

B. Save the Children creates lasting change for children in need, in the United States and around the world, through government intervention. Save the

Children helps provide food, clothing, and medical aid to all children in poverty through government-funded support. The funds that Save the Children raises are managed and administered to children in need through public agencies, especially the U.S. government. These public agencies will use the funds to help children who are in need of food, clothing, and medical care.

Potential donors were polled after reading the two descriptions. They were asked to report their level of affinity toward the charity, their likelihood to donate, and the size of their potential donation. Responses are captured in the following graph.[2]

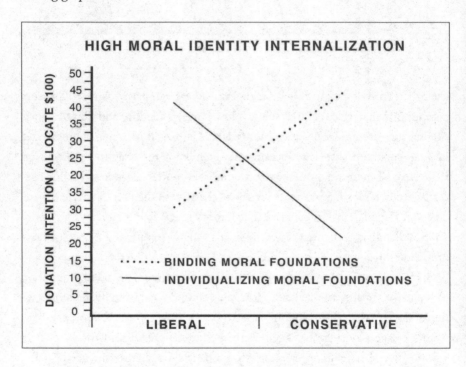

As you can see, those participants with a Social Binding IP responded more favorably to the conservative description of the charity. Those with an Individuist IP responded similarly to the liberal description. Simply accounting for the depiction of the foundation as conservative or liberal predicted the subject's affinity for the charity, and the likelihood of their donating to it.

These results fly in the face of current cause marketing strategies, and strongly suggest that there is more than one path to building appeal. More diversified messaging could easily increase a charity's donor rolls, across a broader population.

Perhaps one of the most overt examples of advertising based on the Care/ Harm instinct is a campaign conducted by the American Society for the Prevention of Cruelty to Animals. Nowadays, it's hard to recall Sarah McLachlan's song, "Angel" without recalling the ad that originally ran in 2007 featuring image upon image of abandoned and abused pets. It was one of the most successful campaigns in history—raising nearly $30 million in donations[3]—yet it could have done even better.

What other clear emotional connections can expand the base of the ASPCA? What about the loyalty that pets are known to engender within us? Or the role that pets play in our families, pulling at our sense of long-standing tradition? (Historically, most presidential families welcome a new dog when they move into the White House.) Even the joy of anticipation a pet brings to a relationship might leaven the seriousness of the Care/Harm thread. Despite their long track record of success, appealing to a single instinctual trigger, if the ASPCA's goal is to maximize their relationship with all prospective donors, there are ample ways to do more. The conundrum for marketers is that when a campaign finds success, it is assumed that the path taken to achieve such results is the only way, *the* answer. However, we contend that it should be seen as the starting point for inquiry.

MAPPING THE JOURNEY

Building customer or donor journeys with coordinated effort has proven to be worthwhile. One can organize a journey by the layers of information presented in any discovery phase of planning. It may be organized like this:

Because we can access a wide range of data sources in today's connected world, we can see that our Instinctual Patterns are expressed in myriad ways. Again, behavioral markers are the most convenient to observe, but also the most variable and difficult to link to a motivational cause. In any customer journey, the closer we get to the IP layer, the more meaningful an observation becomes.

Likewise, if you're a cause or a charity trying to secure new donors, timing is everything, and you should pay particular attention to laying out a sequence of precise and targeted steps to secure a donation. Broadly speaking, there's a predictable path in the acquisition funnel, moving prospects from awareness to con-

THE CUSTOMER JOURNEY ACCOUNTS FOR THE LAYERS OF IDENTITY

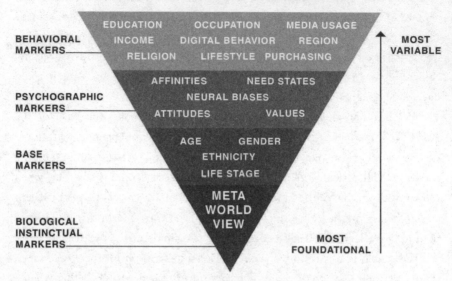

siderations to conversion as comfort levels are established. Would you ask someone whom you'd just met to marry you? In most cases, probably not. Here is one visualization of the Donor's Journey that we have found useful:

1. **Moral Support, or the Icebreaker.** This is when the prospect hears about a cause's good works and signifies moral support for it, breaking the seal on a potential new relationship. A digital "Like" will suffice.

2. **A simple, low-friction donation, likely online.** Perhaps the potential donor is inspired by stories of good deeds shared by the cause.

3. **Deepening participation.** The potential donor joins activities in relevant interest areas. Associating with people of like interests demonstrates that a person is not alone in their willingness to run a race, play golf, dance, or retrieve litter from a stream.

4. **Offer of formal membership.** But only when it's become clear that the cause's values and ethics are in alignment with those of the potential donor. This journey may take ten minutes, ten weeks, or ten years, depending on the cause and target.

5. **Advocacy.** The final stage is when the potential donor extends his or her boundaries to include personal relationships. This includes far more than direct contributions. At this point, the cause becomes an extension of the donor's identity. They volunteer, head donation drives, sponsor events, or share personal stories to drum up support.

The challenge for causes, and for that matter brands, is to customize the journey to the very particular value propositions at the heart of the matter. Typically, there are three steps in applying Instinctual Patterns to this task:

1. DISCOVERY: THE SEARCH FOR WHY

At this stage, it is crucial to understand the value proposition in detail. We generally conduct personal interviews with company leaders to understand the details of their proposition. We review past and current creative materials and collect data about the target population, including information on what their recent responses have been. And we ask the following questions:

- To whom is the value proposition targeted?
- What are the key performance measurements that will let us know that they have received it?
- How do we know if we are successful?

2. ENGAGEMENT ARCHITECTURE:
MAPPING FOR WHY

Next, we lay out the strategy and plan. For this phase of the process, we ask:

- What Instinctual Pattern will we target?
- What media will be used (e.g., direct mail, digital, TV)?
- What's the time frame?
- What's the narrative of the campaign?

3. DEPLOYMENT: MEASURING FOR WHY

Once the campaign calendar is built, including objective measures of success, we can keep track of the deliverables. Depending on the scope, we issue periodic progress reports, which allow for any needed adjustments in real time.

One misconception about Instinctual Patterns is that they are distributed over a population in discreet clusters, signified by common attributes. For a more accurate picture of what IPs can tell us, imagine an array of points, each representing the Instinctual Pattern of a person on the Social Binding Spectrum, the axis upon which we find a distribution of patterns spreading from total Individuist to complete Social Binder. Before our discovery stage, these distributions appear to be random—just points spread across the spectrum. As we learn more through observation and gathering data, we begin to see patterns. The more data we have, the more we see people organize around narratives, interpreting the world in a similar way. The more specific the narrative, the more people it may

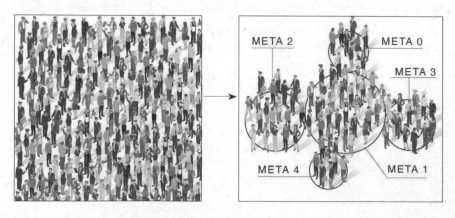

exclude. Likewise, a general narrative may tolerate many people across the spectrum.

When we present the Model of Why, we offer the base narratives applicable to the U.S. distribution. However, marketing or political campaigns can create customized narratives defined by the specific characteristics of brand, cause, or movement. This degree of targeting, based on the characteristics of the narrative, will certainly influence more than just the copy used in a promo. The ultimate impact is measured by how well the narratives conspire to use all available inputs to create the most influence possible. This may reflect how we measure influences, by accounting for the use of more robust measures of success. Consider the relevance of the ways in which Instinctual Patterns intertwine with and influence one's understanding of:

- **Life Stage**: Does the narrative represent an authentic description of the event to the target? How about for a Millennial Individuist? A Boomer Individuist?

- **Gender:** How does a man or woman react to the narrative? How does that look through the lens of an Individuist versus a Social Binder? Remember our discussions about sensitivity to traits like gender perspective.

- **Ethnicity**: Are there differences in the life experiences typical to particular ethnic groups that could cause them to draw different conclusions from the "facts on the ground"? How are people of varying ethnicities influenced by their Instinctual Patterns and life experiences? Stereotypes are typically meant to clump ethnicities into a single homogeneous group.

- **Religion**: How people express themselves through religious practices is likely to be influenced by their Instinctual Patterns as well. Perhaps the specific religion one chooses might have generational influences beyond one's profile, but how you practice that religion may be individually determined.

- **Values:** The values that people espouse are certainly a result of the interaction between one's Instinctual Pattern and life experiences. This is true for ethics, norms, and traditions. Different patterns will determine how one's worldview interprets them.

This model is a way to begin to account for layers of identity and make them accessible to the topic of intersectionality, as discussed earlier in the book.

Brands are very much in the same boat in terms of how they communicate, appeal to, and attract customers via messaging that resonates with a targeted audience. The Rogers Model of Diffusion of Innovation is a well-regarded paradigm that seeks to explain further how ideas, products, trends, and/or behaviors can become more widely adopted. See the progression of stages below. We should note that this model resembles the life stages of groups that we discussed in the previous chapter.

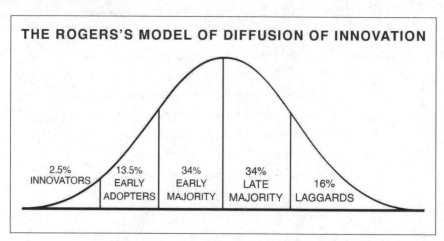

THE ROGERS'S MODEL OF DIFFUSION OF INNOVATION

| 2.5% INNOVATORS | 13.5% EARLY ADOPTERS | 34% EARLY MAJORITY | 34% LATE MAJORITY | 16% LAGGARDS |

This model suggests that different types of people are responsible for behaviors at various points in the cycle. Not surprisingly, our Instinctual Patterns assume different roles, much as they do in the group formation model. Similarly, how a dynamic brand takes shape, moves to the mainstream, and either fades away or rejuvenates over time is a combination of Instinctual Patterns and the Model of Diffusion of Innovation. The most successful brands—like successful organizations, ideas, and causes—rely on the interdependence of the roles various groups (IPs) play as they propel objectives perhaps unbeknownst to them, such as extending a brand's life cycle.

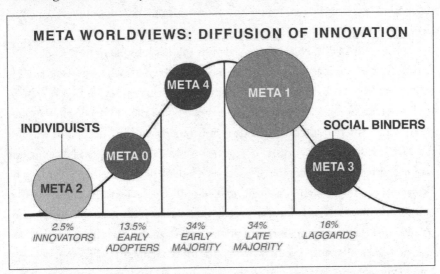

JOURNEY OF NIKE

Not surprisingly, Individuists typically occupy the role of innovators and early adapters. The Meta 0 IP, with its awareness of individual differences, often act as translator to help socialize innovations for their introduction to the mainstream. This is similar to the Meta 4 who act as a gateway to the more mainstream Centrists. This is what most mass-market brands covet. The traditionalist Social Binders act as the laggards, but they can extend a brand's life for a long time before unceremoniously letting it fade away. This reliable collaboration of forces helps to explain how a brand like Nike has stayed not only relevant but hip all these years. The brand history of Nike, found on their website (nike.com), conforms to this model completely.

Consistently one of the most admired brands in the world, Nike has been around for decades. It's remarkable that it has continued to stay fresh and alive for each new generation. Bill Bowerman, Nike's cofounder, was an innovator from the start. As the coach of the University of Oregon's track team, Bowerman always tried to give his runners an edge. Looking to innovate with a purpose, he was responsible for turning a demo shipment of Tiger shoes into his vision of what a track shoe should be.[4] His precursor company to Nike was called Blue Ribbon Sports. By 1970, Bowerman, with his partners Phil Knight and Jeff Johnson, had grown tired of working as a distributor, and they began to design and distribute their own shoes. And a legendary brand was born. Soon, Nike was the market leader, growing to serve the mainstream market not only in America, but around the world.

In the mid-1980s, Nike briefly ceded its market leadership to Reebok,[5] and faced a fork in the road. But rather than double down on what they had always done, they went in a different direction. Consider this response. In 1987, Nike readied a major product and marketing campaign designed to regain their industry lead and differentiate their brand from competitors. The focal point was the Air Max, the first Nike footwear to feature visible Nike Air bags. The campaign was supported by a memorable TV ad set to the original Beatles recording of "Revolution." It was catchy, inspiring, and edgy, to say the least. A year later, Nike built on its momentum from the "Revolution" campaign by launching a broad, yet personally empowering, series of ads with the tagline "Just do it." The series included three ads with a young, two-sport athlete named Bo Jackson, who espoused the benefits of a new cross-training shoe. In 1989, Nike's cross-training business exploded, due to the incredibly popular "Bo Knows" ad campaign. By the end of the decade, Nike had regained its position as the industry leader, and they haven't relinquished it since.

From a detached historical perspective, what Nike did was transform the linear Model of Diffusion of Innovation into a circle. Rather than extending what they had done to reach number one, as many intuitive leaders might have been tempted to do, they recognized that that strategy wouldn't keep them from ultimately falling into the grip of the laggards (the Social Binders)—for a likely false promise of recurring revenue. Instead, they found a way to reintroduce Nike, again and again, to the influencers (the Individuists), whose original defection probably cost Nike their number one ranking early on.

By metaphorically converting this linear model to a circle, Nike demonstrated that a brand, just like a cause, has the potential to develop lasting and robust relationships with its customers or donors.

As recently as 2018, Nike again proved its mastery of cyclical rejuvenation—and its talent for partnering with charismatic and influential athletes.

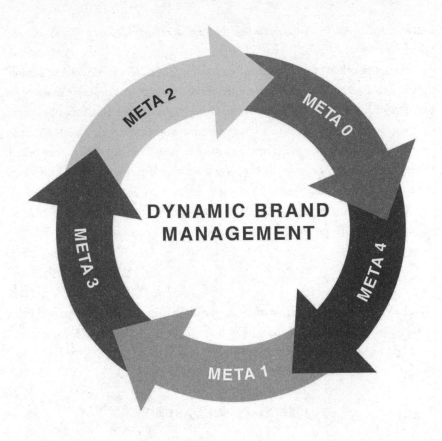

With the football season buckling under the pressure of America's entrenched tribalism, fans faced a choice about what patriotism looked like—and meant—to them. This debate was kick-started by a handful of players, most notably San Francisco 49ers quarterback Colin Kaepernick, "taking a knee" on the field while the national anthem played to the stands. There had been a recent spate of widely publicized killings of unarmed black people by police officers, and the players said they were taking a knee to call out institutional discrimination, racial inequality, and police brutality. Their rallying cry struck a chord, but it was heard differently, depending on the football fan. Even President Trump got involved, taking the side of the Social Binders, naturally. At the time, Nike took the extraordinary (and risky) step of reintroducing its brand to Individuists by making Colin Kaepernick the face of a sweeping new campaign across all media. The results were spectacular. By endorsing the activist, their value judgment remained true to the brand's history, and spoke to its core target audience. By letting the

Diffusion of Innovation system work its magic yet again, Nike enjoyed its best sales year ever.

How can other brands, especially those without Nike's formidable market position, take advantage of this dynamic brand management process? It starts by first defining the value proposition they hope to deliver to consumers, donors, voters, or buyers. For Nike, the original promise was to give their athletes a competitive advantage through innovations in running shoes. Since then, the brand has built on that promise by aligning itself with visionaries who break through not only athletic barriers, but cultural ones.

This combined model points the way to a process that will be invaluable to any brand, cause, or person looking to leave their mark in history.

A FEW CASE STUDIES

Now let's look at a few more current scenarios in which PathSight has had the opportunity to deploy the Model of Why to increase our clients' reach, and expand upon and exceed their target goals.

LIBERTY MAGAZINE ARCHIVE

In March 2015, we got an interesting call from the owner of *Liberty* magazine's archive library. The defunct magazine had been very popular in the U.S. between 1915 and 1951, with a circulation of 3 million weekly subscribers. It had published luminaries from the worlds of literature, Hollywood, science, sports, and popular culture: H. L. Mencken, Tesla, Tolstoy, Einstein, President Roosevelt (who contributed more than twenty essays), and Babe Ruth, who once opined on "What It Is Like to Be a Has Been." The archive's current owner hoped there might be value in reviving the extraordinary library in a multichannel platform.

After reviewing the contents of the library, researching its appeal, and conferring with management, we made a proposal. The goal was to reintroduce the material to the public in a way that would appeal to advertisers, avoid controversy, and stimulate conversation. After some research, we decided that our ideal reader would be a Centrist, with the attendant full-throated support for status quo values, balanced sensibilities, and uncontroversial sensibility. So we reviewed a cross-sample of this group's likes, dislikes, and preferences to define our messaging paradigm and content strategy. Consider some of these observations from 2015 for the Centrist IP.

THE LIBERTY PROJECT			
CAUSES	**ENTERTAIN-MENT**	**LIFESTYLE INTERESTS**	**TOP FEMALE CELEBRITIES**
American Heart Association	Cards Against Humanity	Food	Carrie Underwood
Salvation Army	Monopoly	Music	Beyoncé
Special Olympics	Trivia Crack	Pets	Jennifer Lawrence
Wounded Warrior	Words With Friends	Travel	Taylor Swift
BRANDS	**TELEVISION**	**MOVIES**	**TOP MALE CELEBRITIES**
Coca-Cola	*Breaking Bad*	*Frozen*	Dwayne Jonson
Ford	*The Office*	*Saving Private Ryan*	Jimmy Fallon
Minute Maid	*The Simpsons*	*The Shawshank Redemption*	Justin Timberlake
Nike	*Top Chef*	*Toy Story*	Kevin Hart

The challenge was how to organize the library for consumption. We proposed a conceptual framework of tentpole subjects like Security, Freedom, Love, Well-Being, Culture, Justice, and Purpose. Individual articles from the *Liberty* library were served to the audience under one of these banners, promoted with Centrist-informed headlines to create a consistent appeal for the core audience. Not surprisingly, we found that when words in a headline deviated from the content's primary audience, engagement dipped substantially. For instance, we ran an essay by Einstein with the headline: "Einstein on Security: Why He Refused to Give Up on Humanity." In the article, Einstein couched the benefits of security accruing to humanity in Meta 2 Individuist language. He spoke of humanity being safer, fairer, and more inspirational when it paid attention to the individual and, reciprocally, to the culture as a whole. This headline was misleading, or confusing, to the magazine's Meta 1 Centrist audience.

HEADLINE #1: MISALIGNED

Just to be clear, in the first four days that particular essay ran, it garnered four thousand viewers. But, ultimately, we detected that the headline's reference to "humanity" was more aligned with a Meta 2 Individuist pattern than a Meta 1 Centrist one when we noticed that the tone of the comments on the piece were much more combative and antagonistic than usual. On the fifth day, we changed the headline to one that was thought to be much more in the realm of the Meta 1 Centrist in tone: "It's a Question of Balance, Even for Einstein." As a result, over the next four days, due to the title change, viewership doubled. Even more interestingly, the comments now showed much longer engagements, and they had

HEADLINE #2: ALIGNED

returned to their reciprocal, less confrontational tone. Great results that speak directly to our main premise: When you know whom you are communicating with and how they like to be engaged, you will be heard and acknowledged. Carefully crafting the right headline is essential. Words matter and they're powerful.

We also created a shared content strategy within the marketplace. Given our research, we wanted to create new, relevant content that would complement the archive pieces, so that the experience was not purely historical. This led us to seek out Centrist-leaning communities in areas we knew our audience was interested in: Food, Outdoor Life, Travel, Pop Culture, and Healthy Living. The editors of the Liberty Project tracked conversations on online message boards and social media that might appeal to our audience and align with Liberty Project content. Authors or bloggers from the original communities were offered the opportunity to cross-promote with the Liberty Project's growing audience. The Liberty Project launched in July 2015, and by January 2016 it had generated more than 450,0000 unique monthly visitors. (The principals sold the platform six months later.) So, as you can see, there is ample evidence for the applicability of the model in any format.

NFL TEAM CASE STUDY

One more example, from an NFL team who will remain nameless, was a simple ask: how to improve their fans' email open rates. They were focusing specifically on people who had not responded to marketing messages for at least three years. Armed with ticketing data, we were able to sort them into three IP groups, and resolved to see how modifying the subject lines of the emails would affect the open rates of Individuist, Centrist, and Social Binder groups. For example:

INDIVIDUIST: "Tailgating Like You've Never Seen It"

CENTRIST: "Traditions of Tailgating for Your Viewing Pleasure"

SOCIAL BINDER: "Rich Traditions of Tailgating Revealed"

Open rates are listed below for each compared to the control group.

EMAIL CAMPAIGN TO COLD CASES*

Each subsequent email was sent to those who opened the previous email.
The chart shows the difference in open rates when compared to control emails.
Cold Cases: Have not responded to the client in 3+ years.

EMAIL CAMPAIGN	EMAIL #1	EMAIL #2	EMAIL #3
✉ Invite to Tailgating	+ 62%	+ 31%	+ 31%
✉ New Recipes	+ 22%	+ 18%	+ 18%
✉ Favorite Ring of Honor	+ 45%	+ 35%	+ 28%

Interestingly, the Individuist pattern is typically not targeted by sports franchises. Their positive response might indicate that they are worthy of more marketing attention, or at least a messaging variation within each campaign.

DIRECT MAIL MARKETING CASE STUDY

Another PathSight client, a direct mail marketer with an already established track record for attracting potential customers, was looking for a way to improve on their customer acquisition campaign results. When we evaluated the customer mailing list, we saw that they were appealing to a broad section of the Social Binding Spectrum, but with a single, one-size-fits-all message. More targeted messaging would help conversion. In all versions the messaging needed to make two points: that debt was bad, and that the solution to getting out of debt could be simple. Together, we optimized their campaign with copy, visual aids, and decision-making strategies to appeal to people looking to manage their lifestyle and, ultimately, their debt. Using the brand's existing rate of return as a baseline, we set out to see if we might make a difference.

Our value proposition was simple: an easy plan for restructuring debt, which helped the customer feel successful in managing their finances. Our model revealed that people with different Instinctual Patterns have varying attitudes toward debt and how to handle it. We expressed these differences with assorted messaging based on the IPs.

It's interesting to see how these instinctual differences play out across the spectrum. The Individuists thought of debt relief as the return of freedom, while the Social Binders hoped that it would give them back control. The balanced Centrists believed that there was a way to handle debt that was fair to all parties involved. With these differences in mind, we delivered messages in which the style of the offer relied less on the logic of debt relief (and less on dense blocks of copy also). Our goal was to refer recipients to a call center where they could discuss their individual situation with a customer representative. The result: a threefold increase compared to the baseline results, and an aggregate increase in customer acquisitions.

Putting you
on the road to

financial *freedom*

Dear Jim,
Making plans for the future when that road is full of
pot holes and speed bumps can feel as if you will never
get there. At ▮▮▮▮▮▮▮▮ we believe that
everyone should have access to the help they need.

Ways to
get in touch

📞 1-888-▮▮
✉ info@▮▮▮▮
🌐 ▮▮▮▮▮

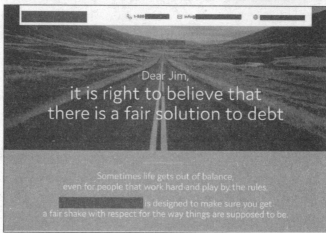

1-888-▮▮ info@▮▮▮

Dear Jim,
it is right to believe that
there is a fair solution to debt

Sometimes life gets out of balance,
even for people that work hard and play by the rules.
▮▮▮▮▮ is designed to make sure you get
a fair shake with respect for the way things are supposed to be.

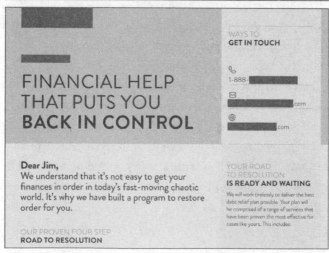

WAYS TO
GET IN TOUCH

📞
1-888-▮▮▮▮

✉ ▮▮▮▮.com

🌐 ▮▮▮▮.com

FINANCIAL HELP
THAT PUTS YOU
BACK IN CONTROL

Dear Jim,
We understand that it's not easy to get your
finances in order in today's fast-moving chaotic
world. It's why we have built a program to restore
order for you.

OUR PROVEN FOUR STEP
ROAD TO RESOLUTION

YOUR ROAD
TO RESOLUTION
IS READY AND WAITING

We will work tirelessly to deliver the best
debt relief plan possible. Your plan will
be comprised of a range of services that
have been proven the most effective for
cases like yours. This includes:

- + 25 percent versus the control
- + 50 percent improved close rate versus the control
- + 40 percent increase in the debt managed versus the
  control group

Even these campaigns, which only use a single media platform like this debt relief client, show how Instinctual Patterns influence the dynamics of behavioral change, regardless of the limitations of the medium. The model can be used to identify targeted customers for a particular company, test the appeal of a value proposition, and generate positive results using only one communications paradigm to convince a customer to purchase a product.

INSURANCE FOR GOVERNMENT EMPLOYEES

In another such case, we worked with a full-service insurance company that serviced employees of the U.S. government. Since all government insurance is required to be portable (so employees can take their insurance coverage to different companies when working for the government) all insurance companies participate in an open enrollment process, usually in November of every year. In this particular case, the client asked if we could answer these three questions:

1. Who is the core customer?
2. Are these customers already being engaged optimally?
3. How do we control for growth?

The trick was, in this particular case, the company did not want to submit any customer data, due to concerns about security and privacy. They also would not let customers respond to questionnaires. So the first phase of our work was significantly more challenging than usual. But by assiduously sorting their customers by age/life stage, gender, region, education, and government employee status, we assembled a sample representative of the core customer base. The distribution was as follows:

The majority of customers were located within the Meta 0 (Balanced), Meta 1 (Centrist), and Meta 3 (Social Binder) Worldview patterns. Among other traits, they shared an ardent preference for the status quo and were found to have an affinity for and reliance on:

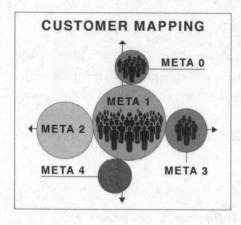

- Authority
- Loyalty
- Security
- Traditions

Additionally, a simple narrative guided their outlook on life: "We work hard and play by the rules. We expect things to work out. There is a right way to do things. We accept that there are leaders and followers, and sometimes winners and losers."

Their customers were motivated by a number of reasons:

MOTIVATORS	
GENERAL MOTIVATORS	• Preserve the cohesion of the social order. • Honoring traditions of the culture. • Protective of the status quo and defender against those seeking to disrupt. • Peace of mind is a goal for living. • Work hard and good things happen.
HEALTH MOTIVATORS	• By following your health protocol, your loved ones and supporters will be at ease. • Following your protocol is the right thing to do, and that is what we do. • Following your protocol will minimize the stress and discomfort for you and all those who care about you. • Relieving the stress on families is just something we know we should do.

In addition to considering these guidelines, management conducted a series of workshops on how to develop marketing materials for the relevant Instinctual Patterns they wanted to target. They sought answers to the following questions:

- How is authority expressed to these customers?
- What are the rules of the road?
- How are traditions referenced?
- What are the loyalty reference points for defining who is the in-group?
- How does security make itself heard? How does the company make people feel safe?

Management and team members participated in the workshops, offering feedback about their own reactions, positive and negative. In the end, they created story-based narratives to capture how any instinct might come to influence a situation in the customer journey. At first, they labored over each touchpoint, but soon it became second nature. This allowed them to reduce their reliance on copy; they found that they could insist upon no more than three customer choices in any Web copy, promo, ad copy, or the like.

As the communications strategy prepared to launch, the insurance company was offered the fortuitous opportunity to conduct a year-over-year study of their work. Prior to the launch, and in anticipation of the fall open enrollment season, they were able to build their budget in a way that mirrored the previous year's budget. They used the exact same promotional radio stations, the same number of promos, the same cost-per-spot calculations, and they standardized the projected CPMs (Cost per Thousands for any advertisement). As many variables as possible were kept the same—except the new messaging strategy. Results were then calculated as follows:

Over the course of two years, website traffic increased by 35 percent. More important, the length of stay for each visit grew by 26 percent. Gross sales improved by nearly 7.8 percent

YEAR / YEAR RESULTS	CHANGE
Website Traffic	+ 34.0%
Length of Stay	+ 26.0%
Sales Growth	+ 7.89%
Customer Satisfaction	+ 4.50%

(this is important, because it shows that they avoided relying on price to sell the product). Product satisfaction also grew by 4.5 percent.

The success of this project also highlighted a common concern in today's multichannel world: how to build consistent communications across all potential touchpoints. A research report from Gartner[6] documents that, in the 1990s, a customer journey typically was made up of three touchpoints (TV, radio, print). Today, it is made up of eight touchpoints (TV, radio, print, website, email, various forms of social media). This same study suggests that if one can manage to coordinate four digital touchpoints (email, direct mail, website banner ads, and social media ads), the campaign will outperform single or dual touchpoint versions of the same campaign by 300 percent. Imagine how much more is possible when we add instinctual relevance to the mix.

SEARCHING, MAPPING, AND MEASURING THE WHY

HOME WARRANTY COMPANY CASE STUDY

Discovery: The Search for Why: A home warranty company with a national footprint and a robust marketing research department was looking to improve their campaigns. They had spent the past nine years modeling and testing their messaging and had grown to a 20 percent market share. They used primarily direct mail, supplementing with digital and social media. The narrative of their current campaign relied heavily on the theme of personal responsibility. Customer files were available in two sets of data. The first one was a nondescript sample of people to which the company sent their marketing materials. The second set was a subset of the first group—the people who responded to the offer and signed up. From this data, we learned that the typical customer was a sixty-year-old male homeowner, susceptible to a message featuring themes of personal responsibility. The data was reviewed, and it was determined that those who responded to the campaign were, not surprisingly, predominantly in the Centrist and Social Binder patterns.

Engagement Architecture: Mapping for Why: Due to the company's commitment to testing results, they preferred to introduce only one variable at a time, hoping to make incremental changes to their existing paradigm. After all, that strategy had already delivered them nine years of success. That is how they had arrived at the targeting of sixty-year-old homeowners susceptible to messages about responsibility. A different company might want to start from scratch, but at PathSight we're happy to let our work be guided by the client's stated needs. In this case, we recommended editing the existing copy to broaden the appeal of responsibility, by positioning it in the context of managing risk. Therefore, the test was between the traditional narrative and one that only made a single change to the copy. Our analysis, in the discovery phase, gave us confidence that there were different pathways to the heart of these customers. We hypothesized that younger homeowners, often less secure in their monthly budgets than older folks, would respond to a different message, for both generational and instinctual reasons. We proposed a narrative focused specifically on budget, and how stressful it would be if they were forced to stretch their money due to an unexpected event. So the important takeaway was about the person and their stress, rather than their (presumed) responsibility for the event itself. This was a pretty clear distinction from the Social Binding point of view, "Is this good or bad?" The message was ultimately applied to recipients under forty years old whom we identified as Individuists. The process took into account the different Instinctual Patterns, but also age/life stage differences, in creating a competing narrative.

Deployment: Measuring for Why: The testing protocol was straightforward. For one set of targets, we deployed a traditional campaign, referencing personal responsibility. For the other set, we deployed the budget stressor campaign. The results were very interesting. Even the traditional campaign returned historic averages for the mailing, while the nontraditional Meta 2 Individuist group yielded a 160 percent incremental increase in response rate. This success instantly qualified the campaign for more testing, including expanding the scope, which had begun with roughly fifty thousand customers, to include hundreds of thousands and eventually millions of people. The really exciting thing was that the nontraditional respondents represented noncompetitive, incremental growth; they did not cannibalize the traditional campaign's results. We can map the results as follows.

Clearly, there is room for more than one campaign to reach success. The only question is: How many different campaigns might be justified to get to 30–40 percent market coverage?

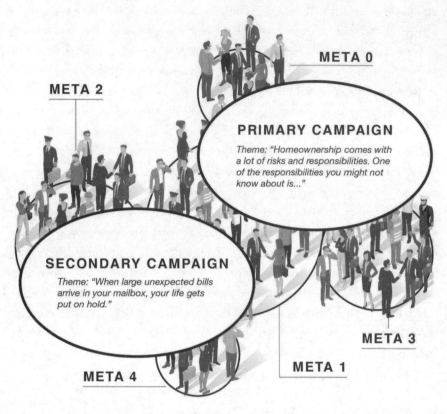

FINDING THE WHY IN AN ORGANIZATION

One last, but very important, use of the model is to identify the culture of an organization. If we think of companies as unique populations we enter and exit each day, it follows that they develop their own culture, language, and customs separate and distinct from the general population that hosts them. Accurately diagnosing a company's culture is useful on many fronts—including recruiting for a strong mix of employees to prevent a homogeneous workforce and identifying roadblocks to performance. To this end, we have used this model to articulate and map the complex infrastructure of large and small companies.

An organization has many different layers—departments, teams, and so on.

Accurate and timely communication across the board is essential—especially when it comes to a company's vision and values. Leadership must inform and inspire; managers must pass this knowledge along to their employees and employees must be the face of those values and processes to the customers. Customers are seen as part of the ecosystem, because they provide feedback about how well the organization executes its plan.

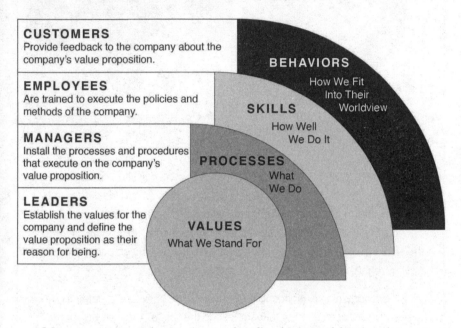

Many corporations have company handbooks created by their human resources department that outline their company's history, mission, core values, and the rules, policies, and expectations for employees. These rules essentially translate the values of the leadership into executable value propositions for the entire company and serve as an excellent recruitment and retention tool. PathSight recently worked with a large domestic manufacturing company looking to revise their personnel policies for a sales department. In the process, we organized a dashboard of information about people and the demands of their jobs. Below is a snapshot of how we envisioned the task.

From this breakdown, we were able to see how skills were organized across the department. They appeared to be well suited to their function. For a department that engaged mainly in sales, the concentration of Balanced and Centrist Instinctual Patterns made sense. The departmental leadership had a healthy

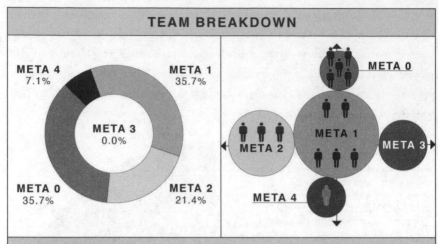

TEAM BREAKDOWN

META 4
7.1%

META 1
35.7%

META 3
0.0%

META 0
35.7%

META 2
21.4%

META 0

META 2

META 1

META 3

META 4

GROUP CHARACTERISTICS

The general shape of this department appears to be well situated for the demands of their positions. The concentration of Meta 0 and Meta 1 for a department that traffics in process and regulations seems to make sense. Those centrist characteristics can be seen as supporting an appeal for the status quo while balancing a temperament that shares empathy with a healthy regard for the role of systems and order.

With the leadership having found their way into the Individualist category, they surely will account for a forward lean to the group. They will be open to new ideas and yet will not be untethered from the realities of their group. This balance should be a virtue of the group's performance.

The group generally regards itself as smooth functioning, which is supported by Key Objective evaluations. When hiring they are faced with a choice — the next hire might be similar to the group, centrist with a lean to the Individualist, however, there could be a push to expand in the social binding traits. This would allow for them to build a more solid skill set for process and order with a muted sense of compassion that their enforcement responsibilities might benefit from. This is a choice point for the group and one that senior leadership should weigh in on.

proportion of Individuists, giving a forward lean to the group; they were open to new ideas, yet not untethered from the realities of the job. The balance of skill sets was considered a key driver of the department's team performance.

In reading the key objective evaluations of the employees in the HR department, we discovered that they each felt they were part of a smoothly functioning team. In future hiring, department heads were faced with a choice: hire someone similar to the group—Centrist with a lean toward Individuist—or expand the team with members who demonstrated complementary skills, in this case Social Binding traits. Perhaps they could better communicate with customers who had a muted sense of compassion and demanded attention on process and order, a task well suited to a Social Binder.

TEAM MEMBERS	META	CARE	FAIRNESS	LOYALTY	AUTHORITY	PURITY
Edward D***	2					
Kaitlyn T*****	0					
David L*****	1					
Leigh R*****	4					
Matthew V*****	0					
Spencer K*****	2					
Annette W*****	1					
Alexis C*****	1					
Brian F*****	0					
John P*****	1					
Michael S*****	0					
Robert L*****	2					
Sandra L*****	1					
Drew L*****	0					

SPENCER K*****

To facilitate this type of analysis, we created a grid showing the profile of every person in a given department or group (names are not actual people). Not only did it display the spread of Instinctual Profiles, it also noted the specific strength of each instinct in each person. This dashboard also provided a summary of personal characteristics, and an example of a personal narrative.

In the beginning of this book, we discussed the question of nature versus nurture and which is more influential in determining one's path. A career that seems to pivot on this question is sales. Some people think of it as a career that one is born to do, that it requires certain inherent personality traits. Others think sales is just like any other career, that it can be taught and that diligence breeds success. Either way, if an Individuist and a Social Binder both set out to find suc-

PROFILE CHARACTERISTICS

This group is instinctively inclined to value individuality, compassion, fairness, and justice. People are given sway in their personal behaviors unless they harm others or treat them unfairly. They have an intuition to protect and nurture those who are vulnerable or unable to provide for themselves and are not especially judgmental as to personal choice. They tend to prefer a life of variety, stimulation and personal freedom. A sense of pride is generated by being first to find and endorse a trend or new product which satisfies the urge to move beyond the status quo. This is distinguished from achieving an elevated status from owning expensive signifiers.

NARRATIVE

"When I look at the world, around me I see one that is filled with new things,lots of choices and ways to express yourself. We get to push the boundaries with new technologies in almost every facet of life. That is thrilling to me and something I embrace. It is easy to get carried away when the world is at your fingertips. I happen to love art and music and can explore it easily and in every conceivable form. What I am concerned about is how judgmental the world is too. I see a whole section of society that wants everyone to do things their way or the highway. That concerns me because I say, if it isn't affecting you, then you should keep your opinions to yourself. People have a right to be able to express themselves as they see fit. For example, I look around and see there are lots people who find themselves in a bad way, and I don't think we do enough to make sure that everyone has a safety net beneath them. There are also too many examples of people not having equal protection under the law and that is just not right. It is our obligation to make sure that is not happening."

cess in sales, they would certainly face different challenges, and bring different innate strengths to bear.

In one sales department PathSight recently worked with, the leadership had a proprietary sales matrix that they used to evaluate candidates. It included a sales skills survey, a lifestyle and aptitude questionnaire, and an optional skills

ARCHETYPAL SALES PROFILES: STRENGTHS AND CHALLENGES

META WORLDVIEW 2	META WORLDVIEW 3
Sales Profile Strengths: • A general curiosity with the world. • New and emerging trends are stimulating. • Empathy for others typically comes naturally. • Relationships are often a strength. • Flexibility and unstructured problem solving are often common traits. • There tends to be a natural instinct toward fairness and reciprocity in their relationships. • Often "discovers" new ways to do things that can lead to unexpected outcomes. • Instinctual triggers are: Caring, Fairness, Justice.	**Sales Profile Strengths:** • Operates well in organizations that clearly articulate rules and responsibilities. • Has comfort within hierarchical authority. • Generally has an instinct to build teams around the social order. • Sees the efficient functioning of the group as more important than the "feelings" of the individual. • Likely to thrive in situations that are transactional in focus. • Values systemic processes or rules based solutions. • Self-starter, disciplined within structure and enjoys marked accomplishments. • Happy to embrace "our way" of operating.
Sales Profile Challenges: • Resistance to convention may be a natural reaction. • Structure may be seen as arbitrary and / or rigid. • The sanctity of "we" may not come naturally. • May be erratic in record keeping. • Procrastination may surface. • Routines may be boring. • The urge to find a "new way" may conflict with "this is how we do it."	**Sales Profile Challenges:** • May be difficult to break with traditions and embrace change. • While structure may be comforting it can also be limiting. • Accomplishments can become the only record of worth. • Initiative to expand the scope of responsibility can be limited. "Not my job." • Hierarchical order (e.g., leaders vs. followers, winners vs losers) may become rigid.

interview. PathSight created an analysis of the various requirements of the sales positions. We found that its sales jobs appealed to others in the Social Binding spectrum, not just Individuists or Social Binders. In this situation, given the current makeup of the department (Centrists with an Individuist lean), there was now a way to understand departmental needs and to select candidates with the most job-related skill set and therefore the highest potential for job success.

When this was presented to the departmental leader, the sales manager commented, "That explains it, we have too much empathy in our group. We need to get some of those Meta 3 Social Binders in here, with their sharp elbows." We were pleased to see leadership was not looking for a candidate with the right "fit." Instead they had asked themselves, What perspectives are we missing? Where are we looking to grow as an organization? Given this company's long sales cycle, PathSight recommendations have not been formally evaluated as of yet, so results are not included in this book. However, we have found that the following profiles' predictors of success are typically linked to a combination of Instinctual Patterns and management style and can serve as a model for improving team alignment, productivity, and performance.

One important note—we believe this tool can help hiring managers understand their unconscious biases when hiring someone who "fits" within the company's values and ethos—so that the words "corporate fit" are not used to discriminate or prevent a diverse and inclusive environment from developing. Research shows that racism, sexism, and ageism all play a role in who lands the interview and who ultimately gets the job. People want to hire others that will most gel with them, and they find comfort in surrounding themselves with others who share interests, customs, language, race, and gender. They might hire people whom they'd want for a friend, someone to go to happy hour with, someone who attended the same schools, someone with a family, or without, depending on your status, someone who lives close to work, someone who played the same sports in college as they did, or someone who grew up in the same town—all factors that can lead us to choose one person over another for reasons other than the most job-relevant skill set. And by that we don't mean the person who has the best GPA or work experience. You might make judgments on who's easiest to onboard. The Model of Why helps you add to your decision-making process an understanding of the company that the new hire will be joining. This may be a way to minimize whether age, gender, and racial bias are creeping into decision-

ARCHETYPAL SALES PROFILES: PREDICTORS OF SUCCESS

META WORLDVIEW 2	META WORLDVIEW 3
Matching these profile attributes to the demands of the job:	**Matching these profile attributes to the demands of the job:**
• Sales opportunities that are very reliant on relationship building and management skills could signal success.	• In the case that a sales opportunity has clear objectives, processes, and expectations, it should align well with this group's instincts.
• This group has strong instincts and genuine interest in people and thus relies on relationships as a foundational sales tool.	• This group might be able to sell anything but their instinct for order, team functioning, and goals is a virtue.
• Sometimes could be strategic or be a natural occurrence based on their instincts.	• Once they understand the methods and expectations, this group should be independent within the system.
• Certain sales situations that require problem solving, longer sales cycles, and nonstandard product solutions would be likely to take advantage of these attributes.	• This group could become a resource for ways to optimize group processes.
• Consultive selling is a natural setting for success.	
Management style is also important:	**Management style is also important:**
• If the sales management structure relies upon structures with routine reporting, hierarchical order, and uniform methods, this might stifle some of the enthusiasm and effectiveness of this group.	• If the sales management structure relies upon structures with routine reporting, hierarchical order, and uniform methods, this group will be right at home.
• This group is optimized in a structure that encourages problem solving, supporting nontraditional or idiosyncratic methods.	• Predictability and order are very comforting.
• Providing a variety of challenges, real stimulation, and a chance to go deep in a process would be a great match.	• Solution selling where the sale can be seen as a culmination of personal skills, knowledge, and repeatable process are ideal.
• Variety and stimulation is a motivator.	• Ambiguous or obtuse selling situations that rely on nonstandard solutions may be uncomfortable and a challenge for this group.

making. The model also makes sure that hiring managers are not reinforcing recurring toxic behavior and systemic discrimination by falling into the trap of hiring the "same" people over and over again.

WHAT'S YOUR STYLE?

Teams are not created in a vacuum. It's important that they're built with the company's culture and strategy in mind. Does your strategy demand innovation and exploration, or is it focused on stability and steady growth? If the former, you'll likely look for the Individuists' openness to trying new things and flexibility. If the latter, you'll favor the Social Binders, since they value hierarchy, rules, and consistency. Each type has its merits and its challenges—a good leader knows how to enlist the right type for the right project at the right time.

I've found that the best teams are the ones that are operate cross-functionally, are diverse and inclusive, and mix backgrounds and work experience. Different working styles are key, too, as each person can contribute what they value, how they approach a task, and the way they'd prefer to interact. Some team members seek challenges and are goal-driven; some value teamwork and loyalty, others crave stability and order, while others are inspired by possibility and exploration. Some people are pragmatic, while others push boundaries; others are decisive and authoritative, while others are more cautious and discriminating. Most value trust in an organization. The list goes on. You probably recognize some of these traits in yourself or in your colleagues.

Although all styles are welcome here, there is a natural tension between some of them. This is where clear direction and individual and team expectations are essential. What happens when one team member wants to brainstorm and sketch all possibilities, and another prefers structure and to discuss only what's pragmatically possible? One lives for pie-in-the-sky thinking, the other for organization and detail—and a desire to not reinvent the wheel or waste existing advantages already earned. Or what happens when a person who sees solutions in black-and-white meets a person who believes it's important to merge the views of multiple stakeholders? One will likely debate his or her point and the other will insist on respecting—even encouraging—all points of view. Or, finally, what about the differences between the person who thinks long-term ideal and the one who thinks short-term goals? One feels the other is not thinking sustainably, and the other thinks they have immediate concerns to think about that, if left unanswered, will mean there is no long term. People are more nuanced than this, but you get the picture. We all bring our way of working to the table. The benefit of teams with opposite styles is uncovering new angles and new ways of thinking. The benefit of teams with like minds is people will tend to get along, building trust is easier, and loyalty is almost an inherent quality. The challenge is these teams are more susceptible to groupthink and can foster "us versus them" attitudes.

GETTING THE MOST OUT OF YOUR TEAM

If the goal is to build a team of individuals who think differently, get things done, and work well together, then you want people who represent different worldviews. How do you then manage a mix of folks who have different styles? Broadly speaking, you understand their style and their *why* and make room for them to be heard. For example, for someone who needs to brainstorm, give them a whiteboard and at least a few people to help them sketch ideas. They're not afraid to experiment. In product development, the brainstorming part of a meeting is time-boxed, and then participants each get two to three minutes to respond with feedback. This gives each person on the team an opportunity to talk, but also respects folks in the room not interested in lengthy brainstorming. To solicit new ideas from people who need more structure, give meeting participants a pre-read or a question to think about before a brainstorming session. This helps team members who need more time to make decisions to clarify their thinking or gather information. For people on your team who thrive on competition, give them a challenge. If they thrive on building relationships, give them opportunities to meet and liaise with other teams in your organization.

Most important, I urge you to prioritize the voices of those in the minority point of view. If you don't, you run the risk of the team ignoring new data and doing what they already believe works over and over again. In my experience, once these ideas are introduced, the conversation starts getting interesting! Differences are a resource.

Canadian Banks Marketing Case Study

Here's one last case study that showcases the PathSight Model of Why at work. This is an example of how our model reveals something about every market that we study. We can learn how the organization of that market reflects who makes up the market and how the organization translates to any individual brand in that market. The dynamic interplay between the marketing and communications efforts of any brand is reflected in which Meta Worldviews they attract. By understanding this, these brands can purposefully execute campaigns that seek to appeal to any worldview that they think will value their offering. The marketplace then acts as a scorecard as to how successful they have been.

Our analysis begins with laying out how Canada is organized relative to these Meta Worldviews. As we shared in Chapter 7, Canada has a higher concentration of Meta 1s in their market as compared to the U.S. market; armed with this information, we want to carefully evaluate how successful brands have responded to the marketplace. We then dive into one sector of the banking industry to see, in detail, how the five largest banks are faring in this challenge. When you look at this analysis, take note of how these banks carve out their relationships with the worldviews. Any differences in their appeal to each worldview? Is there any diversity in the financial services market, or are they just splitting up the same audience?

Our analysis was executed post-COVID-19, and we were curious to see how consumers would interact with the brands they'd come to trust. Would they still be trusted? Would any sectors be left intact? Who would resume marketing as it once was and who would need to find a better way to communicate?

Full-service banks in Canada will have some soul searching to do to recapture the way they ran their businesses before the crisis. It's unlikely banks—or any sector or company anywhere—will be able to resume activities as usual. It's important to look at the reactions from inside the rattled nerve centers of the executive suites at any company. We looked at what leadership was doing at the banks. Would they need to move quickly to shore up the debt markets, or would they pursue new opportunities? Working with five different banks, we analyzed each of their customer bases to predict how their customers might react to post-COVID marketing outreach. This analysis also acknowledged that there may be opportunities for brands to reach new customers in our remade world. Overall, we aimed to learn the following:

1. The general characteristics of the Canadian consumer marketplace, as mapped by the Model of Why.

2. How the marketplace for the major full-service banks has organized itself by developing marketing and communications strategies and responding to results.

3. Specifically, how each bank benefits from the particular customer base it attracts (looking across all Instinctual Patterns).

THE CANADIAN POPULATION

The composition of Canadian culture is similar to that of other Western liberal democracies, but of course it has a handful of unique traits. We've identified the same five Meta Worldviews— Meta 0 (Balanced), Meta 1 (Centrist), Meta 2 (Individuist), Meta 3 (Social Binder) and Meta 4 (Fatalist)—that guide people's decision making across the globe, in every culture, style of government, and economic system.

DISTRIBUTION OF META WORLDVIEWS

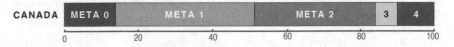

The chart above shows the distribution of the Meta Worldviews—and the size of the market that each represents—across millions of Canadian adults aged twenty to eighty. The smallest group is Meta 4, which reaches 1,948,476 Canadians, and the largest is Meta 1, which reaches 10,025,733l Canadians. This suggests that Canada draws upon the cultural ballast of the Meta 1 and its intellectual flexibility, to consider things from a common-sense point of view. This is not to say that the culture is monolithic, but rather that this common-sense center is core to who Canadians are. This is significant, because many other cultures demonstrate a natural pull toward one extreme or the other.

We analyzed a national consumer population that was asked to rate brands so we could calculate their net-affinity rankings. The consumers were asked to rate a brand between 0 (hate it) and 100 (love it), with 50 as the midpoint of ambivalence. The net-affinity score is found by subtracting the negative score (a score between 0 and 40) from the positive score (a score between 60 and 100). This produces a more useful metric than the raw affinity scores alone. In total, we rated thirty brands, sixteen of which recorded a positive net score and fourteen of which recorded a negative net score. Notably, Canadian Tire, Loblaws Supermarkets, Nestlé, and WestJet led the list of positives.

This list combines several market segments. Unsurprisingly, the consumer brands are more likely to be rated positively than the more B2B enterprises, like energy and transportation. But we can also detect some more subtle patterns within the marketplace. First let's review how the market appeals to Meta 1s.

All of the brands that received a net positive rating on the total brand chart received a positive rating here, too—which makes sense, given that Meta 1 is the most prevalent worldview in Canada. This confirms the Canadian intuition as deeply rooted in consensus.

So you could interpret this data as saying the path to success for a Canadian brand is to get approval from the Meta 1s. This turns out to be partly true, but only partly. If we review the chart below, we will see that the consistent winners of the net-affinity ratings are those brands that have also cultivated a strong relationship with another Meta Worldview group: the Meta 2s. Canadian Tire, Loblaws Supermarkets, Nestlé, and WestJet earned a striking approval from Meta 2s—virtually double the appeal compared to the rest of the marketplace. Typically, this happens when a brand's value proposition is intended to appeal to more than one group and their communications reflect that strategy. Here, the bridge to aligning with the Meta 2s was their shared instinct for fairness. The Meta 2s are instinctually more concerned with how the world affects individuals, as opposed to the community at large.

So while it's important, in Canada, to appeal to the group that most values the status quo, it's equally important to ensure that your value proposition is aimed at more than one Worldview.

THE MARKET FOR FULL-SERVICE BANKS

Let's start by understanding who uses full-service banks and why their customers find them appealing. Banks play an important role in any financial system, by facilitating borrowing and lending. If we examine how Canadian banks proactively support Canadians in their financial decision-making, we can see how well the individual banks are faring.

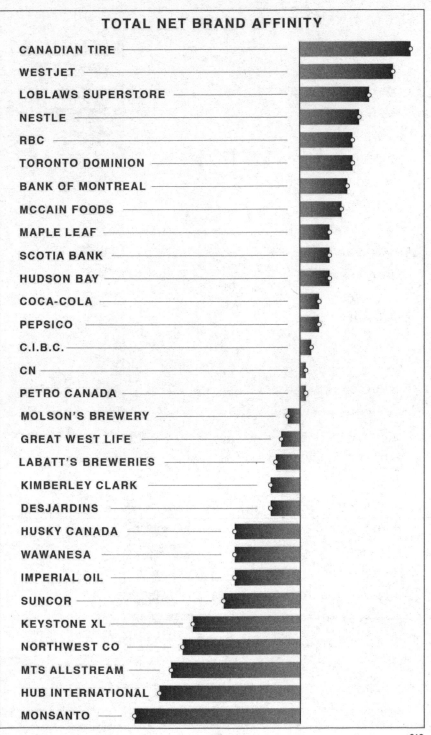

TOTAL NET BRAND AFFINITY

CANADIAN TIRE

WESTJET

LOBLAWS SUPERSTORE

NESTLE

RBC

TORONTO DOMINION

BANK OF MONTREAL

MCCAIN FOODS

MAPLE LEAF

SCOTIA BANK

HUDSON BAY

COCA-COLA

PEPSICO

C.I.B.C.

CN

PETRO CANADA

MOLSON'S BREWERY

GREAT WEST LIFE

LABATT'S BREWERIES

KIMBERLEY CLARK

DESJARDINS

HUSKY CANADA

WAWANESA

IMPERIAL OIL

SUNCOR

KEYSTONE XL

NORTHWEST CO

MTS ALLSTREAM

HUB INTERNATIONAL

MONSANTO

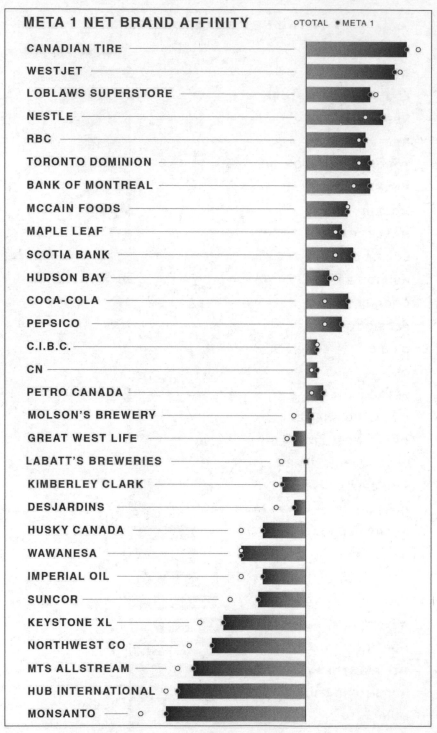

META 1 NET BRAND AFFINITY   ○TOTAL ●META 1

CANADIAN TIRE
WESTJET
LOBLAWS SUPERSTORE
NESTLE
RBC
TORONTO DOMINION
BANK OF MONTREAL
MCCAIN FOODS
MAPLE LEAF
SCOTIA BANK
HUDSON BAY
COCA-COLA
PEPSICO
C.I.B.C.
CN
PETRO CANADA
MOLSON'S BREWERY
GREAT WEST LIFE
LABATT'S BREWERIES
KIMBERLEY CLARK
DESJARDINS
HUSKY CANADA
WAWANESA
IMPERIAL OIL
SUNCOR
KEYSTONE XL
NORTHWEST CO
MTS ALLSTREAM
HUB INTERNATIONAL
MONSANTO

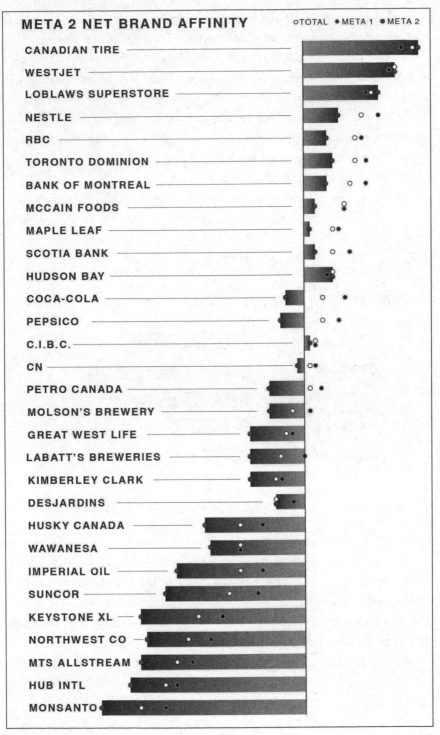

META 2 NET BRAND AFFINITY

o TOTAL • META 1 • META 2

- CANADIAN TIRE
- WESTJET
- LOBLAWS SUPERSTORE
- NESTLE
- RBC
- TORONTO DOMINION
- BANK OF MONTREAL
- MCCAIN FOODS
- MAPLE LEAF
- SCOTIA BANK
- HUDSON BAY
- COCA-COLA
- PEPSICO
- C.I.B.C.
- CN
- PETRO CANADA
- MOLSON'S BREWERY
- GREAT WEST LIFE
- LABATT'S BREWERIES
- KIMBERLEY CLARK
- DESJARDINS
- HUSKY CANADA
- WAWANESA
- IMPERIAL OIL
- SUNCOR
- KEYSTONE XL
- NORTHWEST CO
- MTS ALLSTREAM
- HUB INTL
- MONSANTO

Below is a chart that shows how the full-service banks were rated according to their total-market brand net-affinity prior to the COVID-19 pandemic. We can see that Bank #1, Bank #2, and Bank #3 are tied for the top spot. Bank #5 is next, with Bank #4 trailing noticeably behind. (Note: For the confidentiality of the banks, we will refer to them by these reference numbers only.)

What this chart doesn't tell us is the strategy of the players. Have Banks #1, #2, and #3 settled into the same strategy, or are they implementing different approaches to achieve the same results? Have Banks #4 and #5 embarked on a different strategy, hoping to compete another way?

When we look at rankings for the total net affinity of the five foundational banks that make up the legacy banking system of Canada, we see the following ratings:

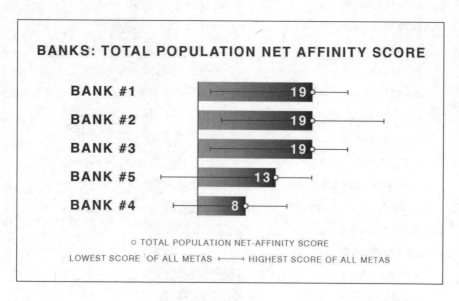

We wanted to see how the ratings might change across various Meta World-views. The chart below shows the results for Meta 1. Bank #1 captures more of their customer base from the Meta 1 group than any other bank. Bank #2 is slightly ahead of Bank #3. Bank #5 has a higher appeal to Meta 1s than their total ratings would predict. Bank #4 is right where the total score would predict.

Clearly, Bank #1 has fully built their appeal on this bedrock of the Canadian marketplace, the Meta 1 Worldview. Conversely, it appears that Bank #4 is lacking that appeal.

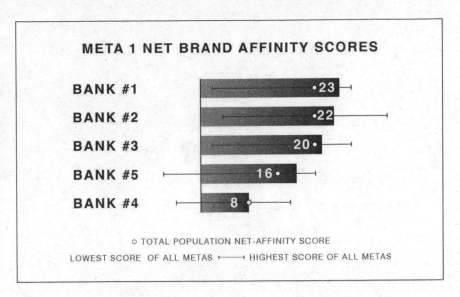

META 1 NET BRAND AFFINITY SCORES

BANK #1 •23

BANK #2 •22

BANK #3 20•

BANK #5 16•

BANK #4 8

o TOTAL POPULATION NET-AFFINITY SCORE

LOWEST SCORE OF ALL METAS ⊢——⊣ HIGHEST SCORE OF ALL METAS

If we now consider the second largest worldview in the Canadian population, Meta 2, we will see some shifts in the relative brand strengths. This analysis reveals a brand appeal that shrinks in size for Bank #1 by nearly 50 percent and for market leaders Banks #2 and #3 by 33 percent. There's a virtual tie now between Banks #2 and #3, with Bank #1 now in a tie with Bank #5. The others appear to not have moved.

(Remember, Canadian Tire, Loblaws, Nestlé, and WestJet appealed to this audience in a way that was significantly higher than their appeal to Meta 1.) The drop in appeal does not bode well for this marketplace. They will likely not find a ready-made audience in Meta 2s even though this worldview is always primed for a new offering, despite not having a history with the brand.

So, to establish a secondary audience for this market, let's look to the worldview that is the ostensible opposite of Meta 2—Meta 3. The Meta 3s consider community sacrosanct and believe no individual is more significant than the group. Life has a natural order—there are winners and losers and leaders and followers and that's okay. Among Meta 3s, Bank #1 achieves almost the same net-affinity rating as with Meta 1s. Banks #2 and #5 are virtually tied. Bank #5 is consistent with how it was ranked with the Meta 1s. Bank #2 is 30 percent lower than its Meta 1 ranking. Bank #4 is in negative territory for this group.

Truth be told, these results are very typical for banks in general. Finance has

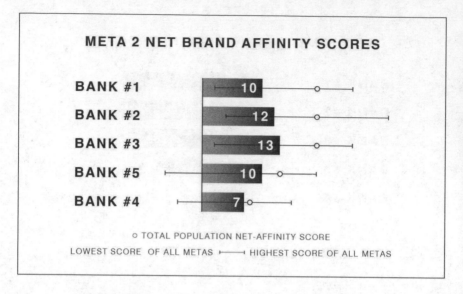

its own vocabulary, and people who are predisposed toward this market tend to have greater fluency in it than others.

Surprisingly, Bank #3 does not appear to be well received by Meta 3s. Their score is off by nearly 90 percent from the total, suggesting that Bank #3 is not positively associated with those core traditionalists of finance. This sector lends itself to comfortably dealing with a worldview that is at ease with the rules of

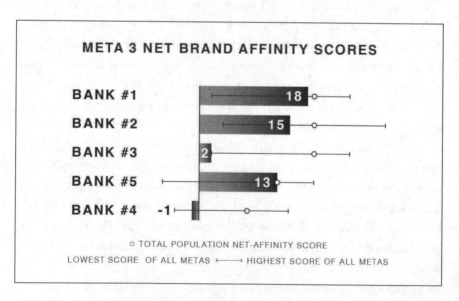

finance, the economy, and the markets. They purport to be dealing with outcomes, not emotions, and there are long traditions to that effect. This is a significant finding.

For now, it appears that Banks #1 and #2 are broadening their appeal to the commonsense worldview (Meta 1s) and to the community traditionalists (Meta 3s). These groups tend to be loyal to the traditional ways of doing business and are averse to change.

The final two groups are unlikely targets for large scale full-service financial services. The Meta 0s and Meta 4s combined represent a total of 5,845,428 Canadians. As such, they're not the core audience, so brand strategists are either ambivalent or hope, at best, to benefit from a halo effect while marketing to their prime customers.

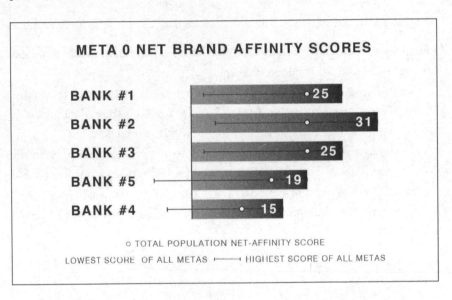

As you can see, the Meta 4s will have a de minimis impact on any one of these brands. However, for a brand that seeks to infiltrate a market heavy on technology and less on social engagements, it would be good to have access to this group. The Meta 0s, however, are in the sweet spot. This worldview is in many ways an offshoot of the Meta 1. These people share many of the same sensibilities but have a particular differentiating trait: Meta 0s find themselves aware of the social boundaries between people. If the Meta 4 is uninterested in social engagements, the Meta 0 is keenly interested in them. When new trends or

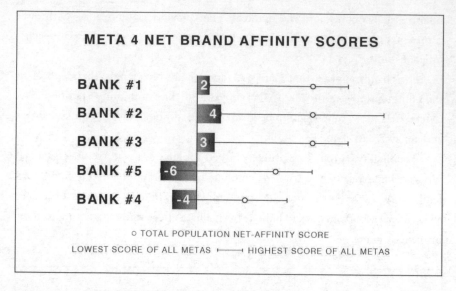

lifestyles are entering the mainstream, Meta 0s are often the group that translates the new trend into the common language.

In this case, Bank #2 earned its highest net-affinity score with this group. Banks #1 and #3 are just behind Bank #2, and in line with their Meta 1 Worldview rankings. Bank # 5 is consistently in line with the total here, too.

In summary, most financial institutions have a strong relationship with the Meta 3s and Meta 0s. You will recall that the Meta 3 Worldview revolves around the Social Binding point of view. Meta 0 is a strong centrist perspective with a keen eye for individual differences. We can conclude the following about each bank:

BANK #1

This brand is very solid in pursuing a classic finance customer base.

- This brand is well positioned to go toe to toe with Bank #2 and Bank #3. Its net-affinity rankings assure it of being able to trade on its loyalty in the marketplace.

- There's a predictable new opportunity to offer the Meta 2s—a new, fair, and equitable offering to a market looking for a guide to help them avoid the traps of a post-COVID-19 world.

BANK #2

This traditionalist full-service bank has established itself in the marketplace with a very conservative appeal to the population.

- A strong primary appeal to a mainstream Canadian (Meta 1s) segment that seeks the balance of a marketplace leader. Further, they have a strong history with those who are inclined to value the stability of the financial sector (Meta 3s). Finally, they are well embedded with the portion of the marketplace keenly interested in how to support the status quo (Meta 0s).

- The tepid relationship with the Meta 2 Worldview could be a weakness in their brand appeal or could be seen as a way to go after a market that generally embraces such opportunities. Perhaps they could build on their annual foundation for this.

BANK #3

A very active bank in the consumer marketplace. Their brand sometimes acts like a traditional financial brand and sometimes not.

- This well-capitalized multinational bank has a good feel for the commonsense middle market (Meta 1s) and also for those who are ready to transact in the status quo (Meta 0s). There is, however, an apparent lack of trust for those who are embedded in the traditions of finance and financial markets (Meta 3s).

- There might be a flexibility in the brand to credibly reach out to the Meta 2 group.

BANK #4

This brand appears to be a value proposition in search of a home. All of the net-affinity ratings are middling, and the appeal of the financial traditionalists is under water.

- There might be a case to build upon their years in the marketplace with outreach to the Meta 2s. This might be the best opportunity to build a strategy with a customer base that is overlooked by the market.

- A strong showing with the Meta 0 market could pave the way for an entry to the mainstream.

BANK #5

For a big five financial institution, Bank #5 has surprisingly not pegged its future on a particular market sector. They continually rate a consistent but underwhelming net-affinity rating in each Meta Worldview grouping.

- Consistency is the word for Bank #5. If they could make a strategic choice for excellence post-COVID-19, they could credibly succeed by choosing a worldview to own.

- There's no downside to creating a strategy that prioritizes a Meta Worldview to build out a commonsense growth plan.

Our review of how Instinctual Patterns have been used in a wide variety of settings has hopefully established our model as a tool that helps us understand *why* we do what we do. We believe these examples have also proven the consistency of the approach and its capacity to be integrated with other models, data sets, and observational behaviors.

Next we turn to how our worldviews shape our positions on many of the most hotly debated topics of our time.

CHAPTER 11

FLIPPING THE SCRIPT: INSTINCTUAL PROBLEM-SOLVING

The very idea of problem-solving may seem paradoxical in a model that presupposes two immovable worldviews at polar extremes. Where to begin? As we start to understand the Social Binding Spectrum, we can measure the emotionality of strongly held beliefs that originate at the poles around complex subjects—for instance, abortion, climate change, guns, and the death penalty. Fortunately, our population curve tells us that only a small percentage of people possess such high degrees of emotionality. Most fall into the Centrist Stack, where views are milder, and may therefore allow more paths toward solutions.

So, if we are not going to logically disarm one side or the other, what is our end goal? Pragmatically speaking, it's to figure out what the majority of people will accept. Implicit in this approach is the belief that successful cultures draw upon the complete range of the Social Binding Spectrum. If we acknowledge the fact that neither side of the spectrum is blessed with moral superiority, we are then in a position to navigate our problems through a process of accommodation: what is best for the most people. Countless communities, countries, and companies have organized themselves around some version of this principle. Think of the Latin phrase "Do No Harm," or Google's original slogan "Don't Be Evil."

Leaders do best when they act in the best interest of the most people. Think of a mayor organizing services for the varied interests of a small town. Or a company's CEO being challenged to consider employees as well as shareholders as the only groups that matter. How might this concept change corporate governance? Or the functioning of Congress?

In the first few years of Mr. Trump's presidency, he and his administration were very clear about whom they consider their coalition. This has been one of the most polarizing administrations in memory, due to their apparent decision to try to govern from that point of view exclusively. This type of governance appears unlikely to change, given the cohesion of traits defining their perspective—a strict adherence to hierarchy, structure, and law and order. Strong opinions regarding a code of religion (High Purity) and a reliance on keeping traditions, or "our way of doing things" (High Authority), signal a restrictive impulse. These Instinctual Patterns act as filters to create a commonality within this community, particularly expressed in their shared beliefs about race, gender, income, and ethnicity. To people who are very aware of such boundaries, it's difficult not to think that these criteria are intentional as governing principles. It seems to be part of their appeal for the in-group, the base. Consider which groups were most impacted by some of the Trump administration's early policy decisions. Regardless of their intent, the result has been that the president has tried to govern with the reliable support of his base of supporters, making him unlikely to reach across the instinctual barriers of the Social Binding Spectrum.

That does not mean that we cannot diagnose the way certain problems became intractable, and try to problem solve, ourselves, as citizens. How can we utilize our understanding of the Instinctual Patterns to encourage collaboration across instinctual types, rather than use those instincts to further divide? Doing so does mean that simply diagnosing the problem will not be enough to solve the problem—that may take the work of a broad contingency of citizens energized to undo the historical scripts that seem to be written into our cultural DNA right now. We often refer to these kinds of efforts as "flipping the script." No better time to start than the present!

Let's first look at how behaviors can serve as proxies for specific worldviews. For example, discussions of racial equity often get hijacked by the stand-ins for Authority, Purity, and Loyalty, which tend to ignore or disguise the importance of a panoply of issues tied to race and ethnicity. Specifically, in discussions of policies used in policing, a frequently used proxy often used is the rule-breaking excuse. For example, in New York City, during the protests of George Floyd's May 25, 2020, death by Minneapolis police—protests meant to focus explicitly on the issue of race, ethnicity, and police brutality—New York City was for a short time put under a curfew. In most instances, if the rallies were peaceful, protesters would be allowed to proceed home. In other instances, NYC police appeared to attack protestors, often without provocation. Their reasoning was that protesters were violating a rule and, thus, the action was justified. This is a perfect example of a substantive issue (race-related policing) being met by a proxy (they broke a rule), which allowed for the authorities to claim that they were just doing their job and not acting in a racially motivated way: "If only the protesters had not broken the rule, we could have acted more humanely."

Another clear example is America's strange relationship with guns.

FINDING THE WHY FOR GUNS IN AMERICAN CULTURE

Our gun laws, and the public's opinion of them, perfectly illustrate the immutability of opinion at the poles of the Social Binding Spectrum. At one end, we see a concentration of instincts focused on Authority, Purity, and Loyalty. These folks tend to support unfettered ownership of firearms, including the ability to carry them most places. However, while vocal, they are nowhere close to a plurality of the voting-eligible population. In fact, their numbers have shrunk over time, though this may inspire even more passion among those remaining. This is the challenge that must be overcome by a higher order of value proposition. Maybe America can accommodate its constitutionally based rights to gun ownership while it preserves the rights of the broader citizenry to a safe and secure community.

The Second Amendment of the United States Constitution provides the legal basis for the right to own guns. However, this protection is inspired by an array of core instincts, to go back to the core instincts of Haidt and Joseph's Moral Foundations Theory. Let's look at the impulse for each.

Authority: There is a legal basis that gives gun advocates support and traditions to uphold.

Purity: This right is encoded in the lexicon of liberty in the United States.

Loyalty: True patriots like them are called to defend this right.

These instincts inform a rationale that shapes a narrative for those adhering to the Social Binding side of the Social Binding Spectrum: "I want the unfettered freedom to own as many guns as I deem fit for use in recreation, sport, and ultimately personal protection. The Second Amendment is a God-given right to freedom-loving Americans, and it will be defended by true patriots."

Key beliefs might include the following:

- "You can't tell me what to do: It is a God-given right."
- "You are not a patriot if you don't agree."
- "If we make any concessions, it's a slippery slope until the government takes all of our guns away."
- "You don't understand gun culture."
- "Real safety means more people owning guns to protect themselves. A good guy with a gun is the best defense against a bad guy with a gun."
- "We have only ourselves to rely on; we can't expect the government to protect us."
- "The government is inherently suspect."
- "We have to own guns in case we need to defend ourselves from the government."

Some facts to consider:

- There is approximately one gun for every American alive today (330 million).
- Only 30 percent of Americans own a gun.
- 3 percent of Americans own 50 percent of the guns.

Individuists, at the other end of the Social Binding Spectrum, have an equal number of instinct-inspired beliefs, or immovable opinions, on the gun debate. They are primarily motivated by Care and Fairness.

Care: The right to bear arms is all well and good, but the sheer number of guns has come to conspire against the safety of all Americans.

Fairness: One's right to bear arms is not fair if it endangers everyone else. The U.S. Constitution is a dynamic document that is meant to conform to today's life circumstances. It's the government's responsibility to provide us with commonsense regulation.

These Meta 2 instincts inform a rationale that shapes a different narrative: "I want to live a life that is free from unnecessary risks for all of our citizens. Reasonable regulation that protects us from the calculated risks of gun ownership is necessary, prudent, and sensible. No one wants to eliminate guns, but like all of our rights, the right to bear arms comes with responsibilities. Your right to own a gun does not trump our right to be safe. Commonsense regulations are our right."

Key beliefs might include the following:

- "The right to bear arms is demonstrably not a carte-blanche right. We already regulate machine guns, tanks, and other instruments of war."
- "The people's right to safety is a primary right that the government is charged with enforcing."
- "It is unreasonable to think that a 'well-armed domestic militia' is necessary today."
- "The right to a gun conflicts with the right of our children to be safe in our schools."
- "90 percent of the American public support commonsense gun regulation."
- "It is only sensible to prevent abusers, terrorists, and the mentally ill from having access to guns."
- "Nobody needs to own an AR-15."

Needless to say, these immovable opinions (as well as the power of gun-industry groups, specifically the National Rifle Association) make it nearly impossible to show effective leadership on the issue of guns in the U.S. Flipping this script will certainly take a broad-based effort of the willing. Sadly, it is not the only example.

FINDING THE WHY *FOR CLIMATE CHANGE*

The U.S. populace has selected climate change as another battleground. Look at how the proxies line up.

PROXIES	
INDIVIDUISTS	**SOCIAL BINDERS**
There are so many things to consider, but we know that science has proven the carbon connection to the climate.	There are cycles of weather, and we will get through these patterns eventually.
Man-made pollution is responsible.	Man is an inconsequential factor.
Climate change is the existential threat.	Eventually we are all going to die.
We have the facts and have to act now before it is too late.	We can't fight progress because of an uncertain risk.
Look around and see the change.	You can't make us do it.

Again, the expressions of our Instinctual Patterns form a perfectly opposi-tional storm of opinions. While there is an emerging shift, in recent years, toward recognizing the reality of climate change, there is still an active debate as to how urgent it is and what should be done about it.

In 2014, more than four hundred thousand people found their way to New York City for the People's Climate March. The visual impact of this moment might have given an outside observer the wrong idea about the level of unity in the movement. Over the next two years, we launched a project to understand how the environmental movement was perceived around the world. Specifically, we looked at the language being used. For instance, we added a question to our IP survey, asking respondents to tell us what they thought of when they heard the word "green." See the range in the list below.

When a leader is faced with one of these quandaries, it is tempting to just choose a side and hunker down (as President Trump has done). But those num-bers rarely work. Whether the issue is guns or the environment, the way forward is always through the center. Inspiration comes from the extremes, but structural

WHAT DOES "GREEN" MEAN TO YOU?	
INDIVIDUISTS	SOCIAL BINDERS
Passionate	Disruptive
Concerned	Reactionary
Caring	Tree Hugger
Benevolent	Risky
Compassionate	Impulsive
Tree Hugger	Disloyal
Enlightened	Radical

change requires building bridges to as broad a coalition of the remaining Instinctual Patterns as possible.

To be clear, this is not about compromising, or watering down, one's principles. It is about finding a value proposition that can appeal to the instincts that drive each IP. Remember, human beings are wired for this. In the time of our distant ancestors, our survival depended on it.

Let's look at potential value propositions for the dilemma of climate change.

A Social Binder's Value Proposition: To live in a way that respects the world's resources, ensures access to clean water and air, reduces reliance on carbon, and promotes the adoption of renewable energy. A foundational principle of conservatism, after all, is conservation.

But, if we understand Instinctual Patterns at play, we might be able to find some common messaging that appeals to the full range of IPs.

The Social Binder's instinctual motivations are to:

- Protect the group.
- Stick to the way we always do things.
- Promote Leaders vs. Followers, Winners vs. Losers.
- Follow the "natural order" of things.

Proxies include:

- No individual outweighs the group.
- The science is equivocal.
- We are responsible for what we do.
- Man cannot affect these outcomes (much).

Effective Social Binder messaging goes something like this:

- "We have a long history of treasuring the world we live in . . . our water, our air, and our natural beauty."
- "Our traditions implore us to leave the world a better place than when we found it."
- "Clean air, clean water: It is our responsibility to make sure we have enough."
- "The science doesn't matter. . . . It is what we should do, morally."

An Individuist's Value Proposition: To live in a way that respects the world's resources, ensures access to clean water and air, reduces reliance on carbon, and promotes the adoption of renewable energy.

The Individuist's instinctual motivations are to:

- Ask if we're treated unfairly as individuals.
- Ask if there's a new way of understanding the climate.
- To resist conformity so they can embrace nontraditional solutions.
- To consider climate change as an existential threat.

Proxies include:

- The science is the motivation to act.
- To put profits over people is unjust.
- Nothing else matters; if we ruin this world, we have no other.
- It is a man-made problem, so we are culpable.

Effective Individuist messaging goes something like this:

- "We know what we need to do."
- "We need to fund whatever it takes."
- "We are in an existential war for the planet."
- "The only question is how fast and how far we need to go."

Obviously, the Individuist will be dissatisfied with the scope and urgency of the response no matter where we land. The messaging to them will need to build in warnings that "perfect is the enemy of good." Luckily, this Instinctual Pattern has a high tolerance for disagreement and dissatisfaction.

Likewise, the Social Binder will need to be presented with a message that is positioned to trigger their proxies: the tradition of valuing our resources, our instinct to be responsible for leaving the world a better place, that we should do this regardless of the cause, and that the motivation should not be contingent on science.

Granted that the two sets of immovable opinions seem to be miles apart, diagnosing the situation this way may at least point us toward a pathway to building a majority, or at least a plurality, of public opinion from which to operate. This is a lesson for leaders looking to find the means of building a governing constituency. By accounting for people's Instinctual Patterns, there is a chance that we can coax citizens out of their tribal corners. This is not to say that the Centrists of the status quo are the instigators of change. On the contrary, the whole ecosystem is required for true, sustainable change to happen.

TURNING THE TIDE ON CLIMATE CHANGE

The whole premise of instinctual problem-solving is to be able to use the Model of Why to consider why relationships between people, groups, companies, and governments get off track. Reality testing can help us break free from old habits and patterns that aren't serving us. Or, at least, it can help us more easily see where we went wrong. This process involves uncovering the underlying elements that define the origins of how and when a problem becomes intractable.

In 2014, I was invited to a retreat in Iceland with a group of scientists, advocates, writers, and NGOs. The agenda was to discuss the fate of the environmental movement. The organizers cited a central question: "Why has the available science not had more of an impact on the issue of climate change?" Does the presence of hard science serve to motivate constructive actions or not?

During the retreat, we heard hours of discussion about the unanimity of the science, and the search for an ignition point that would inspire people to decisive action. Toward the end, I made what I meant to be a flippant comment to the group: "What if the science just doesn't matter?"

To be clear, scientists have been investigating the carbon cycle since way before there was ever an inkling of a connection between carbon and human beings—the nineteenth century, if not before. In the 1930s, the concept of climate cycles was introduced, and 1960 is often referred to as the official historical starting point for measuring the rate of carbon dioxide in the atmosphere. That year, scientist Dave Keeling memorialized Mauna Loa, Hawaii, as the site where he first established the benchmarks of 315 ppm of CO_2, and a mean global temperature of 13.9 degrees Celsius, as the ideal conditions for the earth's survival. In 1967, Syukuro Manabe and Richard Wetherald issued the first warning about the increasing levels of CO_2 in the atmosphere due to human activity and predicted that global temperatures would begin to rise due to a greenhouse effect. Today, it seems that we are destined to hit record temperatures every year, forever.[1]

So our reactions to this scientific narrative have been playing out for a very long time. The resulting opinions are typically not generated by rationally examining a spreadsheet of data, but by our life experience and Instinctual Patterns. The science of climate change is just one strand of data for us to absorb. However strong the science, the calcified opinions of the American public on this topic have evolved over generations and can only be solved within our current cultural context.

By way of comparison, let's look at another dire subject: cancer. In 1971, Congress declared a war on cancer.[2] Unlike now, in 1971 many people did not survive the disease. The role of science, in this case, was as an arbiter of reality. How were we doing in the war? Were we winning or losing? It was easy to assess. The details of the science were shrouded in cancer labs, and the public did not have any meaningful opinions on which trials should be supported or not. There were some brushes with religion, but by and large this research escaped controversy, as long as it was perceived to be making progress. The key public sentiment was a coming together to support victims and to raise money. Even today, there are a plethora of foundations with no political affiliation working to raise billions of dollars for the fight. To be a cancer scientist is to be revered.

Not so for climate science. Consider that at about the same time that we declared a war on cancer, Richard Nixon launched the Environmental Protection Agency.[3] At the start, it was a bipartisan agency, and environmental protection, like cancer, was considered a motherhood issue: in other words, not controversial. But there were some other key differences:

- Climate science was in conflict with one of the most powerful industries in the world: energy, mostly derived from fossil fuels. Naturally, the energy industry did not acknowledge the new findings about climate change.

- The introduction of the EPA affected life choices of people in the present tense, but for results that were promised to come later. This is hard for some people to get behind; it's too abstract. Motivations are easier when they are definitive.

- The science became a public variable to question. Climate scientists could not predict exactly *when* various catastrophes would occur, just that they were inevitable.

- Because the science was promoted as unanimous, any detail to the contrary was cast as an invalidation of the whole endeavor. For instance, a 2020 photograph showed signs that were installed in Glacier National Park predicting that the glaciers would be melted by 2020. Since they are not all gone now, some see that as another missed mark, and more reason to doubt climate change science.

Unlike with the topic of cancer, there was little coming together among Americans to support victims or raise money for climate change. By the time I arrived in Iceland, we had begun to ask why. As mentioned earlier, the instincts on this issue have clear proxies across the Social Binding Spectrum. On the Meta 3 Social Binding end, people who support the forces of small government are resistant to changing our traditional reliance on carbon products, or being mandated to follow any sweeping policy change, regardless of who suggests it. On the Individuist's end, the driving forces are a belief in social justice, the rectification the inequities of capitalism, and the moral high ground of saving the planet. Individuists also tend to believe that with a problem so obvious, marching would be superfluous. Everyone can see it's not only a scientific reality, but also a moral crisis.

At this point, can science reassert itself as an arbiter of reality, speaking as clearly as it did for cancer? The scientists who have authored this scientific record now find themselves in the additional role of advocates for what to do next. Does that complicate our situation? Naturally, we need their expertise. But we must also acknowledge that their advice is still filtered through our Instinctual Patterns and life experiences.

So we can't leave it all to the scientists. We must first demystify why the simple warning of science is not universally embraced—at least not enough to prompt real action. At PathSight, we've found that when we don't link behaviors to a specific set of motivations, it's much easier to convince people to change those behaviors. That is, we need to get more people to do the right thing *without insisting that they do it for what we may consider the "right" reasons*. This chart simplifies the process, and it makes the case for a division of labor within our mission.

Phase 1 references the role that science and scientists play as the arbiters of our reality. Are we winning the war? Phase 2 references matching the elements of that reality with the active interests of the population. Causes that align with the interest of citizens provide an infrastructure for action. As we described earlier, when people align their instincts and values with a cause, they can be motivated to do incredible things. Phase 3 signifies the engagement of citizens as a result of their personal motivations being triggered by a particular cause or interest area.

An interesting article in the online journal *Conversation* discusses how key constituents get consumed by proxy wars that mute our true intentions. In the article "An Inconvenient Truth About *An Inconvenient Truth*," the authors, Dominik Stecula and Eric Merkle, recount the success of the documentary *An Inconvenient Truth* by Al Gore.[4] They identify how the film broadly affected an

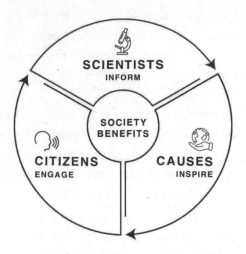

awareness of climate change among Americans. However, the media coverage of the film had unintended consequences, linking the science with the messenger, which muted its impact. Stecula and Merkle write, "We have studied in detail how the media covered the issue of climate change since the 1980s and how it may have played a role in polarizing the American public. The commonly observed pattern is that public opinion tends to follow, rather than lead, debate among political elites."

Voters, particularly in America, tend to harbor strong positive *and* negative attachments to political parties. These form critical components of their social identities. When uncertain about novel political issues, like climate change, they look for signals from political elites for guidance. These signals are, more often than not, carried to them by the mass media.

In our research, we examined the political signals that were present in the coverage of climate change in major, high-circulation daily newspapers, like the *New York Times*, the *Wall Street Journal*, and *USA Today*, as well as the network television channels—ABC, CBS, and NBC—and the cable news channel Fox News. What we found is a nuanced story that sheds considerable light on why the public has become polarized on the subject of climate change. First, politicians became increasingly visible in news coverage on climate change, politicizing the issue as it grew in importance. As a result, the public was exposed to a growing number of messages on the topic from party elites.

Second, Democratic messages have been more common in news coverage and, unsurprisingly, consistently pro-climate. Meanwhile, Republican messages have been fewer in number and, until the Obama presidency, ambiguous in direction. Contrary to narratives often prevalent in the media, only a small fraction of Republican messages on climate change explicitly denied the scientific consensus.

When one side's messages are clear and the other side's messages are muddled, as was the case here, it's plausible that Republican voters took their cues from Democrats. This should not be surprising. In an age of affective polarization, where both Republicans and Democrats each increasingly dislike the other, it makes sense that Republicans may have taken an oppositional stance on climate change at least partly in response to signals from Democratic elites.

So what about Al Gore? Gore was featured prominently in the news media coverage of climate change. This was particularly true when climate change was just emerging as a major concern and Americans were in the process of polarizing. For example, Al Gore was featured in 48 percent of climate change stories on Fox News in 2006, and in 57 percent of the network's stories in 2007. There were explicit references to the movie in 28 percent of the stories in 2006 and 17 percent of the stories in 2007. On the other hand, a leading Republican climate change denier, Senator Jim Inhofe of Oklahoma, was not featured in a single story on Fox News in 2006, and in only 1 percent of the stories in 2007.

The traditional media focused heavily on Al Gore. In 2006 and 2007, the former U.S. vice president was featured in 13 percent and 17 percent of news stories during those years on the subject in the highest circulation newspapers in the United States, and in 16 percent and 23 percent of the network broadcasts concerning climate change. In other words, if you tuned in to news about climate change during that time period, you were exposed to Al Gore and his message. And, even though that message was unabashedly pro-climate and advocating for strong climate action, it likely played a role in turning Republicans against the cause, since to them Gore was simply a Democratic politician whom they disliked."[5]

With insights like these, we should rethink our approach to the most complicated challenges. For instance, at the time of this writing, might Greta Thunberg be on the verge of becoming the new Al Gore? Consider that at Davos in January 2020, Steve Mnuchin, U.S. treasury secretary, was asked a question about Greta Thunberg and her warnings about climate change, to which he responded,

"After she studies economics in college, she can come back and explain that to us." He made an argument about her qualifications rather than commenting on the challenge that our existential predicament presents. By now, shouldn't we expect this kind of response? By now, shouldn't we have an alternative script to inspire our citizens' actions before it is too late?

Is it too late to turn the tide on climate change? Hopefully not. If we can stop demanding that everyone conceive of the problem in the same way and respond with the same solutions, we might succeed in flipping the script. But, as they say, time is being wasted.

CAN THE EDUCATION SCRIPT BE FLIPPED?

Now let's consider education. It is well known that the largest states in the country have an outsize impact on the national curriculum. Two of the biggest states are California and Texas. Recently, Dana Goldstein of the *New York Times* conducted a thorough review of how U.S. history is taught in various schools throughout those two states: "Two States. Eight Textbooks. Two American Stories."[6]

Goldstein writes, "The textbooks cover the same sweeping story, from the brutality of slavery to the struggle for civil rights. The self-evident truths of the founding documents to the waves of immigration that reshaped the nation. The books have the same publisher. They credit the same authors. But they are customized for students in different states, and their contents sometimes diverge in ways that reflect the nation's deepest partisan divides." Students in the United States, depending on where they live and go to school, are learning the same subjects from vastly different viewpoints, the result being that there is diminishing common ground in education. Slavery, the Civil Rights Movement, Watergate, the impeachment of Presidents Clinton and Trump: What is fact? What is opinion? A big part of this is how the various states review and amend the "national" versions, which often pit California against Texas. California has a system that is stacked with professional educators who are entrusted to review and comment on the accuracy of the narratives and the specifics of the text. In Texas, they leave the review to the Republican-dominated State Board of Education, which includes more than just educators. They include parents, Christian pastors, politicians, and business representatives. Often, these reviews end up with very different "State Versions" of these national textbooks. Not every state has the power, determined by population of students, to sway the publishers. This does, however, create different versions for different states, often introducing content far afield from academic accuracy.

The article generated plenty of responses on Twitter, not surprisingly many with opposing views. Consider two below:

Twitter user 1 writes: "National unity has depended on a national narrative and political reality that downplays and erases genocide and slavery to play up an 'idea' only made possible through the subjugation of millions. The belief that there was ever a single national narrative is naive."

Twitter user 2 responds: "National unity depends on their being a national narrative. This is especially so for the U.S. as it is a country based on an idea. The idea of each state fashioning its own narrative is an oxymoron that contributes to our political dysfunction."

Like climate change, this is a problem that we ought to be able to address, but it is continually hijacked by the proxy wars. How might it be rectified by starting over with a process that strives to minimize personalized "state" versions of these texts?

IS THERE A PARTICIPATORY DEMOCRACY SCRIPT TO BE FLIPPED?

What could be wrong with trying to increase the percentage of voters in our elections, when nearly 50 percent of the voting-eligible population chooses not to vote—even in presidential elections? If we start with the literal goal of raising American voting rates, we quickly see the fissures form. Individuists, motivated by care and fairness, believe that voting is a human right, that Election Day should be a national holiday, and (perhaps because they suspect that new voters will side with them) that we should register everyone by mail.

The Social Binders also want to encourage voters to participate. But they have a caveat: Voting comes with responsibilities, just like all rights. They believe that voters should have to prove that they are eligible to vote; they should prove that they are who they say they are, which means showing up in person to vote.

This seems like a challenge made for the times. The gulf between the Individuists and the Social Binders is not nearly as great on voting rights as on guns or climate change. How might it help to put yourself in the shoes of someone who can't vote because they can't get the time off work? Or someone genuinely worried about the corruption of results through fraud? As external crises like the coronavirus force us to consider new models of voting, might they also bring us closer to compromise?

CHAPTER 12

FACING THE FUTURE

W e began this book by exploring what is missing from much of the applied research that surrounds market research, consumer insights, and marketing communications, and how that has come to shape not just the mentality of professional communicators, but also the way we understand one another in the culture at large, considering that the data drawn from base, psychographic, and behavioral markers make their way regularly into popular media. To address that, we explored how our Instinctual Patterns set the hooks from which we eventually hang our personal worldviews. We then explored how those worldviews interact within our ecosystem, and the implications for marketing, advertising, governance, and behavioral change programs. Now let's turn our attention to the many challenges facing us at the population level.

Things like globalization, healthcare, income inequality, terrorism, and pandemics are just a smattering of them. And the answers all begin with how we relate to one another. If we can better organize ourselves to build sustainable and reliable cultures that in turn foster free and representative governments, we could address many of these issues much more effectively.

THE DECLINE OF CIVILITY

Over the last fifty years, there has been a steady decline in American civility. We talked a bit about how it manifests in the extreme polarization of our political parties. But even more worryingly, rates of civic participation—things like organizing, registering, and voting in elections—are trending downward. How might the Model of Why help turn the tide?

Since 2010, Weber Shandwick, a leading public relations firm, has provided an annual review titled *Civility in America—A Nationwide Study.*[1] The first iteration noted, "An overwhelming majority of Americans view the erosion of civility in human interaction today as a major problem, and feel the distressing situation has only been made worse by the recession. Among the many signs pointing to this steady decline are the daily occurrences of cyber bullying, online 'flaming' and nasty blog comments, the venomous bickering taking place on some reality TV shows and between TV news personalities and their guests, and the mean-spirited mudslinging among politicians and their loyal supporters."

In their 2018 update, they also found that "Personal encounters with incivility remain high, as 80% of people report having experienced uncivil behavior at one time or another. The frequency of uncivil encounters per week rose sharply in 2018 and remains at this level, with 10.2 average weekly encounters."[2] This rise is largely attributable to the ever-increasing number of ways we interact with one another. There has been a huge spike in social media use, and Weber Shandwick notes that people hold these platforms accountable for the state of our discourse. The majority also felt that politics was a topic to avoid when trying to be civil.

In 2012, Jonathan Haidt (whose work with Craig Joseph and other Moral Psychology colleagues, as you will remember from the book's first two chapters, established the Moral Foundations Theory that provided the building blocks for the Instinctual Patterns of our Model of Why) and Marc Hetherington sought to broaden the idea of "Uncivility"[3] by looking into the polarization of the U.S. Senate and Congress. In post–Civil War America, Congress was fairly polarized, but it overcame the divide during the First and Second World Wars. Haidt and Hetherington write: "But things started to change in the 1960s and 1970s, as the Democrats became the party of civil rights and the Republicans forged an alliance with the religious right. By the 1980s, the two parties were well on their way to ideological purification: liberals, and more recently moderates, no longer felt at home among congressional Republicans, while conservatives felt unwelcome among congressional Democrats." And it hasn't stopped.

In 2000, the year the dot-com bubble burst, social scientist Robert Putnam of Harvard published his landmark book *Bowling Alone: The Collapse and Revival of American Community.*[4] The book's premise is that we no longer engage with one another in groups, organizations, associations, and teams—all have been steadily declining since the 1950s. As James Fallows remarked in his review in the *Atlantic*, Putnam found that we had become a "group of atomized, dis-connected individuals who owed nothing to one another, and had become a crowd rather than a society."[5]

According to Putnam's research, people were still bowling in the same total numbers, but the nature of it had changed. Rather than going with a regular group of people on a regular basis, they went sporadically, sometimes alone. It was the lack of regularity and coordinated engagement with the sport—and, more important, one another—that had given way. Putnam found the same to be true of engagement in all kinds of group activities, including political parties, civic organizations, and unions.

He posited that the reorganization of our family lives contributed to this decline as well. Small-town life was waning by the end of the 1950s. Across the country, people were moving out of small towns to larger cities. Or they were moving into suburbs, and commuting to work, which is time-consuming and detracts from family life. Putnam quantified that for every ten minutes spent commuting, one reduces overall access to social capital by 10 percent. Think of those all too familiar commutes of two hours or more. Who has time to be sociable when your daily commute creates such a hole in your time bank? On top of long commutes, hours spent at work have increased, too. Working nights and weekends is not uncommon, for those lucky enough to have a regular nine-to-five job, and those in the gig economy suffer even more layers of complication. When juggling so much, there is not enough time to participate in associations, to attend meetings, or to connect. It is no surprise that our challenges have become even more pronounced over the last twenty years or so, as our entertainment choices have become even more isolating. Websites, apps, instant messaging, email, and social media are all touted for their powers of connectivity, yet we become more and more withdrawn as we utilize them.

As you've seen in this book, at PathSight we believe that understanding people's instincts, coupled with their life experiences, can reveal what motivates us—and how we might be inspired to change. If Baby Boomers pioneered the decline of civility, and Gen Xers and Millennials followed suit, that's quite a long drought. Do we even remember how to come together again? What will drive us to reap the rewards of a more united culture?

As we know, changing any deeply ingrained habit is difficult. How often have you ignored pleas to lose weight, eat healthier foods, stop smoking, exercise more? We rarely change our habits, especially the ones we enjoy, just because it's beneficial for us to do so. So how can we marshal our instincts away from the isolating, hyper-personalized worlds we've created for ourselves? How can the cultural stressors we face every day point us toward shared ideals instead of tribal corners? Consider some of the things that we are all trying to sort out now:

- **Pandemics:** Science suggests that global pandemics will be a regular presence in our lives going forward.

- **Globalization:** With the rise of nationalist sentiments around the world, the last seventy-five years of relative peace seems poised to end. International trade agreements and treaties that have held for decades are suddenly in question.

- **Participatory Democracy:** Voting rights are still a fundamental stress on the functioning of democratic institutions. With just a 50 percent participation rate (in America), can our elected leaders really claim to be enacting the will of the people?

- **Opportunity Gap/Future of Work:** The imbalance of opportunity between rich and poor—or even the very rich and everyone else—seems ever more ingrained. Automation and other technological advances are creating uncertainty about the future of work and income and the treatment of already marginalized people.

- **Majority Minority:** This term represents the fact that we are moving toward a majority of our population who are members of one of the minority populations. The Millennial generation is showing us what the Majority Minority future will look like. Older generations are straining to adjust to this new reality.

- **Peer-to-Peer Social Media:** The culture is connected, but how will we save ourselves from the downward spiral of the echo chamber?

- **Localization of Global Stressors:** Global pandemics, climate change, population explosions, terrorism, and the like all present a challenge. How are we going to build a "new normal"? Have historical reference points become obsolete?

In this chapter, I will present two strategic ways that the Model of Why can help you think proactively about these population-level challenges, including incivility:

1. Be Aware of Who Is Talking: The Concept of the First-Person Point of View
2. Experience the Impact of the First-Person POV by Building from the Ground Up

BE AWARE OF WHO IS TALKING: THE CONCEPT OF THE FIRST-PERSON POINT OF VIEW

The Model of Why builds upon our Instinctual Patterns, our "first drafts." Throughout our lives, experience continually edits those drafts. These foundational building blocks influence our view of morality, how we solve problems, what we like, whom we like, and how we interact with the world. As we grow, we construct narratives to guide us through our various journeys. These narratives organize all of the information we receive, and it is through them that we share who we are.

The Social Binding Spectrum of our Model of Why helps us visualize the way very different perspectives can arise, and the resulting discomfort. Each of these ensuing perspectives is valid. None is more valid than the other. An Individuist-only group may brim over with wonderful ideas, but not get anything done. A Social Binder–only group may be efficient and secure, but not enjoy much diversity or peace. A Centrist-only group might be content to just paddle in place, even if the status quo is not serving their interests.

As we discussed, in governing and leadership this flexibility is what enables problem-solving and coalition building. By widening our lens to incorporate as many points of views as possible, we will ensure the maximum number of pathways to the hearts of people. In other words, we may need to invest in understanding who we're talking to, if we want to be heard.

For example, when building a communications campaign for the government, we would want to start by first understanding who the audience is, and given their various Instinctual Patterns, how they might view the service or offering. This understanding must be achieved before an actual campaign goes live. When you know up front how people are likely to respond to a given message, you can build a more effective strategy.

During the COVID-19 crisis, there was a lack of public health communications, especially in Black American neighborhoods. We applied the Model of Why to review this situation, in work done by MEE Productions, a nationally recognized communications and market research firm based in Philadelphia. Their goal was to communicate more effectively about the crucial need for safety measures—wearing a mask, sheltering in place, keeping a six-foot distance between people. There were two choices: to use a general-market approach treated as suspect by many people in the community or try instead to take into account the different voices present within the community.

The value proposition was to produce a series of messages with an Individuist POV ("You are loved by your family, do it for them"), a Social Binding POV ("We have seen worse than this; we will survive"), and a Centrist Stack POV ("Shelter In Place as much as you can"). Considering all these points of view, MEE Productions created a global message that all recipients could see and hear themselves in.[6] This demonstrated the power of first-person communication—when we don't have to interpret messages from another person's perspective.

By purposefully acknowledging other valid perspectives, we may reduce the impulse to see one's own point of view as superior to all others. So much of the incivility in our culture arises from our efforts to get someone else to abandon their viewpoint. As discussed, this is unlikely to happen. Could a movement toward first-person communications aid in the pursuit of a more civil society?

There is a recurring theme in this book: If we become aware of Instinctual Patterns and the ways they can influence our choices, values, and future, we might harness a different type of personal power. With this in mind, we should operate with personal insights as to our own biases, an appreciation of how others see the world, and perhaps the opportunity to understand any gap that might exist between them. If we are able to see and understand these differences, there is potential to discover a pathway to return to civility.

With such an understanding, there may be less of an urge to assume that your worldview is superior to others'. For example, one may see the irrationality in an Individuist's willingness to "try the next new thing." Or one might understand that while a Social Binder can offer a different view of the "facts," they might represent a huge, unforeseen disadvantage. If we are starting with the supposition of equally valid points of view and people can "hear" from differing perspectives, what might that portend? This situation has many barriers to being realistic, but it does provide us with something to aspire to.

In order to achieve this goal, we suggest some ways to promote these habits of thought.

1. When considering policies or strategies, practice writing them from the point of view of each Instinctual Pattern. How do they vary? Are there any insights to be gleaned?

2. Start your evaluation of people with as much of a blank slate as possible. If we are striving for a goal of equanimity in Instinctual Patterns, we should be able to hear a different perspective without first filtering it through a screen of derision before it is considered.

3. Have the courage to say, "I hear you, but I am not convinced." Listening does not mean you will hear anything you can agree with, but the process of listening respectfully will go a long way toward building a relationship.

If we can begin to communicate according to Instinctual Patterns, it will mean a tangible verification of our own and others' existence. Think of communicating about a value proposition in a first-person voice. It is not about shaping the truth, but expressing it in the words, images, and themes of a first-person perspective. It could make a world of difference.

THE HOURGLASS EXPERIENCE

While it's easy to see today's tribalism as the death knell of democracy, there are flickers of hope. A handful of movements are finding their voices as they address the real concerns of real people with whom they share a common space. We suggest that, in these troubled times, you invest your time and energy in these types of efforts for maximum impact. The most successful movements share some key attributes:

1. They make sure to represent a range of people.
2. They start by creating a process that we can trust.
3. They get smart about what they want to do.
4. They are public in their intent.
5. They believe there is no one else to do it.

There are examples of these kinds of initiatives all over the world, with various structures, scopes, and intentions. Here's one example of how to invest social capital for maximum impact, as reported by Thomas Friedman in the *New York Times*. In a July 2018 article titled "Where American Politics Can Still Work," Friedman tells the story of the rebound made by the city of Lancaster, Pennsylvania, population 59,322. Like many other small towns across the country, it had fallen on hard times. In the late 1990s, Friedman writes, it was a "crime-ridden ghost town at night where people were afraid to venture."[7] This is while "the county's dominant industrial employer, Armstrong World Industries, was withering."

In recent years, with the help and foresight of the Hourglass Foundation, a nonprofit organization dedicated to fostering growth and development, Lancaster's citizens and business leaders proved that there is indeed a way to manage the chaos by going back to the basics. In the twenty-plus years since its founding, the Hourglass Foundation has focused on every malady a small Northeastern city today might suffer: crime, education issues, racism in policing, economic inequality, culture clashes, immigration, and environmental decay. Of course, they haven't solved everything, but in 2018 *Forbes* magazine named Lancaster one of the "10 Coolest U.S. Cities to Visit," saying this "newly hip Victorian city—just three hours from New York—is still one of the U.S.'s best kept secrets." It "boasts a bustling food scene and is quickly becoming a cultural hotbed. The architecture is the real star, so explore the alleys and cobblestone streets by foot, checking out the many repurposed old warehouses that house thriving businesses."[8] This is just one version of how progress is made.

The foundation has been instrumental in turning the town around, spurring growth and positive change, all in a way that fosters community: a perfect example of how the Model of Why can work in different situations. Here's how they have adhered to the principles we have suggested:

1. THEY MAKE SURE TO REPRESENT A RANGE OF PEOPLE.

Friedman describes Lancaster as "the quintessential American small city."[9] It is a primarily white suburban residential ring surrounding a cityscape that is less prosperous, with a more diverse population, including Latinx, Black American, and Southeast Asian residents. The total regional population is about six hundred thousand. Notably, none of the leaders of the Hourglass Foundation are part of the city or county government. As they describe it, they left their political affiliations behind when they decided to get involved with the nonprofit. They're aware they have differences, of course —they just don't bring them to work.

2. THEY START BY CREATING A PROCESS THAT THEY CAN TRUST.

The Hourglass has certainly taken this one to heart. "The key to it all is trust," Friedman explains. "Politically we are all different, and our experiences are different. You can only get progress where there is trust." Ray D'Agostino, president of the Lancaster Housing & Opportunity Partnership in Lancaster, takes it a step further, as quoted in the article: "We still look at things in a conservative or liberal way, but I can work with my liberal friends because we agree on what needs to be done—and it has to get done. I won't vote for them, but I will work with them."[10]

3. THEY GET SMART ABOUT WHAT THEY WANT TO DO.

As the foundation recounts on its website, hourglassfoundation.org, one of their original missions was to tap into the expanding sources of information in the world to ensure that the best decisions would be made for their community.

"The Hourglass Foundation was formed as a think tank to facilitate effective growth management by providing comprehensive research, objective analysis, and fresh ideas on important legacy issues—the tough issues that others often avoid, due to their size and complexity," their mission statement reads. "We are also a community watchdog—monitoring emerging issues, stimulating discussion, and creating high standards for decision making."

4. THEY ARE PUBLIC IN THEIR INTENT.

Actions (and reactions) are documented and shared transparently. The Hourglass regularly communicates with the community through biweekly publications, surveys, and an invite-only First Friday forum. This follows the logic of performance-based engagements: listen, act, listen again.

5. THEY BELIEVE THERE IS NO ONE ELSE TO DO IT.

Again, no one in the Hourglass Foundation is an office holder in the local government. Clearly, they know there are no magic bullets. They are leaders without a portfolio, but a lot of accountability—an essential ingredient in any successful enterprise.

THE FIRST NATIONS EXPERIENCE

Another example of a truly inclusive movement comes from PathSight's recent work in Canada. For the past four years, PathSight has been involved in a very different kind of "complex adaptive coalition" in the province of Manitoba. One of the so-called prairie provinces, Manitoba's economy relies heavily on agriculture, tourism, electricity, oil, mining, and forestry. Winnipeg is its largest city, surrounded by a dozen smaller towns and Lake Winnipeg. As does the rest of Canada, they struggle with the cultural dissonance between their First Nations citizens and the federal and provincial governments, as well as the usual issues: climate change, economic mobility, affordable housing, education, and infrastructure.

But unlike the Hourglass Foundation, the participants we worked with in Manitoba were elected officials. They were all committed to solving the challenges of the region by dealing primarily with local or regional government—specifically, those directly accountable to the voters. In 2016, we were invited to Winnipeg by Colleen Sklar, the director of a not-for-profit coalition in the capital region of Manitoba, to help forge an understanding of constituents' attitudes toward the environment. The coalition, including the mayors and reeves (Canadian parlance for local officials) of Winnipeg and surrounding areas, were interested in understanding how Canadians thought about climate change, since the eutrophication (an excessive growth of algae resulting in oxygen depletion) of Lake Winnipeg had been a big concern in the region for a long time.

PathSight set to work, conducting a research study of Canada and the prairie provinces around the issues of climate change, using our Instinctual Pattern model. We then applied this working knowledge of the region and country to our work in Manitoba. The complex adaptive coalition there, called the Collaborative Leadership Initiative, was led by Sklar, Merrell-Ann Phare (a lawyer and founding director of the Centre for Indigenous Environment Resources, or CIER), and Michael Miltenberger, a former mayor and town council member of the town of Fort Smith in the Northwest Territories. These three brought together decades of experience in the areas of economic development, conflict resolution, water rights, indigenous rights, and community activation.

The initial value proposition of the CLI was to address the challenges of climate change, economic mobility, affordable housing, education, and infrastructure. But they decided to start with the region's most intractable problems. Chief among these was a 148-year-old impasse between the government of Canada and the First Nations. That's how long it had been since there were direct discussions of any kind between the Manitoba municipalities and the chiefs of the First Nations. Clearly, we had our work cut out for us. The value proposition was pretty straightforward:

1. **Regional economic development.** Expand the concept of economic development to include the whole region, not just individual municipalities.

2. **Elevating the quality of life for the resident.** Accurately measuring quality of life requires reality-testing everyone's perception of the facts.

3. **Preserving water.** Water and other resources are the basis of survival, and any meaningful long-term value proposition of the province must include them.

As you might guess, trust between these groups was not operating at a peak level. To assemble a team of willing participants, the CLI met one-on-one with every chief, mayor, and reeve they thought might be interested. They were frank about their fears and expectations, as well as the problems they foresaw. It turns out that 148 years is a lot of distrust to work through.

It was interesting to chart the process by which the instinctual issues surfaced in this trust-building process. Both groups of leaders—the chiefs and the mayors/reeves—were identical in the way they parsed each of these instinctual concerns.

- **Loyalty Went First:** Each side felt the need to clarify who they were representing in this process. It may seem obvious, but it was important that they said it out loud to each other.

- **Authority:** Once the loyalty issue was cleared, they wanted to test out the process for going forward—essentially, the rules of the road. They were quite explicit in poking at vague language. For example: "When you say X, what does that mean, and when I say Y, what do you hear?" This mutual exploration helped them dispel some of the most pervasive myths that continued to provoke distrust. We realized it was important to allow ample time in the process, to establish predictability.

- **Fairness:** Once expectations were understood, everyone could challenge them to see if this process was fair. The seriousness of this focus on trust paid off immediately. First, not one of the chiefs, mayors, or reeves dropped out of the process. Second, on March 2, 2019, the participants signed a Memorandum of Understanding, committing them to participate in collaborative regional economic development. It is the only such agreement in all of Canada. The year 2020 has brought a host of projects to the fore that are testing the will of these twenty-six leaders.

In addition to using these instincts to track the trust-building process, we used the Model of Why in shaping our public profile. To do this, we analyzed three different communications platforms with track records in the community and consistently spoke to each community in their instinctual voice.

- The first platform focused on the indigenous and NGO communities. In reading their historical communications, we noticed that the Individuist voice was dominant.

- The second platform targeted the business community, trade associations, and service sectors. It was apparent that the Social Binder voice was dominant for them.

- The third platform, including mainstream sources such as newspapers, radio, Facebook, Twitter, and Instagram, revealed that the Centrist voice dominated their conversations.

We embarked on building relationships with each community by sharing what transpired in the instinctual voice of each platform. As in most relationships, we started by introducing the principals—the chiefs, mayors, and reeves—

to the whole community. Then we told them what we'd be talking about (regional economic development) and why they should care (quality of life).

To fuel the content pipeline, each meeting of the CLI was filmed and spliced into a forty-five-minute documentary. We scheduled a screening of the first installment in Winnipeg, so the leaders could talk directly to the community about their hopes for the process. This solitary journey of twenty-six leaders, who had begun on opposite sides of a cultural divide 150 years ago, was now fully public.

Ever since, people have begun noticing that something special is happening in Manitoba. After twenty years of failed advocacy, Colleen Sklar and her coalition hosted a sold-out luncheon, where the Winnipeg and broader Manitoba business community heard Dr. Robert Murray, a leading authority on public policy and regional economic development, present his analysis of how Manitoba can manage climate change, economic mobility, affordable housing, education, and infrastructure. The key takeaways were as follows:

1. Embark on a path toward strategic regional economic development
2. Commit to the full inclusion of the First Nations in that effort
3. Protect the environmental resources of the region

It's not surprising how closely these points mirror the value proposition the CLI developed three years earlier. How often do we learn that leaders without power often see what needs to be done before the "authorities" do? That is why we always bet on the leaders who derive their authority from the success of their labors.

HOW CAN YOU BE HEARD?

It strikes me that a lot of the challenges we face today boil down to not being heard. By that I don't mean being misunderstood when we give someone directions or ask what color goes with our complexion or even what car to buy. I am talking about moments in life when it is important that what we are saying is accurately and unambiguously heard by another human being. Those moments of understanding—of successful communication—should be regarded as a victory for humanity.

But a victory over what? When we are not able to succeed at performing the most basic function of communication accurately and unambiguously with another human being, we have been known to, at times, get angry, feel powerless and underappreciated; we fall out of friendships, become depressed, or we talk louder. If miscommunication persists, we might resort to insults, assume the moral high ground and troll online, talk really loud, shun "others," get physical, convince ourselves that people just don't get it, only spend time with *real* friends, fight the constant angst of being in a perpetual battle, and sometimes resort to violence to ourselves or others. These are big stakes—and why we should consider it a victory for humanity when we do, in fact, succeed.

Currently, the cards seem stacked against us. We have talked about the complexity of the depressed opinion in our country toward our institutions, the dizzying array of media platforms to navigate, the peculiarities of technology, and the crises of defining the common good as we grapple with a pandemic, economic fragility, and the persistent racism in our culture.

What's making everything seem more fraught and will surely affect our ability to move forward is the tribal nature of our realities and the language we're using with one another. As I write this book, a new Cato Institute poll of two thousand Americans found that 62 percent of Americans say the political climate prevents them from sharing political views because others might find them offensive.[11] What's that old saying? Never discuss politics or religion in polite company. All bets are off. But, in reality, we do need to discuss politics and religion, and any other heated topic. We do want to encourage open and spirited civil discourse. Disagreement is critical. It only becomes a problem when we're not heard. We know when our point of view is rejected, our brain influences us to reject the rejector, and our conversation gets nowhere. As we have discussed throughout this book, in many ways today's tribalism is set up for these conflicts.

We choose a team that aligns with our worldview, and we stick with it. We vote for our team because a loss for the team is a loss for us personally. We are all looking for evidence to confirm our beliefs, and we retreat to the moral high ground to preserve it. The ease with which we find groups that think just like us further solidifies our positions. Algorithms that deliver more and more personalization make it easier to live in a bubble. You can almost go about your life and never come face-to-face with anyone who disagrees with you. We have to govern with a shared set of beliefs that allow us to trust in the outcomes of our disagreements. If that can happen, then we do not have to abandon our cherished beliefs. We can keep our worldview intact as we agree to work on shared outcomes. Too often, today's conflicts are carried out in a "you win, I lose" manner, and that has taught us to hold out for a "lose/lose" proposition.

In order to break through this maze of complex issues, here are some suggested steps to follow:

1. **Determine the purpose of the communication.** This is a critical first step. Begin by differentiating whether the communication is something that pertains to a matter of general conversation or if it represents a deeply held belief by you or the other person. In the first case, as in most communications, we can proceed as usual, with the provision that confirmation is always key in any dialogue. Asking for confirmation of details should be standard operating procedure. For example, if you are going to provide a ride to an event, asking the other person to confirm details you've discussed is always a simple, good habit to deploy.

   But, if the topic is related to a deeply held belief by you or the other person, we suggest taking some additional points of care. For example:

   - Do you have a relationship with this person?
   - Is this a person with whom you would like to cultivate a relationship?
   - Is this a person with whom you would like to cultivate a professional relationship?
   - Are you indifferent to the outcome?

   If your answer falls within the first three categories, we suggest that you consider number 2. All of our relationships benefit from care and continual cultivation. Communication is key.

2. **Being heard is not a solitary activity.** There are senders and receivers in the process. When we are in need of being heard, we should understand that the other person has a stake in the process, too. We will leave you to manage the personal versus professional element of the relationship, but these situations all begin with understanding the goals of the communication first. If you are trying to engender a better understanding of your worldview, it's important to give some thought as to the Instinctual Pattern of the person you're speaking to. Consider the following:

- Is there an alignment between the two of you?
- You are not sure.
- You are pretty sure you're not aligned, but you aren't dissuaded.
- You can't be bothered.

There are countless ways to get a bead on someone's Instinctual Pattern, beginning with asking directly about their views on a hot button topic and/or listening, as they describe certain situations, for trigger words that connote their set of values. Either way, understand that however you choose to proceed, the other participants will shoulder some of the responsibility for success in the communication.

3. **What are your motives?** This is really the key to being heard and to hearing someone else. In very many relationships these days, while communicating, we are continually trying to sort out whether someone is friend or foe, team member or not, or someone to be trusted. We do this almost involuntarily, rather than simply listening to what is being said. Thus, in so many situations we lose out on the opportunity to be heard by short-circuiting the process. As we've discussed several times in this book, there is neurological evidence to support this process of reacting to challenges of our deeply held beliefs by protecting

or discounting this evidence from consideration.[12] We might anticipate this reaction. It could be helpful if we learn to separate what is being said from a judgment as to who is saying it. If we separate the value judgment of the person—whom we may or may not like—it allows us to evaluate both. We can reject what is being said, or not. We can reject the person, or not. It is not easy, but we think that it's important in today's partisan times to be able to separate the two.

For example, we envision a conversation about the economy between Mr. Meta 2 and Mr. Meta 3: They both agree that the economy is going to be in trouble for at least the near term as a result of the COVID-19 pandemic. Both arrive at the real problem: the way the public health portion of the crisis was been handled.

Mr. Meta 2 believes that the reopening was the culprit; it was too soon, too rapid. Mr. Meta 3, though, thinks that point of view is so far off the truth as not to be believed. He thinks that the economy is the key to revitalization and that we have to realize that less than 5 percent of the country will get sick with the virus; most people will recover quickly. He believes that we have to protect the trillion dollars of economic loss, just as we have done during every other epidemic. Clearly, each opposing view could be seen as an assault on the other's set of deeply held beliefs. The choice point has arrived.

Could the two of them avoid a meltdown by confirming to each other that the ultimate goal is to get to a reset on the country's strategy to manage the health crisis *and* the economy. Of course, this would require a sizable reframing of their instincts to take the easy way out and resort to personal insults. But I have seen this work and result in a better outcome when people have a chance to be heard. By choosing to actively work on being heard and listening to others, we can avoid the powerlessness and despair that come from feeling misunderstood. Let me also say that I have not witnessed world peace breaking out after any of these conversations. But I have witnessed some real conversations that promised to be revisited another day.

SO, WHAT HAVE WE LEARNED?

In today's interdependent world, the most complex node by far is the human interface. By pulling the lens back to include many different starting points, rather than just our own, we can envision new pathways to connect people to things they really value. Inspired by decades of research on biological instincts, the Model of Why is our attempt to apply these learnings in the service of increasing empathy and solving big problems by making communications more inclusive of our Instinctual Patterns and the way they operate. In an increasingly complex marketplace and primarily digital communications landscape, helpful data is more readily available to us now than ever. In our communications, we can integrate the strategic use of base-marker, psychological-marker, and behavioral-marker data. By adopting a more complex, nuanced method for understanding one another as individuals before we seek to engage one another, we can help life proceed more smoothly. And by accepting that successful cultures need to access a full array of viewpoints, regardless of how intoxicating the moral high ground may feel, we take one step closer to becoming the country (and the world) we want. If this era of incivility proves to be only a temporary glitch in the long sweep of history, it will be because we found a way to celebrate our virtues, not dwell upon our differences.

NOTES

INTRODUCTION

1. Davide Castelvecchi, "Neutrinos Reveal Final Secret of Sun's Nuclear Fusion," *Nature* 583, no. 7814 (2020): 20–21, doi:10.1038/d41586-020-01908-2.
2. Arthur Stanley Eddington, *The Internal Constitution of the Stars* ((Cambridge, UK: Cambridge University Press, 1999).
3. Campbell Leaper, "More Similarities Than Differences in Contemporary Theories of Social Development?," *Advances in Child Development and Behavior* 40 (2011): 337–378, doi:10.1016/b978-0-12-386491-8.00009-8.
4. Robert D Putnam, *Bowling Alone* (New York, NY: Simon & Schuster, 2007).
5. Ibid.
6. Thomas L Friedman, *Hot, Flat, and Crowded* (New York: Farrar, Straus and Giroux, 2008).
7. "Adhocracy," English Wikipedia, 2020, https://en.wikipedia.org/wiki/Adhocracy.
8. Arnold P Goldstein and Norman Stein, *Prescriptive Psychotherapies* (New York: Pergamon, 1976).

CHAPTER 1: WHY ASK WHY?

1. Robert M. Sapolsky, *Behave: The Biology of Humans at Our Best and Worst* (New York: Penguin, 2017).
2. "ISI Foundation," 2020, https://www.isi.it/en/home.
3. Ibid.
4. Sapolsky, *Behave*.
5. "History of Microscopy—Timeline," Science Learning Hub, 2016, https://www.sciencelearn .org.nz/resources/1692-history-of-microscopy-timeline.
6. Ibid.
7. Daniel Kahneman, *Thinking, Fast and Slow* (New York: Farrar, Straus and Giroux, 2013).
8. Michael S Gazzaniga, *Who's in Charge?: Free Will and the Science of the Brain* (New York: Ecco, 2011).
9. Robert Wright, *The Moral Animal* (New York: Vintage Books, 1995).
10. Ibid.
11. Gazzaniga, *The Ethical Brain*.
12. "Nielsen Global Connect | Nielsen Global Media," Nielsen.Com, 2020, https://www.nielsen .com/us/en/.
13. Point Bleu Design, "The Evolution of the Coca Cola Slogans: Delicious and Refreshing," retrieved 2020 from pointbleudesign.com.
14. "An Introduction to Market Basket Analysis," *Megaputer Intelligence*, 2000, https://www .megaputer.com/introduction-to-market-basket-analysis/.
15. Simon Sinek, "How Great Leaders Inspire Action," Ted.Com, 2009, https://www.ted.com /talks/simon_sinek_how_great_leaders_inspire_action.

CHAPTER 2: LAYING THE FOUNDATION: BIOLOGIC INSTINCTS

1. "Nielsen Global Connect | Nielsen Global Media," Nielsen.Com, 2020, https://www.nielsen .com/us/en/.
2. Jonathan Haidt, *The Righteous Mind: Why Good People Are Divided by Politics and Religion* (New York: Pantheon Books, 2013).

3. Jesse Graham, Jonathan Haidt, Sena Koleva, Matt Motyl, Ravi Iyer, Sean P. Wojcik, and Peter H. Ditto, *Moral Foundations Theory: The Pragmatic Validity of Moral Pluralism* (University of Southern California, New York University, University of Virginia, University of California, Irvine, 2014).
4. Ibid.
5. Ibid.
6. "Moral Foundations," Moral Foundations Theory, https://moralfoundations.org/.
7. Gary F. Marcus, *The Birth of the Mind: How a Tiny Number of Genes Creates the Complexities of Human Thought* (New York: Basic Books, 2004).
8. Graham et al., *Moral Foundations Theory*.
9. Haidt, *The Righteous Mind*.
10. Graham et al., *Moral Foundations Theory*.
11. Oliver Scott Curry, Matthew Jones Chesters, and Caspar J. Van Lissa, "Mapping Morality with a Compass: Testing the Theory of 'morality-as-cooperation' with a New Questionnaire," *Journal of Research in Personality* 78 (2019), doi:10.1016/j.jrp.2018.10.008).
12. Gary J. Lewis and Timothy C. Bates, "From Left to Right: How the Personality System Allows Basic Traits to Influence Politics via Characteristic Moral Adaptations," *British Journal of Psychology* 102, no. 3 (2011), doi:10.1111/j.2044-8295.2011.02016.x.
13. Allison Lehner Eden, *The Influence of Moral Behaviors on Person Perception Processes: An MFRI Investigation*, Michigan State University dissertation, 2011.
14. Marcelo R. Roxo et al., "The Limbic System Conception and Its Historical Evolution," *Scientific World Journal* 11 (2011), doi:10.1100/2011/157150.
15. Lisa Feldman Barrett and W. Kyle Simmons, "Interoceptive Predictions in the Brain," *Nature Reviews Neuroscience* 16, no. 7 (2015), doi:10.1038/nrn3950.
16. Joe O'Connell, "Researchers Pinpoint Epicenter of Brain's Predictive Ability," *News@ Northeastern*, Comments, June 2, 2015, accessed August 27, 2020, https://news.northeastern.edu/2015/06/02/researchers-pinpoint-epicenter-of-brains-predictive-ability/.
17. Barrett and Simmons, "Interoceptive Predictions in the Brain."
18. Jeremy Frimer, "Moral Foundations Dictionary," OSF, August 19, 2018, https://osf.io/2vpzu/.
19. Ibid.

CHAPTER 3: BUILDING THE MODEL: THE FIVE META WORLDVIEWS

1. Allison Lehner Eden, *The Influence of Moral Behaviors on Person Perception Processes: An MFRI Investigation*, Michigan State University dissertation, 2011.
2. Jesse Graham, Jonathan Haidt, Sena Koleva, Matt Motyl, Ravi Iyer, Sean P. Wojcik, & Peter H. Ditto, *Moral Foundations Theory: The Pragmatic Validity of Moral Pluralism* (University of Southern California, New York University, University of Virginia, University of California, Irvine, 2014).
3. Dan P. McAdams, "The Development of a Narrative Identity," *Personality Psychology* (1989), doi:10.1007/978-1-4684-0634-4_12.
4. Andrea V. Breen, Christine Scott, and Kate C. Mclean, "The 'Stuff' of Narrative Identity: Touring Big and Small Stories in Emerging Adults' Dorm Rooms," *Qualitative Psychology* (2019), doi:10.1037/qup0000158.
5. Robert Shiller, "Economics and the Human Instinct for Storytelling," Chicago Booth Review, May 8, 2017, https://review.chicagobooth.edu/economics/2017/article/economics-and-human-instinct-storytelling)
6. Jesse Graham, Jonathan Haidt, and Brian A. Nosek, "Liberals and Conservatives Rely on Different Sets of Moral Foundations," *Journal of Personality and Social Psychology* 96, no. 5 (2009), doi:10.1037/a0015141.

CHAPTER 4: TO EACH THEIR OWN: THE INDIVIDUIST WORLDVIEW

1. Dana R. Carney et al., "The Secret Lives of Liberals and Conservatives: Personality Profiles, Interaction Styles, and the Things They Leave Behind," *Political Psychology* 29, no. 6 (2008), doi:10.1111/j.1467-9221.2008.00668.x.
2. Ece Sagel, "Age Differences in Moral Foundations Across Adolescence and Adulthood," thesis, 2015, http://etd.lib.metu.edu.tr/upload/12619122/index.pdf.
3. Cheryl Staats, "Understanding Implicit Bias—What Educators Should Know," *American Educator*, 2015.
4. Patricia G. Devine et al., "Long-Term Reduction in Implicit Race Bias: A Prejudice Habit-Breaking Intervention," *Journal of Experimental Social Psychology* 48, no. 6 (2012), doi:10.1016/j.jesp.2012.06.003.
5. Walter S. Gilliam, PhD, et al., "Do Early Educators' Implicit Biases Regarding Sex and Race Relate to Behavior Expectations and Recommendations of Preschool Expulsions and Suspensions?," Yale Child Study Center, September 28, 2016, https://medicine.yale.edu/childstudy/zigler/publications/Preschool Implicit Bias Policy Brief_final_9_26_276766_5379_v1.pdf.
6. Kimberlé Crenshaw, "Mapping the Margins: Intersectionality, Identity Politics, and Violence Against Women of Color," *Stanford Law Review* 43, no. 6 (1991), doi:10.2307/1229039.
7. Angela Allan, "What 'Norma Rae' Understood About Unions and Racial Solidarity," *Atlantic*, March 2, 2019, https://www.theatlantic.com/entertainment/archive/2019/03/norma-rae-40th-anniversary-racial-solidarity-unions-labor-movement/583924/.
8. Allison Lehner Eden, *The Influence of Moral Behaviors on Person Perception Processes: An MFRI Investigation*, Michigan State University dissertation, 2011.
9. Jonathan Haidt, *The Righteous Mind: Why Good People Are Divided by Politics and Religion* (New York: Pantheon Books, 2013).

CHAPTER 5: BETTER TOGETHER: THE SOCIAL BINDER WORLDVIEW

1. "U.S. Census Bureau QuickFacts: United States," Census Bureau QuickFacts, https://www.census.gov/quickfacts/fact/table/US/PST045219.
2. Vincent Canby, "The Screen: 'Patton: Salute to Rebel'," *New York Times*, February 5, 1970.

CHAPTER 6: A FINE BALANCE: THE THREE CENTRIST WORLDVIEWS

1. Tiffany Green, "Forrest Gump Facts No One Saw Coming," *Collider*, July 20, 2020, https://collider.com/galleries/forrest-gump-behind-the-scenes-facts/).
2. Bill Keveney, "How Lovable 'Big Bang Theory' Pals Matured (Well, Not Always) over the Show's 12 Seasons," *USA Today*, May 8, 2019, https://www.usatoday.com/story/life/tv/2019/05/08/thebigbangtheory-chuck-lorre-actors-praise-character-evolution/1126047001/.

CHAPTER 7: BREAKING IT DOWN: THE FIVE INSTINCTUAL PATTERNS, DECONSTRUCTED

1. Erving Goffman, *The Presentation of Self in Everyday Life* (New York: Anchor Books, 1959).
2. Ibid.
3. "Motivational Educational Entertainment," MEE Productions, https://www.meeproductions.com/.
4. Ibid.
5. A. Tversky and D. Kahneman, "The Framing of Decisions and the Psychology of Choice," *Science* 211, no. 4481 (1981), doi:10.1126/science.7455683.
6. Ibid.
7. Richard H. Thaler and Cass R. Sunstein, *Nudge: Improving Decisions about Health, Wealth, and Happiness* (London: Penguin Books, 2009).

8. Cass R. Sunstein and Richard Thaler, Elizabeth Kolbert, and Jerome Groopman, "The Two Friends Who Changed How We Think About How We Think," *New Yorker*, December 7, 2016, https://www.newyorker.com/books/page-turner/the-two-friends-who-changed-how -we-think-about-how-we-think.
9. Ibid.
10. David Brooks, "Five Lies Our Culture Tells," *New York Times*, April 15, 2019, https://www .nytimes.com/2019/04/15/opinion/cultural-revolution-meritocracy.html.
11. Shalom H. Schwartz, "An Overview of the Schwartz Theory of Basic Values," *Online Readings in Psychology and Culture* 2, no. 1 (2012), doi:10.9707/2307-0919.1116.
12. Erik Lundegaard, "Truth, Justice and (Fill in the Blank)," *New York Times*, June 30, 2006, https://www.nytimes.com/2006/06/30/opinion/30lundegaard.html.
13. G. Feldman, "Personal Values and Moral Foundations: Towards an Integrated Perspective by Examining Meaning, Structure, and Relations," DOI: 10.13140/RG.2.2.32570.49600/1.
14. Schwartz, "An Overview of the Schwartz Theory."
15. Ibid.
16. Feldman, "Personal Values and Moral Foundations."

CHAPTER 9: THE REACH OF WHY

1. Jonathan Haidt, *The Righteous Mind: Why Good People Are Divided by Politics and Religion* (New York: Pantheon Books, 2013).
2. Donelson R. Forsyth, *Group Dynamics* (Belmont, CA: Wadsworth Cengage Learning, 2014).
3. Steve Stoute and Mim Eichler Rivas, *The Tanning of America: How Hip-Hop Created a Culture That Rewrote the Rules of the New Economy* (New York: Gotham Books, 2012).
4. Jonas T. Kaplan, Sarah I. Gimbel, and Sam Harris, "Neural Correlates of Maintaining One's Political Beliefs in the Face of Counterevidence," *Scientific Reports* 6, no. 1 (2016), doi:10.1038/srep39589.
5. Lisa F Barrett, Nathan L. Williams, and Geoffrey T. Fong. "Manual for the Defensive Verbal Behavior Ratings Scale," Interdisciplinary Affective Science Laboratory, 2002. https://www .affective-science.org/pubs/2002/FBWilliamsFong2002.pdf.
6. George Lakoff, "Why Trump?," March 03, 2016, https://georgelakoff.com/2016/03/02/why -trump/.
7. Ibid.

CHAPTER 10: HOW TO USE THE MODEL

1. Karen Page Winterich, Yinlong Zhang, and Vikas Mittal, "How Political Identity and Charity Positioning Increase Donations: Insights from Moral Foundations Theory," *International Journal of Research in Marketing* 29, no. 4 (2012), doi:10.1016/j.ijresmar.2012.05.002.
2. Karen Page Winterich, Vikas Mittal, and Karl Aquino, "When Does Recognition Increase Charitable Behavior? Toward a Moral Identity–Based Model," *Journal of Marketing* 77, no. 3 (2013), doi:10.1509/jm.11.0477.
3. Zach Morrow, "Guilt Appeals in Nonprofit Marketing: How to Do It Right," The RoundUp App: Donate Your Change to a Nonprofit, https://roundupapp.com/guilt-appeal-fundraising/.
4. "Which Came First: Nike's Cortez or Onitsuka Tiger's Corsair?" Sneaker Freaker, https:// www.sneakerfreaker.com/features/which-came-first-nikes-cortez-or-onitsuka-tigers-corsair.
5. Douglas C. Mcgill, "Nike Is Bounding Past Reebok," *New York Times*, July 11, 1989, https:// www.nytimes.com/1989/07/11/business/nike-is-bounding-past-reebok.html.
6. Anwar Majda, "26 Statistics on Why You Should Consider Omni Channel Marketing," Business 2 Community, January 26, 2017,https://www.business2community.com/marketing/26 -statistics-consider-omni-channel-marketing-01765352.

CHAPTER 11: FLIPPING THE SCRIPT: INSTINCTUAL PROBLEM-SOLVING

1. "The Discovery of Global Warming," Global Warming Timeline, January 2020, https://history.aip.org/history/climate/timeline.htm.
2. "National Cancer Act of 1971," National Cancer Institute, https://www.cancer.gov/about-nci/overview/history/national-cancer-act-1971.
3. "The Origins of EPA," Environmental Protection Agency, https://www.epa.gov/history/origins-epa.
4. Dominik Stecula and Eric Merkley, "An Inconvenient Truth About *An Inconvenient Truth*," *Conversation*, https://theconversation.com/an-inconvenient-truth-about-an-inconvenient-truth-81799.
5. Ibid.
6. Dana Goldstein, "Two States. Eight Textbooks. Two American Stories," *New York Times*, January 12, 2020, https://www.nytimes.com/interactive/2020/01/12/us/texas-vs-california-history-textbooks.html.

CHAPTER 12: FACING THE FUTURE

1. *Civility in America—A Nationwide Study*, Weber Shandwick, 2010, https://www.webershandwick.com/uploads/news/files/Civility_2010_SocialMediaImplications.pdf.
2. *Civility in America 2018: Civility at Work and in Our Public Squares*, Weber Shandwick / Powell Tate / KRC Research, 2018, https://www.webershandwick.com/wp-content/uploads/2018/06/Civility-in-America-VII-FINAL.pdf.
3. Jonathan Haidt and Marc J. Hetherington, "Look How Far We've Come Apart," *New York Times*, September 18, 2012, https://campaignstops.blogs.nytimes.com/2012/09/17/look-how-far-wevecomeapart/?mtrref=undefined&gwh=C64931A1E8E44EAE92AF8E012EE3EB8D&gwt=pay&assetType=REGIWALL.
4. Robert D Putnam, *Bowling Alone* (New York, NY: Simon & Schuster, 2007).
5. James Fallows, "First Bowling Alone, Now Vaulting Together," *Atlantic*, March 15, 2015, https://www.theatlantic.com/national/archive/2014/09/first-bowling-alone-now-vaulting-together/380481/.
6. "Motivational Educational Entertainment," MEE Productions, https://www.meeproductions.com/.
7. Thomas L. Friedman, "Where American Politics Can Still Work: From the Bottom Up," *New York Times*, July 3, 2018, https://www.nytimes.com/2018/07/03/opinion/community-revitalization-lancaster.html.
8. Ann Abel, "The 10 Coolest U.S. Cities to Visit in 2018," *Forbes*, February 26, 2018, https://www.forbes.com/sites/annabel/2018/02/26/the-10-coolest-u-s-cities-to-visit-in-2018/#5bc95197663b.
9. Friedman, "Where American Politics Can Still Work."
10. Ibid.
11. Emily Ekins, "New Poll: 62% Say the Political Climate Prevents Them from Sharing Political Views," Cato Institute, July 22, 2020, https://www.cato.org/blog/poll-62-americans-say-they-have-political-views-theyre-afraid-share.
12. Jonas T. Kaplan, Sarah I. Gimbel, and Sam Harris, "Neural Correlates of Maintaining One's Political Beliefs in the Face of Counterevidence," *Scientific Reports* 6, no. 1 (2016), doi:10.1038/srep39589.

INDEX

J

Jackson, Bo, 186
Janssen, Hans, 4
Janssen, Zacharias, 4
job search process, 151–52
Joseph, Craig, 21–25, 27, 33–35, 127, 227, 244
Judge Judy (TV program), 18–19

K

Kaepernick, Colin, 187–88
Kahneman, Daniel, 6–7, 118–21
Keeling, Dave, 234
King, Martin Luther, Jr., 16

L

L.A. Daily News, 89
Lakoff, George, 167–68
Lancaster, Pennsylvania turnaround story, 250–52
Latinx:
family and, 116, 117
as Fatalists (Meta Worldview 4), 102
as Individuists (Meta Worldview 2), 54–59
intersectionality of base/demographic markers, 57, 59
as Social Binders (Meta Worldview 3), 74–77
Trump Effect and, 170
Leaper, Campbell, xi
Lewis, Gary J., 28
liberalism, Individuists (Meta Worldview 2) and, 47, 178
Libertarian Party, 164–66
Liberty magazine/The Liberty Project case study, 188–92
life stage, *see* age/life stage
lifestyle, attributes, and attitudes, 111–18, 136–41, 142, *see also* entertainment exemplars; musical genres; voting patterns
Loblaws Supermarkets, 212, 213–15
Lorre, Chuck, 103
loss aversion tactic, 121
Loyalty/Betrayal instinct:
in Canadian First Nations climate change project, 254
described, 26
emotional responses to, 26
gun control/Second Amendment rights and, 227–28

in Moral Foundations Theory (MFT), 21, 24, 26, 227
racial equity and, 226
of Social Binders (Meta Worldview 3), 70, 78, 227–28
triggers for, 26
"us vs. them" dynamic in, 26, 70, 209
voting patterns and, 172

M

Madison, James, 162–63
majority minority, 246
Manabe, Syukuro, 234
Marcus, Gary, 25
Marcuse, Herbert, 164
marketing and advertising:
affinity scores in, *see* net-affinity scores
behavioral change and, 13–15
Care/Harm instinct in, 176–79
in charitable fundraising, 176–84
customer journey mapping in, 179–88
data science modeling in, 8–9
digital technology in, 8–9, 20
engagement planning, *see* engagement planning
evolution around social listening, 12
group dynamics in, 161–62
individual differences in, 10–13
market basket analysis model in, 11, 15, 42
Model of Why in, *see* applications of the Model of Why
motivation to buy and, 11–12, 15–16
in network television, 17–20
public service announcements (PSAs), 121, 142–44
research in, 17–20
role of customer insights and research in, 9–13
segmentation models in, *see* segmentation models
tactics used in, 121
why people buy things and, 15–16
Mass Appeal, in group dynamics, 159–62
mass media:
in marketing and advertising, 15, 17–20
political signals on climate change, 237–38
McAdams, Dan P., 37
McLachlan, Sarah, 179
MEE Productions, 19, 112–13, 248
Mercedes-Benz, 111–12
Merkle, Eric, 236–37